D0291285

About the cover illustration

In the enclosed space of an egg a double-headed hermaphrodite stands upon a winged and fire-breathing dragon, which in turn is perched upon a winged globe. Inside this winged globe is the uniting of the square of the four and the triangle of the three.

The image is described by Titus Burckhardt this way:

> . . . from Basilius Valentinus' *Aurelia Occulta Philosophorum* in *Theatrum Chemicum, Argentorati,* 1613, vol. IV. – The Hermetic androgyne stands on the dragon of nature, which lies on the winged sphere of materia prima. The compass and setsquare in the hands of the androgyne correspond to heaven and earth, to the male and female powers. On the male side are Venus, Mars, and the sun, and on the female side are Saturn, Jupiter, and the moon. At the top is perfect Mercury.
> *Alchemy*, Burckhardt, Penguin Books, 1972, page 194

The man/woman figure is a Rebis (Latin, *re bis* = "thing twice") and a pointer to Rubeus Hagrid, an alchemical androgyne in *Harry Potter* who loves dragons (see page 114). The winged sphere, the quintessence or prima materia, is clearly a Golden Snitch, the aim of Quidditch seekers like Harry. Penguin Books used this 17th century image as the cover of the most popular edition of Burckhardt's *Alchemy*, a book that almost certainly was part of the "ridiculous amount about alchemy" Ms. Rowling admits she read "in order to set the parameters and establish the stories' internal logic."   (see page 46 for the complete Rowling quotation).

This book has not been prepared, approved, or licensed by any person or entity that created, published, or produced the *Harry Potter* books or related properties. Harry Potter, characters, names, and related indicia are trademarks of Warner Bros. and
Harry Potter Publishing Rights © J. K. Rowling

UNLOCKING HARRY POTTER
Copyright © 2007 John Granger
Wayne, Pennsylvania

All rights reserved. Except in the case of brief quotations embodied in critical articles or reviews, no part of this book may be reproduced or transmitted in any form or by any means, electronic or mechanical, including photocopying, recording, or by any information storage or retrieval system, without written permission of the publisher.
For information, contact Zossima Press www.Zossima.com

Zossima Press titles may be purchased for business or promotional use or special sales.

Book design by Robert Trexler

ISBN 0-9723221-2-4
Printed in the United States of America

10 9 8 7 6 5 4 3

UNLOCKING HARRY POTTER

FIVE KEYS FOR THE SERIOUS READER

JOHN GRANGER

Zossima Press

UNLOCKING HARRY POTTER

FIVE KEYS FOR THE SERIOUS READER

All references are to the Scholastic editions of the books.

The following shorthand is used when referring to the books: *Harry Potter* 1 (HP1) I call *Stone*, HP2 *Chamber*, HP3 *Prisoner*, HP4 *Goblet*, HP5 *Phoenix*, and HP6 *Prince*.

Table of Contents

An Introduction and Invitation

The subtitle of this book – "for the Serious Reader" – strikes even me as elitist. I chose it because I want to be up front about who will benefit from this book and who won't.

C. S. Lewis once explained that there are two types of readers, "the unliterary man" ("the majority") and "those who read great works."

> In the first place, the majority never read anything twice. The sure mark of an unliterary man is that he considers 'I've read it already' to be a conclusive argument against reading a work. We have all known women who remembered a novel so dimly that they had to stand for half an hour in the library skimming through it before they were certain they had once read it. But the moment they became certain, they rejected it immediately. It was for them dead, like a burnt-out match, an old railway ticket, or yesterday's newspaper; they had already used it. *Those who read great works, on the other hand, will read the same work ten, twenty or thirty times during the course of their life.*
>
> (*An Experiment in Criticism*, 1961, p. 2, added emphasis)

Many readers of the *Harry Potter* novels enjoy them as I enjoy an éclair – a light treat of sensual pleasure to be enjoyed and then forgotten. For these readers, *Unlocking Harry Potter* will not be very enjoyable. It may even seem silly. "Why unlock *Harry Potter*? It's only a kid's book or a 'beach-read.'"

People I call "Serious Readers," like Lewis' literary man and woman, not only reread books they love but want to know more about their favorites and why they love them. Beyond reading what they can about the author, serious readers read reviews and published reflections of other serious readers. *Unlocking Harry Potter* allows these friends of Harry and Ms. Rowling a greater understanding of books and the world in which they live. Most notably:

1

- **An Appreciation of the Artistry and Achievement of Ms. Rowling's Writing:** It may seem pedestrian or overly curious to pull a spring-wound watch apart and re-assemble it with the help of a watchmaker, but only someone who has done this work sees and knows the genius of the watch's design and operation. Until you have looked at the *Harry Potter* books closely to see what makes them tick as literature, it is not likely you will appreciate what Ms. Rowling has done and is doing.

- **An Understanding of "Potter Mania:"** Even casual readers have to be curious about the unprecedented and near-universal fascination with Ms. Rowling's stories, a popularity that social observers call a "mania." If we insist that the superficial story line is the only relevant story, we fall short of grasping "why we love Harry." Digging below the surface to the workings of the story reveals the "why" of Potter-mania.

- **Answers to Difficult Questions:** Ivory Tower culture mavens have, in patronizing fashion, dismissed the *Potter* books. Many Christian believers have condemned the books as "gateways to the occult." Is *Harry Potter* "really just slop" as Yale's Harold Bloom tells us? Are children reading these books in greater danger of joining dangerous cults than those who do not? Reading the books in context and in depth reveals answers to these questions as well as the reason these books upset both the intelligentsia and the true believers (who, it should be noted, are odd bedfellows!).

- **A Pick to Ms. Rowling's Lock:** The five keys discussed in *Unlocking Harry Potter* can be used to force the locked door that stands between us and the concluding novel of the series.

Thinking the Way the Author Thinks

Understanding *Harry Potter*, as you'd expect, means trying to think like the author and recognize the patterns and the tools she uses. The only sure way to do that is to immerse oneself in Ms. Rowling's books, read the interviews she has given, become familiar with news stories about her past, and keep up with her life outside of books.

Introduction

I'd love to say that everything in this book was written based exclusively on interpretation of Ms. Rowling's novels. Frankly, I'm extremely wary of speculation based on media interviews or other "celebrity" type "news."

Having said that, it's important to note that interviews with Ms. Rowling have revealed two things about how she thinks. She's a planner and she's a pattern writer.

About the planning, we know she planned the seven books in detail for five years before even finishing the first book. From the archives of the invaluable *Accio Quote!* website:

> KING: Do you know, J.K., where you're going?
> ROWLING: Yes.
> KING: You do? You plot it out?
> ROWLING: Yes, I spent five years – it was five years before – between having that idea and finishing the first book and during those five years I was planning the whole seven book series, so it's already written in stone. That's how it's going to happen.
> www.accio-quote.org/articles/2000/1000-cnn-larryking.htm

We know, too, that she spends two months re-planning the new novel she is working on before she begins writing it:

> AjXTee: How long does it take you to plan a book before you even start writing? Or do you just plan as you go along?
> JK Rowling replies: It's hard to say; book six has been planned for years, but before I started writing seriously I spend two months re-visiting the plan and making absolutely sure I knew what I was doing.
> www.accio-quote.org/articles/2004/0304-wbd.htm

Planning is one essential difference between good writers and bad.

> ALEXANDRA LE COURTEUR WILLIAMSON for the South Australian Advertiser: When you start, do you do a complete plan before you start writing, or do you just have an idea from the start and then just keep writing?

JK ROWLING: I do a plan. I plan, I really plan quite meticulously. I know it is sometimes quite boring because when people say to me, "I write stories at school and what advice would you give me to make my stories better?" And I always say and people's face often fall when I say "You have to plan," and they say, "Oh, I prefer just writing and seeing where it takes me". Sometimes writing and seeing where it takes you will lead you to some really good ideas but I would say nearly always it won't be as good as if you sat down first and thought: Where do I want to go, what end am I working towards, what would be good, a good start? Sorry, very dull.   www.accio-quote.org/articles/2005/0705-edinburgh-ITVcubreporters.htm

She even said in August, 2000, that she wasn't about to make market driven changes in the books and "throw away 10 years' meticulous planning."

I got asked the other day, "Given the huge success of your books in America, are you going to be introducing American characters?" And I thought, "You're an idiot. I am not about to throw away 10 years' meticulous planning in the hope that I will buck up to a few more readers."
   www.accio-quote.org/articles/2000/0800-ew-jensen.html

The *Harry Potter* books are meticulously planned. There's very little that is accidental or spur-of-the-moment about them. This is especially important to remember because of the way Ms. Rowling's mind works.

And how can we know how her mind works, how she thinks?

Well, for the answer to that question, we have her six *Harry Potter* books for models and examples that I'll be talking about for the rest of the book – and we have a bizarre fact about how she likes to spend her free time. The woman loves to play a computer game called "Minesweeper." In fact, I think it's safe to say she is an addict because she says as much herself. From her web site:

Introduction

> Just thought you might like to know that my personal best
> for Expert Level Minesweeper is now ninety-nine seconds.
> This goes to show how much time I have been spending at
> this computer, typing 'The Half-Blood Prince'. To those
> who suggest that I might get on even faster if I stopped
> taking Minesweeper breaks, I shall turn a deaf ear. It's either
> Minesweeper or smoking, I can't write if I have to give up
> both.
>
> www.jkrowling.com/textonly/en/extrastuff_view.cfm?id=17

If you don't know what Minesweeper is, it is a popular game that comes loaded on every computer with Microsoft Windows. I have had to remove it from every computer in my home and workplace because I wanted to finish this book. The parallel Ms. Rowling makes with smoking is not accidental; the game is a life-stealing pleasure.

The surprising thing about her post isn't that she plays – millions do. What is startling is how good she is.

Ninety-nine seconds on the Expert board is phenomenal. A quick check at the rankings at metanoodle.com/minesweeper shows this time (which has probably improved since she posted it late in 2004) makes her number 27 on the Women's All Time Best list. For a game that is on almost every computer and is played competitively worldwide, from New Delhi to North Dakota and back to the Netherlands, being ranked in the top 50 players is a resume item. They'd probably give her a full scholarship and stipend at Microsoft University if she'd agree to play Minesweeper on their Division 1 team.

A ninety-nine second Expert board also represents an astonishing investment of time. I have played Minesweeper many more hours than I want to admit or than I want my wife and students to know. I blush to admit that I thought I was pretty good. On the Expert board, I have broken 500 seconds twice. My children that play (and who secretly curse me for having deleted it from our computers) as a rule do not play the Expert board because it is too hard for them to finish within the 999 seconds allowed.

So what? To break the 100 second barrier is only possible if a player has a gift for the type of thinking the game requires, if the player has invested hours of playing time over years, or, most likely, both. Even if

Ms. Rowling has given up Minesweeper since 2004 via hypnosis therapy or Minesweepers Anonymous meetings, her aptitude on the electronic game board tells us a lot about the way she thinks – and how we should think if we want to figure out the magic of her stories.

What does Ms. Rowling's love of and gift for Minesweeper tell us?

Minesweeper is essentially a game of logic with an element of luck. As one Minesweeper program tutorial explains it:

> The grid of squares represents a minefield. Mines are distributed randomly in the cells. Initially, all cells appear as blank tiles. The player clicks on a cell. If the cell contains a mine, the game is over. If the cell does not contain a mine, the application computes the number of adjacent mines. If there are no adjacent mines, the application does the calculation for all the adjacent cells, expanding recursively whenever a cell is examined with no adjacent mines. A player can use logic to make informed decisions on which cells to examine, though it is possible for there to be a situation when the player has to guess. The game is timed.... The goal is to click on all the cells not containing mines. http://newmedia.purchase.edu/~Jeanine/games/minesweeper.doc

The game requires spatial reasoning and logical elimination of possibilities based on the information given on cleared squares. A good Minesweeper player quickly eliminates possibilities and discovers openings and bombs on all points of the grid. A great player instantly recognizes geometrical patterns of possibilities that reveal what is hidden beneath multiple squares.

And here is the clue we're looking for. "Recognizing patterns."

Thinking like Ms. Rowling, Minesweeper extraordinaire, means working with patterns based on tangential or diagonal lines of possibility. How does she think? Answer: "She plans meticulously and she sees things in patterns as part of her cranial hard-wiring." The patterns she chooses to write with, because she plans her novels so carefully, are our surest means to understanding her books, why millions of people around the world love them (and why others despise and fear them), and how the series may end.

Introduction

Painters, film makers, poets, sculptors, dramatists, and novelists all make choices of medium, genre, color, technique, shading, and of form, which choices determine how they make the points they wish to make with their audience. Joanne Rowling is not the exception that proves this rule. The deliberate and repeated patterns in her *Harry Potter* novels are the weave and woof of the tapestry she is creating. To get at the beauty and power of this arras in progress, the challenge is recognizing Penelope's patterns.

Remember faux Moody's trunk in ***Harry Potter and the Goblet of Fire***?

> Dumbledore walked over to the trunk with seven locks, fitted the first key in the lock, and opened it. It contained a mass of spellbooks. Dumbledore closed the trunk, placed a second key in the second lock, and opened the trunk again. The spellbooks had vanished; this time it contained an assortment of broken Sneakoscopes, some parchment and quills, and what looked like a silvery Invisibility Cloak. Harry watched, astounded, as Dumbledore placed the third, fourth, fifth, and six keys in their respective locks, reopening the trunk each time, and revealing different contents each time. Then he placed the seventh key in the lock, threw open the lid, and Harry let out a cry of amazement.
>
> (***Goblet***, Chapter 35, pp. 680-681)

Think of Ms. Rowling's books as magical objects very much like this trunk. To get inside you have to have a set of keys. The keys we need are the patterns she uses so deliberately.

If you're here to get those keys, you're reading the right book. *Unlocking Harry Potter* is an explanation of five important patterns Ms. Rowling uses, namely, literary alchemy, the hero's journey, postmodern themes, narrative misdirection, and traditional symbolism. These patterns are the five keys the serious reader needs to get to the heart and magic that make these "kids' books" the treasures they are.

A real quick look at each:

The **hero's journey** is the primary and most obvious scaffolding on which Ms. Rowling builds her story (to give the weaving metaphor a rest). Each year's adventure has been built on the same story line or skeleton, that of Harry's trip to Hogwarts, his solving a mystery there with the help of his friends, and his return home. Ms. Rowling makes some significant changes to the classic hero's journey formula but she adheres strictly to her own formula year after year. We'll look at this cycle of journeys Harry makes as well as examining her most oft-repeated story elements.

Paralleling the hero's journey is the **alchemical cycle** Harry repeats each year and the "Great Work" his seven-year education is about. Alchemy, the traditional science of creating a Philosopher's Stone that will change lead to gold and produce the elixir of life, is a series of seven cycles and three sequential stages, usually described in the colors black, white, and red. Ms. Rowling uses the English tradition of literary alchemy for its themes, symbols, and structures, all of which create the backdrop of Harry's adventures at Hogwarts.

She also is the master of the mystery novelist's specialty, namely, **narrative misdirection**, a skill she learned from her repeated readings and close study of Jane Austen. By controlling what we see of the story, restricting it to Harry's perspective and thoughts, she creates the illusion that we know what is happening when in fact the greater part of the story (what Voldemort, Snape, and Dumbledore, just for example, are doing and thinking) is always off our screens. Ms. Rowling's signature surprise endings "happen" because of this book-long deception. Even Ms. Rowling's characters practice narrative misdirection, it is so much a part of her thinking.

We cannot forget that Ms. Rowling is a woman of her times, which is to say, that she is a **postmodern** writer. Her books have the concerns and slant, if you will, of almost all writers of our historical period, especially screenwriters and the authors of popular fiction. Her war on prejudice, celebration of the under-dog, and her genre-bashing mélange of story – detective fiction, Gothic romance, manner-and-morals fiction, among quite a few others – reveal the common sense fact that she lives in the 21st century and her works reflect the concerns and beliefs of our historical period.

Add to this her philosophical realism and facility using **traditional symbols**, quite a departure from "orthodox" postmodernism, and you have the explanation of her global popularity as well as the reason both academics and religious culture warriors despise *Harry Potter*. Ms. Rowling writes books that resonate simultaneously with the *Zeitgeist* and the transcendent longings of the human heart. No small thing.

The aim of *Unlocking Harry Potter* is to explain to serious readers how to match each of these keys to the locks in Ms. Rowling's novels. The remarkable benefits of this key-to-lock exercise make what effort is involved seem a great investment of a little time reading. There are two obvious benefits beyond just having a lot more fun while reading and gaining a greater appreciation of what Ms. Rowling has done and is doing. First, you can use these five keys in combination to try to force the lock on the trunk for which we don't have a key, namely, the one opening the seventh book, *Deathly Hallows*, we're all waiting on.

My experience talking and corresponding with serious readers about Harry makes me think learning about and using these keys will help you in one more way. By reflecting on Ms. Rowling's choices and her artistry, you may gain a new perspective on reading and art in general that opens other books and films and poems and plays.

But that's extra curricular activity. The main point here is unlocking *Harry Potter*, just like the title says. Here is how I hope to present these five keys so you're sure to get a good grip on each.

How this Book is Organized

The organization of this book is simple. I will introduce each pattern/idea and suggest how it may explain what happened out-of-sight in *Half-Blood Prince* or what may happen in *Deathly Hallows*. The goal is to have fun with the story and its possibilities while unwrapping the major patterns.

The first chapter will be everything you wanted to know about narrative misdirection. The chapter could be subtitled 'What We Missed in *Half-Blood Prince*' because its unresolved narrative misdirection is what has us sitting on the edge of our seats waiting for the last book. I suggest at chapter's end that Dumbledore and Snape may be using Harry in *Prince* to practice narrative misdirection on the Dark Lord (and all of us watching the story unfold over Harry's shoulder).

The next chapter is everything you need to know about literary alchemy, even the alchemical arithmancy of the stories (why there are so many sevens, fours, and twos). This means we have to look at things like Shakespeare and the Metaphysical poets – or almost exactly the opposite of how we see things today. Ms. Rowling's use of alchemical images and scaffolding in a postmodern epic may be the most important key you'll get here. It certainly unlocks a lot of what has happened and what must happen in *Deathly Hallows*, the seventh alchemical cycle and the red stage or Rubedo of the "Great Work."

The third chapter is a lot lighter. After going through the heavy thinking about literary alchemy comes a review of the roller-coaster ride experienced in each book: Harry's hero's journey cycle and the several repeated elements that should be red-flags demanding our attention. This is a forehead-slapping chapter ("How obvious! Why didn't I see that!") rather than a trip into new conceptual territory.

Looking at Our Eyeballs

The fourth chapter is all about looking at our postmodern eyeballs. This is no small trick. Imagine looking at your own eyeballs. Studying postmodernism is learning about the peculiar way we all think and the unexamined myths we share as truth. I'll introduce the twelve things found in almost every postmodern story, book, film, play, or poem – and then we'll look at *Harry Potter* as a PoMo myth. You may be surprised to see how the world's favorite books resonate with the predominant concerns and beliefs of our time.

In my experience, all the good literature professors, the ones that are able to get you to see the genius and magic of a book, begin the same way. They provide an overview of the historical beliefs, prejudices, and concerns of the era when the book was written and how the specific writer conformed or did not conform with these beliefs – especially important when studying books, plays, or poems written a long time ago.

This can be really helpful or it can be a disaster. The disaster is when the teacher decides everyone writing in that period was a homophobe or a racist chauvinist lap-dog and the reading descends into group judgment of our ignorant ancestors. The helpful part is when the historical introduction opens up your thinking to an entirely different perspective on the world than the one we bring to the text, a light that helps with the more obscure ideas in the book.

Introduction

I had this experience when I took a Shakespeare course my senior year in high school. Our teacher, Henry Ploegstra, made us read a thin book called *The Elizabethan World Picture: A study of the idea of order in the age of Shakespeare, Donne, and Milton* by E. M. W. Tillyard. We had to read it before we began reading the plays. We were reading every Shakespeare play in one semester and I really didn't think we needed to read one more book "to get ready."

Wow. Was I wrong.

Without Tillyard's little book, I wouldn't have understood the little bit of Shakespeare I did understand back then and I certainly wouldn't be reading and studying the Bard today for pleasure. Tillyard's book was my first introduction to the fundamentals of literary alchemy (four elements, four humors, quintessence, etc.). Without the 109 pages of *Elizabethan World Picture*, I would have been projecting my conceptions into the text and ignoring whatever didn't fit.

Historical understanding of worldview is where the good literature professors begin. Common sense tells us it is just as important in unlocking the meaning and artistry of *Harry Potter* as it is when reading Shakespeare. If anything, though, it's harder and more important for a contemporary writer.

Understanding our historical period requires that we acknowledge that we live in an "Age" with its own peculiar beliefs and prejudices, just like the Elizabethans and the Victorians did. Most people in our times, like most people in every time, imagine that they live at the end of time and the height of progress, which to them means that the way we see things now is the way they really are. C. S. Lewis, a contemporary and friend of Tillyard, called this disdain for the past and faith in the present time "chronological snobbery."

Beyond acknowledging that we live in a historical period, looking at the beliefs of a contemporary author also means looking at the predominant beliefs of our time.

I said a few paragraphs back that good literature profs start the same way – with the historical information needed to escape our own historical prison. They end, though, by explaining what is timeless or transcendent in the poem, play, or novel we're reading. The fifth chapter explains Ms. Rowling's philosophical realism, evident in her stories' symbolism, themes, and storyline. This is where she breaks with more orthodox postmoderns – and wins our hearts completely.

After that, all that's left is the practical exam. The keys we'll have mastered by then are best used for interpreting books, of course, but when discussing a book that isn't finished they should help us make intelligent guesses about how they might end. The postmodern realism and literary alchemy in the sixth chapter provide some straightforward (and reckless) predictions about things like "Will Harry die?" and "How will Lord Voldemort be vanquished?" Some of these reasoned guesses about *Deathly Hallows* will seem far-fetched. At the very least, refuting my crackpot ideas should be an excellent test of what you've learned in the previous chapters.

My goal is not to ruin the ending for readers but to offer thoughtful possibilities within a challenging critical perspective. This is an exercise in stimulating readers to think in new directions and at a different, greater depth about *Harry Potter*.

Some people who read this book will glory in refuting the ideas here and proving their expertise. I welcome this approach and zealotry, only asking that my instructors will be charitable and kind in correcting my silly mistakes. Please write me at john@zossima.com – and I'll do my best to get back to you promptly. I look forward to learning what *Harry Potter* means to you.

Fraternally,

John

"We've got to catch the key to the door!"

"But there are hundreds of them!"

Ron examined the lock on the door.

"We're looking for a big old-fashioned one –
probably silver like the handle."

Stone, p. 280

Chapter One, Key One

Narrative Misdirection

"D'you get the feeling Hermione's not telling us something?"
Ron asked Harry (***Prisoner***, Chapter 7, p. 130).

"They didn't see what they thought they saw!" said Black
savagely, still watching Scabbers struggling in Ron's hands
(***Prisoner***, Chapter 18, p. 351).

"I expect what you're not aware of would fill several books,
Dursley," growled Moody.
(***Phoenix***, Chapter 38, p. 869)

Let's start our adventure in unlocking ***Harry Potter*** with a thought
problem.

Imagine you've been inspired to write the best-selling books of all
time, at least the best-selling books not inspired by God or written by
Chairman Mao. You sit down with your legal pad if you're Ms. Rowling
or in front of your blank white screen and you begin planning what this
story will look like.

What is the first and most important decision you have to make?

It's not what you'll name the four houses of your magical subcreation's
school or the several patterns with which you'll build the books, layer
by layer. The details and structures of your series will be essential to its
blockbuster success, but there is a bigger choice that has to be made first
or none of the later decisions will come off as planned.

Got it? Not yet? Take your time and scratch your head. Or just
read on.

The point of this exercise is that we have to remember writers have
choices. When planning their books, especially if they plan with the
care and attention to form and detail we know Ms. Rowling does, one
of the first choices they have to make when beginning a story is the
"voice" they will use when writing. No, I don't mean alto, soprano, or
bass voice. I mean who will be telling the story, how it will be told.

Believe it or not, this decision determines flat out how we as readers will experience the book and what we'll get out of it. Good writers choose a voice that doesn't get in the way of their story. Great writers use a voice that drives home much of what they are trying to tell us in a story. Ms. Rowling's choices qualify her as at least a "Great Writer Wannabe."

So who tells the *Harry Potter* story?

Like every book, the author is telling the story, but through whom the author tells the story is critical. *Moby Dick*, to leave Harry for a minute, is told from the perspective of Ishmael the survivor, not from the perspective of Herman Melville the author per se. Ishmael speaks for himself as "I" or "me" so this perspective is called "First person narration" (because in grammar "I" and "We" are first person, "you" singular and plural are second person, and "he/she/it" and "they" are third person).

The Chase-the-White-Whale story would be completely different if another person told the story (Ahab? Queequeg?) from their equally limited first person perspective or if the story were told from high above the top sail from which God-like height everything can be seen. This God-perspective is called "Third Person, omniscient" because it is a "see all" perspective not restricted to any person's isolated view.

These are the two big options an author has when writing a novel. "Do I tell it from a narrator's experience of the tale a la Dr. Watson in the Sherlock Holmes cases? Or do I tell it as God sees it unfolding in time?" Open up any anthology of detective fiction (I love the *Oxford Book of British Detective Stories* and their *American Detective Stories* volume, too) and quickly check to see whether a story is told either by a fictional narrator in the "I saw this" and "then we did that" perspective or if the story comes from the author in the role of an all-seeing god. It's usually one or the other.

There are a few variants on these two options, and the one relevant to our getting beneath the narrative surface of *Harry Potter* is the perspective in which Jane Austen wrote *Emma*. This "narratological voice" is called "third person, limited omniscient view" and telling the story this way is how Ms. Rowling pulls off her stunning end-of-story surprises.

Think for a minute about how the *Potter* novels are told or flip open any one of the six books in print. With very few exceptions (most notably, the first chapter of the first book and the opening chapters of *Goblet* and *Half-Blood Prince*), the stories are told not from Harry's perspective talking like Dr. Watson or Ishmael: "Ron and Hermione and I then pushed our way through the door and saw a wild three-headed dog!" The stories aren't told by God floating above the Astronomy Tower, seeing and telling all: "Then Draco went back into the Room of Requirement to pick up where he left off on Vanishing Cabinet repair."

The perspective of these books splits the difference between the "first person" and "third person, omniscient" perspectives. What this split means in practical terms is that we see all the action in the books as if there were a house-elf sitting on Harry's shoulder with a minicam who can also tell us everything Harry is thinking and feeling in addition to what he sees around him. We don't see any more than Harry sees (hence the "limited" in "limited omniscient") but because we're not restricted to Harry's narration it seems as if we're seeing a larger bit of the story than if Harry just told it himself.

This last bit of seeming is critical because this allows for what literary geeks call "narrative misdirection." If you have to remember one thing about how Ms. Rowling writes, make it "narrative misdirection," your key for the first big lock on Harry's magical trunk. It's how Ms. Rowling writes her books so they end in a surprise. Narrative misdirection is also the reason *Half-Blood Prince* was a satisfying story with all the clues we need without "giving away" how the last installment will end.

All "narrative misdirection" amounts to is our being suckered into believing, because the story is not being told by Harry himself, that we are seeing the story as God sees it. Of course this isn't the case but over the course of the tale our looking down on Harry and friends (and enemies) from "on high", even if "on high" means only from a few feet over Harry's head, we begin to think we have a larger perspective than we do.

We don't, of course; we never have anything but the smallest fraction of information about what is going on with Voldemort, Dumbledore, or Snape. Of all the perspectives on the story Ms. Rowling could have chosen to give us, she chose to give us the relatively clueless angle on events in the Wizarding World. Harry doesn't know that much about what's going on.

Check out the following diagram. The surrounding rectangular area of the page represents all knowledge that can be had about what's going on at Hogwarts. Only Ms. Rowling and God know this much, with her boxes of back story on every character and very clear idea both of how the story will end and why. The circle with horizontal stripes represents what Dumbledore knows, the checkered one Voldemort's knowledge, and the vertical-lined circle everything Snape has been told or figured out.

For the purpose of this illustration, let's assume that these three circles are all roughly the same size but they cover different things. Severus is confidant to both the Dark Lord and the Hogwarts Headmaster, to varying degrees. As each wizard is an accomplished Legilimens and Occlumens, they are careful to shield their thoughts from one another and to learn what they can from those whose minds are open books to them, relatively speaking.

The darker circle that rests pretty much in the intersection of these three wizards' understanding of things represents what Harry sees and thinks. This, because of Ms. Rowling's choice of third person, limited omniscient view, is all we get. Harry, as the prophesied vanquisher of Voldemort, is a subject of great interest and probable scrutiny by all three of the other circles. It is possible that Harry knows information and has ideas that Voldemort, Dumbledore, and Snape do not know about, but, frankly, I doubt what he learns on his own is very important compared to what the other three know.

The trick of the limited omniscient view works because we like Harry and sympathize with him and his struggles. In short, we begin to identify with how Harry thinks and feels, and, because Harry is not telling the story, we think we have come to this position of sympathy and identification with the hero because of our unprejudiced view.

When you've arrived at this position – and, confess, we've all been there, this woman is really good at what she's doing – Ms. Rowling has you wrapped up. She can take you anywhere she wants to take you and make you think almost anything she wants about any character because, by and large, "what Harry thinks" has morphed into "what we believe."

Remember our confusion of Professor Snape and Quirrell as the servants of the Dark Lord in *Philosopher's Stone*? I do. I swallowed Harry's conviction that Snape was evil and made it my own belief.

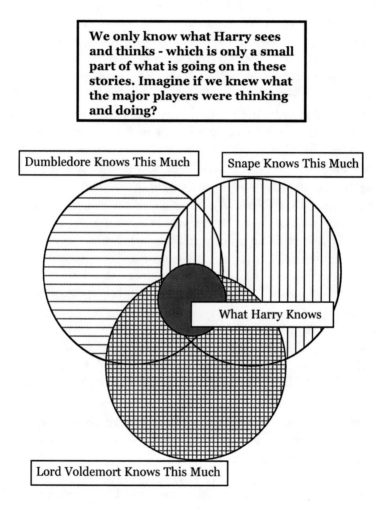

**We only know what Harry sees
and thinks - which is only a small
part of what is going on in these
stories. Imagine if we knew what
the major players were thinking
and doing?**

Dumbledore Knows This Much

Snape Knows This Much

What Harry Knows

Lord Voldemort Knows This Much

I had all the information that pointed to Professor Quirrell as the black hat – Ms. Rowling plays by the rules, y'know, if she doesn't give enough evidence to convict – but I back-shelved that information as I rushed through the underground obstacles with Ron and Hermione in support of Harry to get to the Mirror of Erised and Snape. Severus, of course, wasn't there. He turned out, in the world-turned-upside-down denouement (when Dumbledore tells us the view from on high…), to have been a white hat, despite appearances.

This deception was possible because of our identification with the orphan boy living under the stairs who was treated horribly by his Aunt and Uncle. We sympathized with him and took his view as our own, though it wasn't his view or an all-knowing one. Pretty embarrassing, but Ms. Rowling uses this same trick in every book. In *Chamber of Secrets* she even shows us Harry being suckered by a writer's narrative misdirection. Shame on us for not catching on to what is happening.

In Chapter 13 of *Chamber*, 'The Very Secret Diary,' Ron and Harry find a diary in the girls' bathroom where Moaning Myrtle "lives." Ron tells Harry not to pick it up or read it because books can be dangerous. Harry laughs that warning off, picks up the diary, and is not satisfied until he learns how to "read" it. I wrote in *Looking for God in Harry Potter* that *Chamber* is largely a book about how to read books and how to discern what makes a book good and what makes a book dangerous. In Chapter 13 of *Chamber* we learn that books can be dangerous, if not exactly for the reasons Ron gives. Trusting the narrative line, Harry shows us, can make us believe things we shouldn't believe.

'The Very Secret Diary' is a Horcrux we learn in *Prince,* but even in *Chamber*'s finale "miles beneath Hogwarts" we find out that this diary is a reservoir for Lord Voldemort's memory. He's not a bad writer, as he tells us; "If I say it myself, Harry, I've always been able to charm the people I needed" (*Chamber*, Chapter 17, p. 310). We see him charm Harry right out of his core beliefs when Harry agrees to enter into Riddle's diary, in much the same way as Harry later drops into Dumbledore's Pensieve.

Inside Riddle's diary we experience along with Harry the turning of the story on its head via the author's telling the story so (1) we see only what the writer wants us to know of the story which, (2) because of our mistaken belief or leaning, leaves us thinking we know something that we didn't see. Nothing that Riddle tells Harry about his turning

Hagrid in as the Heir of Slytherin and the wizard whose monster killed Moaning Myrtle is untrue; Riddle shows Harry these facts, however, so selectively and out of context that Harry exits the diary believing that Hagrid, his best friend among adults at Hogwarts, is a monster and a murderer. Harry believes this because he knows Hagrid loves monsters and does not suspect that Riddle, the author of the story, has an agenda.

That's what choosing the right voice can do to a reader not looking out for narrative misdirection. The writer can make you believe almost anything by concealing or disguising information and playing on your prejudices.

Rowling does this in every book. In *Chamber*, we're convinced for more than half the book that Draco is the Heir of Slytherin before, along with Harry, we fall into Riddle's (and Rowling's) trap. In *Prisoner*, not knowing what Lupin and Dumbledore know about Sirius, we believe with everyone and especially with Harry that his godfather is a monstrous criminal who betrayed the Potters. In *Goblet*, Harry's faith in Dumbledore's friend, Alaister "Mad-Eye" Moody, is a faith we share until the scales fall from all our eyes in his office.

In *Phoenix*, too, we're suckered along with Harry into Voldemort's trap; why didn't he force the issue at the beginning of the school year with Dumbledore? I confess I didn't think of that until Sirius was dead and Harry was tearing up the Headmaster's office. I didn't think of it because once again I accepted Harry's view of things as a comprehensive view or, if not comprehensive, then at least a "greater than marginal" view. Wrong again.

This is so much Rowling's way of writing that almost all her savvy characters are adept at it. In addition to Tom Riddle's diary in *Chamber*, we see Snape in *Phoenix* (Chapter 28) trick Harry by loading the Penseive with his "worst memory" to give a deceptively one-sided view of Harry's father (for reasons discussed in Chapter 6). Hermione in *Phoenix* (Chapter 32) uses Umbridge's conviction that Dumbledore is plotting against Fudge to get her into the Forbidden Forest.

And narrative misdirection is almost all Voldemort is doing in *Phoenix* – and Dumbledore knows it! The Dark Lord tries to tempt Harry into the Department of Mysteries by a persistent dream he plants in Harry's head because he assumes Dumbledore has told him about the

Prophecy. Dumbledore hasn't told him just so Harry won't be tempted into the Prophecy vault and sets up faux Occlumency lessons to show Voldemort that he knows the Dark Lord's plans. Voldemort succeeds in getting our young hero into the Ministry basement by activating Harry's people-saving reflex. Once that button is pushed, it's hard to hold Harry back.

Not to mention Lord Voldemort lies low the whole year because he knows his remaining out of sight, when combined with everyone's desire to believe he has not come back, will result in few people believing Dumbledore or Harry about his return. The Dark Lord understands narrative misdirection and hoodwinks almost the entire magical world because the story he writes by his inaction confirms what those readers want to think is true.

Half-Blood Prince: Super Narrative Misdirection

Narrative misdirection is a key to all the books but nowhere does Ms. Rowling do it more brilliantly than in *Half-Blood Prince*, even though there really isn't a surprise ending in the sixth book.

How she did it is fascinating.

First, she turns off the voice we're used to hearing. In the opening of *Prince*, instead of a house-elf with minicam on Harry's shoulder, we have an elf on the Muggle Prime Minister's shoulder reading his mind in Chapter 1 and another on Bellatrix's shoulder in "Spinner's End." By the time we get to Harry in Chapter 3, we're ready to resume our comfortable position on our friend's shoulder – someone we like. If you liked the Muggle Prime Minister and Bellatrix more than Harry and identified more with them than with him, I'm sorry. The ten million of us who gladly leapt onto Harry's shoulder were already deeply hooked into buying his view as God's view or "the truth."

But for you hard-core readers determined not to identify with Harry, Ms. Rowling had another hook or undercurrent to suck you into delusion with the rest of us. For 28 of the 30 chapters, everyone thinks Harry is a nutcase for believing Draco is a Death Eater and that Snape is helping him with his mission from the Dark Lord. If we are resistant in believing Harry to be right in these beliefs, we are in good company; Ron, Hermione, Remus Lupin, Nymphadora Tonks, Mr. and Mrs. Weasley, even Albus Dumbledore also think Harry is just determined to believe the worst of Malfoy and Snape – and that he is wrong (again).

But events confirm everything Harry has thought since the book's beginning! Malfoy *was* on a suicide mission from the Dark Lord! Snape *is* his willing comrade and a man capable of killing the beloved Headmaster. And everyone in a wave in the Infirmary conclave around Bill apologizes to Harry for doubting him and for believing the best of others like Dumbledore when they should have been hating Snape and Malfoy. Harry is a Prophet!

You're a better reader than I am if the traction of this current didn't pull you off your feet and send you downstream. This isn't just "narrative misdirection." This is judo and Ms. Rowling has a black belt, third dan, in this martial art.

The Judo Throw at the Finish of *Half-Blood Prince*

If you don't know anything about judo or its cousin, aikido, let me explain what I mean. The point of these martial arts is to use the force or direction of the opponent to subdue him or her. If someone tries to punch or kick you, the judo response is to "encourage" them to continue in their unbalanced direction and lock them up. Ms. Rowling's judo move is to get us leaning exactly the way we want and then push us over in that direction.

We come into the story as careful readers who have been duped, by and large, five times. We've all taken oaths, publicly and privately, not to be fooled a sixth time. Everyone else in the book is on our side. "Sure, Harry," pat on head, shared glance with Dumbledore and Hermione, "We know. Draco's the youngest Death Eater ever and you know best about Snape – like all the other times you've been right about Snape. Which would be 'never, ever right about Snape.'" As much as we love Harry, we're not going to be kicking ourselves again at book's end for buying into Harry's jaundiced view. We lean way back from Harry.

But it turns out he is right! And everybody that was with us in leaning away from Harry is on the floor apologizing for not trusting in his discernment. This is the crucial difference between the ending of *Half-Blood Prince* and every other *Harry Potter* book. In every other book's finale we're swearing we won't identify with Harry's view again. We take solemn oaths that next time we'll be more like Hermione and we'll see this is one of Harry's mistakes, his "saving-people-thing."

At the end of *Half-Blood Prince*, though, we weren't saying, "I was suckered again! Doggone it!" We were saying, "Wow. Harry was right. Snape killed Dumbledore as part of the plan that the Dark Lord had for Malfoy to 'do in' the Headmaster. Time to line up behind Harry and go Horcrux and Snape hunting on our white hippogriff and in our white cowboy hats."

Ms. Rowling has spun us around from the position toward which we were leaning contra-Harry and forced us into the identification and sympathy mode for Harry's perspective that we swore we'd never accept again.

If Harry were Hermione, he would have asked questions about what was going on. Harry's perspective, alas, is largely an unquestioning perspective. When Dumbledore explains how Severus saved his life after he tried to destroy the ring Horcrux, Hermione would have asked, "How did he do that?" or "Why isn't it treatable more than it is? How serious is this injury?" Harry doesn't blink at the Headmaster's explanation or ask the obvious questions you or I might of a man with this bizarre a wound who was saved by a wizard we believe to be a black hat. Harry also assumes the man he is speaking to is Dumbledore, although the man openly teases him that this is a mistake (*Prince*, Chapter 4, p. 61).

When we accept Harry's non-questioning posture, we're already being swept into narrative misdirection. We think we're learning important information. All we're really getting is a surface explanation. The narrative line actually raises more questions in *Half-Blood Prince* than it answers. As much as we tried not to be suckered, Ms. Rowling has "rowled" us over again.

And not just in the ending! Think of Harry and what he sees and what we believe in the chapter called "After the Burial." Harry, more than half desperate to get the Slughorn memory, finally takes a swig of Felix Felicis potion. With the liquid luck in his veins, everything goes his way. Ron and Lavender have a row and Dean and Ginny begin the fight that ends their relationship before Harry is out of Gryffindor Tower. Everything is going his way and we are beginning to believe as much as Harry does that nothing can go wrong tonight.

Whenever you think this in a *Harry Potter* novel, red flags should go up in your brain-housing unit to signal you that you are in serious trouble. Harry runs into Horace Slughorn – just the man we are looking for – and in our excitement and surety that this is all good luck, especially getting the necessary Horcrux memory, we skip over all the information we pick up along the way or have learned before.

We forget that Horace is a more than competent wizard and no slouch at drinking. Are we to believe he doesn't notice that Harry isn't drinking while refilling their glasses? Sure, Horace is excited about the Acromantula venom and unicorn hair sales he's about to make, but enough to forget how to drink and be duped by a sixteen year old drinking novice? Wouldn't Hermione be asking "What else could he be doing with that venom and unicorn hair?"

And those greens he's getting from Professor Sprout? Every class we've seen Slughorn teach has been a minimum of real work on his part and the maximum load of "Let's see what you've been able to figure out on your own." Is this the sort of professor that goes to gather greens for his Third Year students at dusk because they will make their potions especially "efficacious"?

And he needs to "change his tie" for Aragog's funeral? He's already said he needs to get some wine, why the second excuse? He needs to check a tie, I think, and maybe ask instructions from someone now that he is close to having the ingredients he needs for his own potions work. Can he feign drunkenness now and give up the memory to Harry?

We never think to ask.

Why not suspect there is more to Slughorn than meets the eye? Outside of Lupin, every new teacher at Hogwarts has been either dangerously self-involved or downright dangerous or both. Why don't we assume Slughorn is more than a social parasite? Because that's all Harry thinks he is – and when we see him doing even remarkably suspicious things, we're under the spell of Rowling's real world, literary Felix Felicis, the magic potion of narrative misdirection.

Two Penetrating Reader Questions

What don't we learn because of Dumbledore's death that he might have told us? After first reading *Half-Blood Prince*, I decided to play "twenty questions" with the text. In less than ten minutes I had a list of twenty questions raised in *Prince* by explanations of events in the story line rather than answered (you can find these questions and the discussion of Evil!Slughorn in the first chapter of *Who Killed Albus*

Dumbledore?). The two best examples of narrative misdirection and of Ms. Rowling's providing important clues to be discovered under the surface story are:

(1) Why does Dumbledore behave so strangely and differently in *Half-Blood Prince* than he did in *Order of the Phoenix*? and

(2) What is Lord Voldemort up to this year?

If you recall, the Headmaster is largely absent from Harry's life in the fifth book of the series. Except for an appearance in Harry's defense before the Wizengamut and a forced meeting when Harry sees the attack on Mr. Weasley through Nagini's eyes, Dumbledore avoids seeing Harry or even making eye contact with him. He asks Harry at book's end why he didn't ask him about this:

> "But did you not wonder why it was not I who explained this to you? Why I did not teach you Occlumency? Why I had not so much as looked at you for months?"
>
> Harry looked up. He could see now that Dumbledore looked sad and tired.
>
> "Yeah, " Harry mumbled. "Yeah, I wondered."
>
> "You see," continued Dumbledore heavily, "I believed it could not be long before Voldemort attempted to force his way into your mind, to manipulate and misdirect your thoughts, and I was not eager to give him more incentives to do so. I was sure that if he realized that our relationship was - or had ever been - closer than that of headmaster and pupil, he would seize his chance to use you as a means to spy on me. I feared the uses to which he would put you, the possibilities that he might try and posses you. Harry, I believe I was right to think that Voldemort would have made use of you in such a way. On those rare occasions when we had close contact, I thought I saw a shadow of him stir behind your eyes.…. I was trying in distancing myself from you, to protect you. An old man's mistake…"
>
> (*Phoenix*, Chapter 37, pp. 827-8)

Key One: Narrative Misdirection

Hence Harry's disbelief when Dumbledore sends him a message in the first weeks of his summer "vacation" at the Dursleys, a message that he says he will be picking him up. After Side-Apparating to Budleigh Babberton, the neighborhood in which Horace Slughorn is hiding, the strangely exuberant Dumbledore asks Harry about his scar and if it has been hurting him:

> "No," he said, "and I've been wondering about that. I thought it would be burning all the time now Voldemort's getting so powerful again."
>
> He glanced up at Dumbledore and saw that he was wearing a satisfied expression.
>
> "I, on the other hand, thought otherwise," said Dumbledore. "Lord Voldemort has finally realized the dangerous access to his thoughts and feelings you have been enjoying. It appears that he is now employing Occlumency against you."
>
> (*Prince*, Chapter 4, p. 59)

Harry swallows this whole. This sudden switch, however, is unfortunately either one of the few instances of necessarily poor explanations to retain mystery and planned action in her books (akin to Dumbledore's feeling unable to ever share with Harry anything about the prophecy because this boy who has saved the world several times from Lord Voldemort couldn't handle it...more on this in a second) or there is something Dumbledore doesn't tell us. Maybe Severus told Lord Voldemort something that made him worry that Dumbledore planned on using Harry to spy on the Dark Lord. Either way, the answer is too pat.

Because, no doubt about it, the Headmaster does a 180 degree flip between *Phoenix* and *Prince*. It's not just the amount of time Harry spends in tutorials and on adventures with the greatest wizard living, it is how the master alchemist acts. Dumbledore is no less than a saint and a guardian angel with his Hogwarts students, forever patient and charitable with them (even the real stinkers) and sacrificial in his care for them. In *Half-Blood Prince*, though, he loses patience with Harry twice, once when Harry questions whether Dumbledore has adequately protected the school, and, more surprisingly, when Harry failed to get the Horcrux memory from Professor Slughorn.

This task, against a resistant Slughorn, is impossible. Yet Dumbledore shames Harry in a series of biting, rhetorical questions for not turning all his energies to this impossible task, though he gave Harry not one clue as to where he should begin. Harry is humiliated by Dumbledore's evident disappointment and shocked by the threat that the tutorial session he was in would be the last until he had the necessary Slughorn memory (**Prince**, Chapter 20, p. 428).

What's the hurry? Why the verbal bullying without reasonable explanation or helpful suggestion? Is there a deadline Harry doesn't know about?

This weird behavior and 180 degree change raise other questions about Dumbledore. Just for instance:

What happened to Dumbledore's hand arm? We are told now that the wound was a consequence of Dumbledore's attempt to destroy the ring Horcrux and that Snape saved his life. We don't know what happened to make such a horrific wound (unusual in being incurable and unmaskable) and how Snape saved him. If destroying Horcruxes is dangerous business, shouldn't Harry know this? It is supposedly the task at which his tutorial sessions are aimed.

Why did Dumbledore trust Snape? Why couldn't he tell anyone? The Headmaster doesn't even try to explain until Harry learns that it was Snape who told Voldemort about the Prophecy. Only then does Dumbledore tell Harry that it was the shame and anguish that Snape felt consequent to Voldemort's attack on the Potters that caused him to become a double-agent. Harry thinks Dumbledore was suckered – and Lupin, a man without Harry's "age-old" prejudice against Snape, agrees this is unbelievable. Is there another better reason to have trusted Snape without reservation? Why didn't he tell anyone what it was?

And the Bad Guy?

If Hermione and I had a meeting with the Big Guy in the white hat at year's end (assuming he wouldn't die to get out of answering our questions), we would have asked him about his peculiar behaviors, I'm sure. We might even have tried to figure out if he really was Dumbledore. As important, though, is the elephant-in-the-room question no one seems to say out loud while thinking about all the time. What is Lord Voldemort up to?

Key One: Narrative Misdirection

We learn a lot about Voldemort in *Half-Blood Prince* via Dumbledore's screening of his collected memories in the Pensieve for Harry (none of which memories come from his own head). We do not, however, learn anything about what he is doing in the present time. In the previous books, we learn about Lord Voldemort and what he has been up to in the final battle and Dumbledore's explanation at book's end. Unfortunately, Dumbledore doesn't surface after his drinking binge at the cavern lake and the nightmare on the Astronomy Tower – so we're left wondering.

A quick survey of the previous five books shows us that Dumbledore might have told us, too, about the good guy who turned out to be different than what he appeared to be while he was explaining what Riddle, Jr. was up to that year. Professors Quirell, Lockhart, Lupin, False Moody, Umbridge… they all turned out to be surprises and usually a nasty surprise. It almost amounts to a formula. Look closely at the Defense Against the Dark Arts teacher, the "new guy" – if you look hard enough you'll learn something about the Dark Lord.

With Quirrell, Lord Voldemort was "on board." With Lockhart, the famous author, the bad guy is hiding in a book (Riddle's diary). With Lupin, closeted werewolf and friend of Black and Pettigrew, we learn the Dark Lord is in hiding. Crouch-Moody is Voldemort's servant laboring to deliver Harry to the rebirthing party, and Umbridge, self-important Ministry sadist, is revealed to be sick enough to turn the Dementors loose on Harry in Little Whinging. Voldemort reveals himself in *Goblet* and *Phoenix,* but Dumbledore still has to explain what Harry missed during the year of what Voldemort was doing.

At the end of *Half-Blood Prince*, though, there were no revelations beyond what Harry saw on the Tower. Are all the Good Guys really good - unlike every other story? And what was the Big Bad Wolf (Voldemort, not Greyback) up to all year? I confess to feeling pretty certain he wasn't sitting on his hands waiting for Draco Malfoy to hit a solo home run in his first trip to the plate.

Stoppered Death

It turns out that the questions of what happened to Dumbledore's arm, his bizarre behavior in *Half-Blood Prince*, and why he trusted Severus Snape can all be answered together using clues that Ms. Rowling gives us openly and repeatedly. It all goes back to Harry's first Potions class in *Philosopher's Stone.*

My comoderator in the August 2005 Discussion Room at Barnes and Noble University.com (BNU) was Cathy Liesner from "The Leaky Cauldron," a notable *Harry Potter* fan site. Cathy was struck by the number of references in *Half-Blood Prince* to Harry's very first Potions class way back in *Philosopher's Stone*, Chapter 8, "The Potions Master." Cathy realized that something Snape said in that first class could be an explanation of how Severus helped Dumbledore with his arm. Cathy's idea is called "Stoppered Death" and, with narrative misdirection in mind, it helps us see what we missed because we see things only from Harry's unquestioning viewpoint.

In case you missed the references to this first Potions class, here's a quick review. In *Prince*, Chapter 18, "Birthday Surprises," Harry is half-desperate to think of a way to impress Slughorn and clear the way for his handing over the unedited Riddle-asking-about-Horcrux memory that Dumbledore wants. The Potions Master gives an impossible "Find the alchemical antidote" (yes, he uses the word "alchemical;" see *Prince*, p. 375) class assignment and Harry is clueless about how to go about applying Golpalott's Third Law. His annotated Potions textbook says only:

> And there it was, scrawled right across a long list of antidotes:
> Just shove a bezoar down their throats.
> Harry stared at those words for a moment. Hadn't he once, long ago, heard of bezoars? Hadn't Snape mentioned them in their first ever Potions lesson? A stone taken from the stomach of a goat, which will protect from most poisons."
> (*Half-Blood Prince*, Chapter 18, p. 377)

The shortcut impresses Slughorn who awards Gryffindor ten points for "sheer cheek" and says for the umpteenth time "Oh, you're like your mother," in admiration. It does not smooth the way for a Horcrux memory revelation, however, far from it, and we're left to wonder at this whole protracted Potions class scene and what it meant. We learn why before chapter's end (we think) when Harry saves Ron's life with a bezoar in Slughorn's apartment.

Ms. Rowling, though, doesn't leave it at that. In the first paragraphs of chapter 21, "The Unknowable Room," Harry and Hermione are having another go at it about the Half-Blood Prince textbook that Hermione thinks is dicey, at best.

> "Don't start, Hermione," said Harry. "If it hadn't been for the Prince, Ron wouldn't be sitting here now."
>
> "He would be if you'd just listened to Snape in our first year," said Hermione dismissively.
>
> (*Half-Blood Prince*, Chapter 21, p. 447)

This is a curious throwaway comment. Yes, Hermione had done the assigned work in Potions class and had every reason to be miffed at Harry for taking the shortcut, contrary to directions, and earned Slughorn's approval (again). But, knowing that Harry and Ron can't remember anything scholastic without endless repetition or her explanations, it's curious that even in her pique about the Potions class she thinks Harry could have remembered that first class without some prompting like the note from the Prince. Why does she bring up the first Potions lesson here?

Perhaps to get us to go back and look at that first lesson? Severus Snape also makes an aside about his first meeting in class with Harry to Bellatrix and Narcissa in *Prince*, Chapter 2, "Spinner's End," that provides some context for what we should look for in that lesson. In answer to Bellatrix's question about why Severus has not killed Harry Potter, he says:

> "Have you not understood me? It was only Dumbledore's protection that was keeping me out of Azkaban! Do you disagree that murdering his favorite student might have turned him against me? But there was more to it than that. I should remind you that when Potter first arrived at Hogwarts there were still many stories circulating about him, rumors that he himself was a great Dark wizard, which was how he survived the Dark Lord's attack….
>
> "Of course, it became apparent to me very quickly that he had no extraordinary talent at all…. He is mediocre to the last degree, though as obnoxious and self-satisfied as was his father before him." (*Half-Blood Prince*, Chapter 2, p. 30-31)

"It became apparent to me very quickly." Say, in the first Potions lesson? What happened in that class in the dungeons?

In a nutshell, Severus insults Harry during roll call, gives a short speech on the wonders of Potions (that he believes will be lost on these dunderheads), and then quizzes Harry on the ingredients for the Draught of Living Death (which Harry produces for Slughorn in Sluggo's first class using the *Half-Blood Prince*'s directions…), on bezoars, and Monk's Hood. He takes two points from Gryffindor for Harry's attempt at humor during this harassment and, later, because Harry didn't prevent Neville from melting his cauldron. Harry is astonished by the evident hatred the Potions Master feels for him and discusses the problem with Hagrid later that afternoon.

So what?

Well, we see in the harassment Severus gives the child Harry that he is looking to see, not so much if Harry is a great Dark Wizard in embryo as he claimed in *Half-Blood Prince*, but to see if he was a Potions genius like his mother who had been able to absorb all of the first year's text as Lily probably did (whose image we have in Hermione who frantically tries to answer Snape's questions?). Or maybe he is just trying to convince Harry and the children of Death Eaters present that he is a certifiable "Harry Hater." Severus begins the attacks and borderline sadism that define his exchanges with Harry until his departure from Hogwarts at the end of *Half-Blood Prince*.

That this extraordinary beginning reveals the character of their relationship, though, isn't my point. There are references in this chapter to bezoars and the Draught of Living Death in *Half-Blood Prince*. Some readers think Dumbledore or his stand-in consumed the latter in order to seem dead after his fall from the Tower (see Chapter 6). But it is the speech that Severus gives in his first class that unlocks much of the background in *Half-Blood Prince*.

The class most like an Alchemist's laboratory begins with Professor Snape telling these frightened first year students:

> "As there is little foolish wand-waving here, many of you will
> hardly believe this is magic. I don't expect you will really
> understand the beauty of the softly simmering cauldron with
> its shimmering fumes, the delicate power of liquids that creep

through human veins, bewitching the mind, ensnaring the
senses....I can teach you how to bottle fame, brew glory, even
stopper death - if you aren't as big a bunch of dunderheads
as I usually have to teach."

(*Philosopher's Stone*, Chapter 8, p. 137)

"Bottle fame, brew glory, even stopper death." It is this last comment
about "stoppering death" that is important; it explains many of the
questions that are never explained in *Half-Blood Prince*. In a nutshell,
Professor Severus Snape "stoppered" Albus Dumbledore's death when
the Headmaster tried to destroy the Slytherin ring Horcrux.

The Meaning of "Stoppered Death"

What does it mean to "stopper death"? It isn't saving a life, obviously,
or effecting a cure; it is suspending a death that has already happened.
When Professor Snape asks his Defense Against the Dark Arts class what
the difference is between a ghost and an Inferius (*Prince*, Chapter 21, p.
460), the answer may be "Headmaster Dumbledore." In his stoppered
death, Albus is quite literally a "dead man walking," something between
"a corpse that has been re-animated by a Dark Wizard's spells" and "the
imprint of a departed soul left upon the earth." We miss this clue from
the Potions class, of course, despite it being an off-the-wall question,
because we are caught up in cheering for Harry against the sadistic
D.A.D.A. master.

Notice that this stoppering is not an indefinite process nor does
it change the reality of Dumbledore's demise. Dumbledore, as Ms.
Rowling told us in 2006, is "definitely dead." Severus Snape does not
have the cure for death. By stoppering the Headmaster's death for,
let's say, at least a month or one year or more, however, Dumbledore
and Snape are forced to be much more aggressive than they might
otherwise be in Harry's sixth year. I think we can assume "suspended
de-animation" doesn't last forever or allow for a lot of dramatic or
melodramatic activity. Dumbledore may not even be on the Tower at
book's end.

We were wondering about Dumbledore's arm and why the
Headmaster trusts Severus. The "Stoppered Death" theory explains,
of course, what happened to Dumbledore's hand at least partially

illuminates why Dumbledore trusts Snape without reservation and why he doesn't explain his trust. If the man we think is Dumbledore in *Prince* is Dumbledore, this man cannot share this secret with anyone who is not an accomplished Occlumens because its discovery will mean instant death for the Potions genius. Nonetheless, what reason could the Headmaster have for doubting Severus' loyalty when, except for his Potions genius, he would not be present to doubt him? Dumbledore says as much to Harry when he finally explains what happened to his hand:

> "Had it not been — forgive me the lack of seemly modesty — for my own prodigious skill, and for Professor Snape's timely action when I returned to Hogwarts, desperately injured, I might not have lived to tell the tale."
> (*Half-Blood Prince*, Chapter 23, p. 503)

It answers, too, why Severus would take the Unbreakable Vow with Narcissa even if he knew that Draco's mission was to kill Dumbledore. For the same reason that he had no qualms about blasting the Headmaster with the Avadra Kedavra curse on the Astronomy Tower. As Albus said to Draco on the Tower, "He cannot kill you if you are already dead" (Chapter 27, p. 391).

Why would Dumbledore give Snape the cursed Defense Against the Dark Arts post, knowing that no one had lasted more than a year in this teaching position? Was it because they both knew that the death Severus had stoppered would be evident to everyone before the year was out? If Snape is to survive Dumbledore's staged death, however, and continue to help the Order defeat Voldemort, the Potions/Defense professor has to leave Hogwarts, and, worse for Severus, cannot be known as the man who "saved Dumbledore's death" for a year or more. He has to be known as "the man who killed Dumbledore." A one-year appointment with an orchestrated, seemingly murderous finish, is perfect.

"Stoppered Death" also suggests why Dumbledore did a 180 degree turn from his hands-off approach to Harry in *Phoenix* and begins tutorial lessons with him. If the clock is ticking on his stopper or if he plans to "take a dive" at year's end, the Headmaster didn't have the leisure to let Harry mature and live a relaxed life. This suggests, too, reasons why Horace Slughorn had to be brought on to the Hogwarts faculty and why Dumbledore was absent from Hogwarts for such long stretches. He had to get as much information about the Dark Lord's Horcruxes – and get them to Harry – as soon as possible. "Stoppered Death" accelerates if it doesn't outright cause most of the action behind the scenes in *Half-Blood Prince*.

Voldemort's Invisible Year

"Stoppered Death" gives us the peek behind the narrative that explains much of the mysterious goings on at Hogwarts during *Prince*. It does not, however, give us a cohesive idea of what Voldemort has been up to this year and what his part in the Astronomy Tower murder was.

Before trying to explain this, though, let's be sure to note that Voldemort is all but invisible this year. We know that he gives Draco Malfoy a suicide mission to kill Dumbledore, a mission in which he is to die either in the attempt on Dumbledore's life or at the hands of the Death Eaters for failing. His mother understands this to be an assignment to punish the Malfoys for Lucius' mistakes with the diary Horcrux and in failing to recover the Prophecy. Dumbledore echoes her understanding in a later passage.

> "Ah, poor Lucius… what with Voldemort's fury about the fact that he threw away the Horcrux for his own gain, and the fiasco at the Ministry last year, I would not be surprised if he was not secretly glad to be safe in Azkaban at the moment." *(Half-Blood Prince, Chapter 23, p. 508)*

Beyond this "fury" and his attacking Lucius by throwing away the life of his son (and torturing both in the process), we see nothing of the Dark Lord. The natural assumption, however illogical or incredible, is that he isn't doing anything this year because we don't read about it.

It's happened before. We didn't see Lord Thingy in *Phoenix* either and assumed he was sitting on his hands. Out of sight, out of mind – and "out of luck" is what we were in figuring out that the Dark Lord had been setting up the trap in the Department of Mysteries' Prophecy vault through his own use of narrative misdirection.

If we assume that Lord Voldemort was at least as active in *Half-Blood Prince* as he was in *Phoenix*, unlike Harry, we should be thinking he had more on the stove than punishing the Malfoys with Draco's suicide mission or breeding Dementors like Aunt Marge breeds bulldogs. We can think all we like, but I doubt we'll get much of an answer.

The only way we have learned what Voldemort was doing in the previous books, after all, was because he either told us himself in a face-to-face confrontation as in **Stone, Chamber, Goblet**, and **Phoenix** or because Dumbledore explained it to us in his private one-on-one with Harry at story's end. In **Prince**, though, Voldemort leaves the Tower drama to his stooges, so we don't learn from him ex cathedra what he's been up to. The Headmaster, unfortunately for Harry and for us, takes a powder and misses the end-of-book date with his protégé. He goes to his funeral instead, so we are left without the explanation we want.

Looking back at the diagram of perspectives above and thinking about 'Stoppered Death' and narrative misdirection suggests Ms. Rowling is up to something bigger than just fooling Harry and us. If Snape and Dumbledore understand narrative misdirection as well as Riddle did in **Chamber**, perhaps the white hats are staging a drama to fool Harry and, through Harry, to fool Voldemort. We're talking a big twist here.

To understand the importance of 'Stoppered Death' and why Dumbledore doesn't mask the injury to his arm in any way, we need to talk about Jane Austen.

Jane Austen, Joanne Rowling, and 'The Big Twist' as Holy Grail

Ms. Rowling is a "first-time author," something we tend to forget because of her remarkable accomplishment with **Harry Potter**. The only thing every first-time author says when asked by obliging media mavens what he was trying to do when he set out to write his wonderful book is say, "I wanted to write a book like those I like to read."

The press or television reporter then inevitably and as a reflex asks, "Who is your favorite author?" and "What is your favorite book?" Those who read through Ms. Rowling's many interviews, every one of which is posted at www.accio-quote.org, have seen this exchange enough times that they can play Ms. Rowling's and the reporter's parts without cue cards.

Her answers to these two questions are always the same: "Jane Austen" and "**Emma**."

Key One: Narrative Misdirection

It is important to understand the narratalogical voice in which these stories are told. This voice, "third person, limited omniscient," creates narrative misdirection, the surprise ending, and the postmodern effect of making you doubt your own understanding because of postmodernism's inclination toward believing what it expects to be true (the metanarrative). Ms. Rowling didn't make this up; she's borrowing it (and using it masterfully) from Jane Austen whose *Emma* is written in this style. Really, Ms. Rowling's debt to Jane Austen, always acknowledged by her, is such that Austen's heirs might deserve a piece of the *Potter* pie and a second helping.

Here are some quotations and citations that confirm the influence of Austen on Rowling.

In 1999 and every year since Ms. Rowling has said at least once: "My favorite writer is Jane Austen and I've read all her books so many times I've lost count." http://www.accio-quote.org/articles/1999/0099-amazon-staff.htm Sarah-Kate Templeton wrote in 2000 that "Ms. Rowling describes herself as a "squat, bespectacled child" and admits that she was as obsessed with Jane Austen as many of her readers are with her tales of *Harry Potter*. But while Rowling's fans might whiz through *Harry Potter and the Prisoner of Azkaban* just to start reading it all over again, Rowling ploughed through Austen's *Emma* at "least 20 times." http://www.accio-quote.org/articles/2000/0500-heraldsun-templeton.html

In case you think Rowling is freakish in having read *Emma* "at least twenty times," not unlike her legions of fans reading her much longer books, you should know that Benjamin Disraeli, English Prime Minister (and accomplished novelist), was said to have read Austen's *Pride and Prejudice* seventeen times. C. S. Lewis in his much neglected *Experiment in Criticism* makes the important point that the first and best test of a good book is whether it is something readers will return to again and again. Serious readers are distinguished from book consumers, too, by their rereading favorite texts repeatedly and profitably.

There are dozens of references to Austen in Lewis' letters who first mentions reading her novels at age 16. Lewis once wrote of Austen: "Her books have only two faults and both are damnable. They are too few and too short" (*Collected Letters of C.S. Lewis Vol. 2*, Hooper, p. 977).

More than twenty readings of a book should make a strong impression, and, sure enough, even if we didn't have Ms. Rowling's testimony in her interviews, the direct allusions in her books might be sufficient to bring us to the same conclusions about the importance of Jane Austen in understanding *Harry Potter*.

- The caretaker of Hogwarts Castle, Mr. Filch, has a cat named "Mrs. Norris," the name of a busybody aunt in Austen's *Mansfield Park*.

- Percy Weasley's letter to his brother Ron in *Order of the Phoenix* in which he advises him to break off relations with Harry Potter (*Phoenix*, Chapter 14, pp. 296-298) is almost dictated from Mr. Collins' letter to Mr. Bennet in *Pride and Prejudice*. Mr. Bennet is advised in that letter to "throw off your unworthy child from your affection forever" (Volume III, Chapter VI).

- Mr. Knightley's comic change of heart about the villainous Frank Churchill as he learns that Emma will consider and accept Mr. Knightley's proposal of marriage (*Emma*, Volume III, Chapter XIII) is echoed inversely but to similar humorous effect in Harry's altered opinion of Cedric in *Goblet* (Chapter 22, p. 398).

This is important for thinking about *Prince* and the last book, lacking Dumbledore's and Voldemort's perspective on events, because of what Ms. Rowling thinks is so great in her favorite author and book. It's not just narrative misdirection. It's "the twist."

> "The best twist ever in literature is in Jane Austen's *Emma*. To me she is the target of perfection at which we shoot in vain." http://www.accio-quote.org/articles/2000/1200-readersdigest-boquet.htm

What's a "twist"?

We're not talking Chubby Checker here. A "twist" is the delicious surprise and turnaround at book's end consequent to brilliantly executed narrative misdirection in the lead-up to the story's climax. What you believed to be the case is not; what you never expected turns out to be the forehead-slapping truth (the self-punishment is the result of realizing how you overlooked the several now-very-obvious clues in the storyline). The stunning reversal of what appeared to be true, of course, is Ms. Rowling's signature. It's what she loves in Austen's *Emma* and, in her words, this "best twist" is the "target of perfection" she's shooting for in *Harry Potter*.

Nothing earthshaking in this, I suppose. Her readers all know too well the delightful twist in each book: Quirrelldemort in *Stone*, Voldey-in-the-Diary in *Chamber*, Wormtail Scabbers in *Prisoner*, Crouch-Moody Jr. in *Goblet*, the Prophecy trap in Harry's head at *Phoenix*'s end, and Assassin Severus on *Prince*'s Astronomy Tower. The big twist that reveals our preconceptions to us is, as I discussed in *Hidden Key to Harry Potter*, a large part of how Ms. Rowling delivers her prejudice theme to each reader personally. As we'll see in Chapter 4, it is her poststructuralist message as well about our inability to judge correctly from our restricted view of things.

But, wait a minute. The end of *Prince* wasn't really a surprise, however bad we may have felt when the man-believed-to-be-the-Headmaster took the Avadra Kedavra blast in the chest. Harry has been telling us for six books without a break that Severus Snape was not to be trusted, and, c'mon, the guy has been nominated for "Classroom Sadist of the Year" at Hogwarts every year we've been there. How surprising should it have been that the Head of Slytherin House, when push came to shove, knocked the helpless Headmaster off the Tower?

Not very.

Ms. Rowling's love of the "twist" when joined with the absence of a surprise or revelation-contra-expectation at the climax of *Half-Blood Prince* points to two things we have to expect in the series' last novel.

> • First, we will learn, sooner or probably later, everything we missed in *Prince*, all the things that Albus Dumbledore in the other books explained at story's end.

> • And, second, we should anticipate a dose of jaw-dropping, head-shaking astonishment at all the things we missed and misunderstood because we have no idea what Dumbledore and Snape have been doing all these years.

Our focus, consequently, in trying to figure out how we were duped by narrative misdirection in *Prince* should be on looking for the biggest and best twist in English literature. Piece of cake.

My bet is that it comes down to Dumbledore's horrifically scarred arm – and I don't think 'Stoppered Death' is more than a partial explanation of that arm – and that other scar, the one connecting Harry and the Dark Lord.

"Scar-O-Scope Harry:" The Ultimate in Narrative Misdirection

Look back at the chart of perspectives and review the passage from *Phoenix* in which the Headmaster explains why he didn't talk to Harry in his fifth year:

> "You see," continued Dumbledore heavily, "I believed it could not be long before Voldemort attempted to force his way into your mind, to manipulate and misdirect your thoughts, and I was not eager to give him more incentives to do so. I was sure that if he realized that our relationship was – or had ever been – closer than that of headmaster and pupil, *he could seize his chance to use you as a means to spy on me. I feared the uses to which he would put you, the possibilities that he might try and possess you.* Harry, I believe I was right to think that Voldemort would have made use of you in such a way. On those rare occasions when we had close contact, I thought I saw a shadow of him stir behind your eyes…. I was trying in distancing myself from you, to protect you. An old man's mistake…"
>
> (*Phoenix*, Chapter 37, pp. 827-8, emphasis added).

The wizard who picks Harry up from the Dursleys at the beginning of *Prince*, in contrast, tells Harry this is no longer a concern. He says everything is hunky-dory now because "It appears that [Voldemort] is now employing Occlumency against you" (*Prince*, Chapter 4, p. 59). This is either, 1): poor plotting from a master planner – the reason for the tragedy in *Phoenix*, that is, what kept Dumbledore from speaking with Harry is no longer a live issue in *Prince* because of what? – or, 2): this dramatic change in Harry's ability to communicate with Dumbledore is a pointer to something funky going on.

Try this on for a twist:

Let's assume from our perspective chart above that after *Goblet* the Dark Lord really has the ability to look through Harry's eyes and read Harry's mind. Harry doesn't notice this unless Lord Voldemort gets excited, neglects his Occlumency, and stirs the figurative serpents inside Harry. Let's imagine, just for a minute, that Voldemort is reading the same book we are reading. Impossible? As Severus explains to Harry in *Phoenix* during their first Occlumency lesson:

> "Time and space matter in magic, Potter. Eye contact is often essential to Legilimency....The usual rules do not seem to apply to you. The curse that failed to kill you seems to have forged some kind of connection between you and the Dark Lord. The evidence suggests that at times, when your mind is most relaxed and vulnerable – when you are asleep, for instance – you are sharing the Dark Lord's thoughts and emotions....The important point is that the Dark Lord is now aware that you are gaining access to his thoughts and feelings. He has also deduced that the process is likely to work in reverse; that is to say, he has realized that he might be able to access your thoughts and feelings in return –"
> (*Phoenix*, Chapter 24, pp. 531-533).

If Harry has become a walking minicam for Lord Voldemort and Dumbledore and Severus know this, the sixth book becomes a play-within-the-novel for the Dark Lord to watch through Harry's eyes. The "biggest twist in English lit prize" that Ms. Rowling is shooting for is the revelation that Snape's sadistic act is just that, an act, albeit an act he has no trouble playing. The Headmaster and his apprentice are writing an alchemical drama for Voldemort's viewing and to deceive him.

Dumbledore wasn't lying when he told Harry:

> "Did I believe that Voldemort was gone forever? No. I knew not whether it would be ten, twenty, or fifty years before he returned, *but I was sure that he would do so*, and I was sure too, knowing him as I have done, that he would not rest until he killed you"
> (*Phoenix*, Chapter 37, p. 835, emphasis added).

He was sure that the Dark Lord wasn't truly dead probably because he knew about the Horcrux possibility, which Joyce Odell has surmised is probably one of the few spells that cause the facial disfigurement that had so changed Tom Riddle's appearance. Dumbledore has one ace in the battle that must be waged when Voldemort returns: Severus Snape. As long as everyone believes the Potions Master's loyalty to Dumbledore is somehow questionable – and that everyone believes Snape hates Harry Potter – Severus' value as a spy in the coming VoldeWar II is retained. Hence Snape's bizarre and constant without-fail meanness to Harry and his favoritism for Harry's enemies.

When the Good Guys, with a "gleam of triumph," realize at the end of *Goblet* that Harry is forever bugged by his very "handy" scar, (*Stone*, Chapter 1) and then Dumbledore's death seems inevitable despite a temporary stoppage the month after *Prince* ends, what are they to do? Three things seem reasonable, given these premises:

1.   Create a Dumbledore stand-in that Harry and Voldemort can believe is the real thing;

2.   Write a drama for Harry's sixth year at Hogwarts that Harry and Voldemort will believe is real Order of the Phoenix activity in resistance to the Dark Lord, preparing Harry for his inevitable battle with He-Who-Must-Not-Be-Named; and,

3.   Most important, act out the climax of this drama in which Dumbledore's death at Snape's hand is staged realistically and the "murder" is witnessed by Harry, Voldemort, and Death Eaters alike.

The horribly scarred arm is a stage prop that the Potions Masters and Dumbledore realize will act both as a token of Dumbledore's identity and as a distractor, consequently, that will divert any attention to the impostor's unusual behaviors. And Snape as Dumbledore is unusual, no? He baits the Muggles by barging into their home and banging drinks against their heads before beating them up verbally for being abusive parents. Not very Dumbledoresque. Then he pokes his wand hard into a piece of furniture he thinks is a wizard in disguise? Weird.

In fact, as I wrote above, the *Prince* Dumbledore is clearly a different man in several ways than the Headmaster we met in the first five books. Ms. Rowling plays fair. Three times in the first five chapters she makes the point to us through Harry that we shouldn't believe that people are who they say they are (the flyer from the Ministry, Dumbledore/Snape's discussion of same with Harry, and the conversation between Arthur and Molly Weasley on his return from work). This is overdone if there isn't someone important who isn't what he or she seems to be.

Of course, that's a recurrent theme in Ms. Rowling's books. No one is who he or she seems to be, Good Guys and bad (more on this in the coming chapters). And Polyjuice potion as often as not is at the root of the deception. We've seen students brew it in *Chamber*, the very Bad Guys use it in *Goblet*, and Slytherin student Bad Guys are disguising themselves with it in *Prince*. The only folks we haven't seen using it to good effect are the Potions Masters who would seem to be the ones most likely to use it. Professor Slughorn has a cauldron full at the ready in time for Harry's first N.E.W.T level Potions class (*Prince*, Chapter 9, p. 185).

The Giant Squid and Dumbledore?

I understand this is a giant stretch to most readers. Harry's scar a portal Voldemort can look through to see what Harry sees and thinks and feels? Dumbledore stoppered death, dying, or Draught of Living Death comatose off-stage? Snape and Slughorn conspiring with Hagrid to take his place through all of *Prince* – to include the drama on the Astronomy Tower? This is a supertwist well beyond the offstage action and narrative misdirection of Austen's *Emma*.

Is the fact that Dumbledore is never seen with Snape, Slughorn, or Hagrid in *Prince* after the Sorting feast important evidence for a substitution? Steve Vander Ark, the genius and comic responsible for the online *Harry Potter Lexicon*, told me last summer that it was as likely that the Giant Squid was Polyjuicing Dumbledore in *Prince*. "The Giant Squid," Steve explained, "is never seen with the Headmaster."

I like the theory despite its unlikelihood and introduce it in this discussion of narrative misdirection for one reason. "Scar-O-Scope Harry," to give this theory a name, is impossible even to understand as a possibility without seeing the significance of Ms. Rowling's decision to tell the story from the third person limited omniscient view. Severus playing Albus in *Prince* from Privet Drive until the Tower scene (where Horace plays Albus if the Headmaster is truly incapacitated) is only credible if Severus and Albus, with Hagrid's and Horace's help, are doing to Harry (and, through Harry's Scar-O-Scope, to Voldemort) what Riddle, Jr., did to Harry with the diary-memory in Chapter 13 of *Chamber* – and what Ms. Rowling does to us in every book.

She presents the facts in such a way that we believe we have all the facts when we really only have a narrow perspective on what's happening. Everything we think we know, we learn at the end of the first five books, can be understood differently, often in the opposite way, when we have a larger view of things. True or not as a theory, "Scar-O-Scope Harry" is intriguing because it makes Ms. Rowling's signature as an author, narrative misdirection consequent to masterful plotting, the way the heroes of her story manipulate and deceive the villain in order eventually to destroy him and save Harry.

So far, I have tried to explain what narrative misdirection is and to share two big-twist possibilities that we can see by looking at the text diagonally or with narrative misdirection in mind. Why Ms. Rowling chose the narratological voice she did is as important as the what because it points to one of the reasons these books are so popular.

Conclusion

Again, we have to ask, "So what?"

Well, having grasped that Ms. Rowling's best tool is her masterful use of the narratological perspective from Austen's *Emma*, we have stepped back and looked at *Half-Blood Prince* to see where we may have been misled. Dumbledore died sometime this year, sometime before he could explain his weird behavior and injury and before we learned what Lord Voldemort was doing behind the scenes.

We came up with two theories from things we know are true and that Harry has misunderstood or not put together. "Stoppered Death" and "Polyjuiced Dumbledore," taken together, explain what happened to Dumbledore, why he trusts Snape (heck, he is Snape), and why the Headmaster seemed to be in a time crunch in Harry's sixth year. It may be the biggest twist in English literature.

The odds are pretty good that neither theory is true, given my track record for predicting, however interesting and challenging each one is to prevalent notions.

Key One: Narrative Misdirection

But if I'm not a true believer in "Stoppered Death" and "Scar-O-Scope Harry," committed to winning all readers to my point of view about what really happened in *Prince*, why did I drag you through all that?

To illustrate and demonstrate the questions and possibilities the narrative line never explores. As serious readers we have to get a firm grip on the misdirection that (1) keeps us from asking those questions and (2) keeps us almost as oblivious as Harry is that we really are clueless about what the greater players in this drama are doing. Take a look back again at the chart of perspectives early on in this chapter. Remind yourself that Harry and those of us who only know what Harry knows are in the dark with respect to what Dumbledore, Snape, and Voldemort are thinking, planning, and doing. We don't know nuthin'.

Lord Voldemort is up to something, of course. Dumbledore and his allies are on a tight schedule and working to counteract the Dark Lord's agenda, and we don't know what we need to know about the Potions Master or the Defense Against the Dark Arts teacher. If "Stoppered Death" and "Scar-O-Scope Harry" aren't the answers, they certainly highlight the breadth of our ignorance consequent to Ms. Rowling's artistry. Which was the point of this chapter.

I do love the play-within-the-play possibility of Harry's being a Voldemort minicam creates, if only because it has the white hats doing to Voldemort what Ms. Rowling does to her readers in every book. I'll expand on variants of this theory in coming chapters on the other four keys and at length in Chapter 6's big wrap-up. Remember Sirius in The Shrieking Shack crucible: "They didn't see what they thought they saw!" Ms. Rowling works in every book except *Prince* to stun us in the end by the "tricks we missed" because we trusted Harry's view of things. What a delight if Severus, Albus, Horace, and Hagrid, taking a page from the author's narrative misdirection playbook, have hoodwinked Harry, Voldemort, and all of us with the same trick.

But this is more than just trickery. This is the substance of our lives, believe it or not, and our ability to understand narrative misdirection is one indicator of the quality of human life of which we are capable. Really.

Most of us, including myself certainly, walk about in confusion about how we see things. If we ever stop to think about it, we know that our individual perspectives are just that, "how I see things." The problem is, as a rule to which only personal tragedies force exceptions, we don't think about.

We confuse, consequently and constantly, "first person, ignorant," which is our real view, with "third person, omniscient," which is the "all-seeing" view. We act as if we know what's really going on when we haven't a clue about what any of the players in our lives are doing and thinking. Just like Harry.

Reading *Harry Potter* is a delightful introduction to the importance of striving to understand how little we are seeing through our eyeballs and how much our prejudices cloud even what we think we are seeing. Can't get much more important than that. The Greeks called it, "Gnothi Seauton," Know Thyself.

Segue to Literary Alchemy

As important and fascinating as I find the ideas of perspectives and penetrating the surface story to find out what is really happening in these books, I doubt my first questions to Dumbledore's painting in his old office would be about narrative misdirection. Albus Dumbledore's greatest achievements on his frog card are his defeating a dark wizard in 1945, his figuring out the twelve uses of dragon's blood, and his accomplishments as an alchemist. I suspect, with some reason, that all three are joined and the important piece is the alchemy. I'd be asking Albus about his work with Nicolas Flamel.

Why? Because the *Harry Potter* books are built on a traditional structure called "literary alchemy" about which you are a very rare bird indeed if you know much, if anything. It runs through English literature from Shakespeare to Lewis and Tolkien and gives the *Harry Potter* books a host of powerful images and relationships to draw on. Much of Ms. Rowling's great achievement is the way she uses symbols of personal transformation as powerfully as she has. It certainly is difficult to understand the power of love in the books and nigh on impossible to get at what *Deathly Hallows* will be about without an introduction to alchemy.

Narrative misdirection is critical to understanding the *Harry Potter* books because it shows us how the author is manipulating our understanding of the story's events. Before jumping from the plot points to any conclusions, though, let's take a long look at Ms. Rowling's most traditional artistry and real magic…the Alchemy in **Harry Potter**, a three part course.

"I've never wanted to be a witch, but an alchemist, now that's a different matter. To invent this wizard world, I've learned a ridiculous amount about alchemy. Perhaps much of it I'll never use in the books, but I have to know in detail what magic can and cannot do in order to set the parameters and establish the stories' internal logic."

J.K. Rowling – December 7, 1998

http://www.accio-quote.org/articles/1998/1298-herald-simpson.html

Chapter 2, Key 2, Part 1

Alchemy 101

I have a good friend in Washington State who lives in Bellingham, a city north of Seattle. He's in his 70s and a big man, well over six feet, and he really enjoys *Harry Potter*. He made his living for decades as a book distributor, with a special emphasis on Christian books. We met when he read my *Hidden Key to Harry Potter*.

As a businessman who knows books, readers, and what will sell or not sell, my septuagenarian, more-than-half-giant friend has consistently given me the same advice. "John," he says, "I know you think the literary alchemy is really important. But nobody is going to get it. Just talk about the other stuff everyone will understand."

My friend is no fool. He's heard me talk several times in bookstores and at schools, and he's right. Whenever I start talking about the alchemy, one of the two most important and difficult patterns for understanding the series, a lot of the audience rub their eyes, squirm in their seats, and check out mentally for a minute or two.

But this is a book for serious readers, right? You simply cannot have a real grasp of what these books are about without digging into the alchemical structures and symbols on which these stories are built. We have to, as popular idiom would have it, "go there."

But, in acknowledgement of my west coast mentor's point, I'm going to stage this discussion in three parts. The first part of this chapter will be an introduction to alchemy, and especially literary alchemy as it relates to *Harry Potter*. Call it "Alchemy 101." With these basics under your belt, we'll step it up a bit in the next part for an "Alchemy Advanced Placement" course with a big helping of Arithmancy.

And then we'll have a "Practical Exam" and put all that theory to the test in a look at what we should expect in *Deathly Hallows* as the alchemical finale. Ms. Rowling is a formula writer and the alchemical potion she's brewing is evident from the title of the first book, *Harry Potter and the Philosopher's Stone* to the wedding we're invited to at the end of *Half-Blood Prince* that will take place in the summer before Harry's last year.

Sit down, then, grab yourself a cuppa, and begin your three-part education in the real magic of great writing, literary alchemy.

Socrates' Challenge

Anyone talking to a 21st century group about alchemy finds himself in the position of Socrates in his *Apology* before the Athenian jury. Socrates was charged with corrupting the youth of the city and for supplanting the gods of the city with gods of his own invention. He was found guilty, despite his remarkable speech in his own defense, and put to death. He complained in the opening of his defense that he was not so much afraid of the charges brought against him in the trial as he was of his "earliest accusers" who "took hold of so many of [the jurors] when [they] were children and tried to fill [their] minds with untrue accusations against [him]", most notably Aristophanes in his comedy, 'The Clouds.'

Socrates told the jurors his biggest problem was that "I must try, in the short time that I have, to rid your minds of a false impression which is the work of many years" (*Apology*, 19a). I recognize Socrates' challenge – and I have to hope for a better or, at least, a less lasting verdict from you. What modern people know of alchemy is almost always wrong and, frankly, horribly wrong, so wrong that the use of alchemical imagery in English Literature from Chaucer to Shakespeare, Donne to Blake, from Shelley and Yeats to C. S. Lewis, Joyce, and Robertson Davies – not to mention Ms. Rowling – must seem absurd.

So, I have three tasks before me.

• First, to explain quickly and clearly what alchemy is and what it isn't (despite what your chemistry teacher, pastor, guru, or Jungian analyst may have told you).

• Next, do a hurried survey of the English 'Greats' to document their usage of alchemical imagery through the centuries and explain why the language of this supposedly material or scientific procedure was so fit for expression of grand themes and meaning.

• And, last, explain how and why Ms. Rowling uses alchemy in the *Harry Potter* novels, because that's what this game is all about, no?

Alchemy: What It Is and Isn't

I grew up in 20th century America and, like my peers, was indoctrinated by inoculation with the popular misconceptions that define our age (as popular ideas, cosmology, and blind-spots define every age). Perhaps the most important spell or charm that entrances us as modern people is the belief that nature, and specifically, matter and energy, are all that exist. This belief, sometimes called 'scientific materialism' or 'naturalism' is what thinkers like Phillip Johnson have called "the de facto state religion of the United States."

As a good student and child of my era, I was a confirmed naturalist and held the physical sciences – biology, physics, and chemistry – in the highest regard. Though I was a Classics major in Prep School and in College, I also studied AP Chemistry and college chemistry at university. I knew the scientists were the high priests and power brokers, and I struggled to learn their language and their secrets.

One of the first things you learn in chemistry classes, by asides and by osmosis, is that chemistry grew out of a kind of medieval voodoo called alchemy, which pseudoscience tried to isolate a philosopher's stone that could turn all metals to gold and bestow immortality on the alchemist. This is still the predominant idea of alchemy in the popular mind, which, if written as a bumper sticker, would read "alchemy is stupid chemistry."

Publicity for a book released in November, 2003, *The Last Sorcerers: The Path from Alchemy to the Periodic Table* by Richard Morris (Joseph Henry Press, 2003) puts it plainly:

> What we now call chemistry began in the fiery cauldrons of mystics and sorcerers seeking not to make a better world through science, but rather to make themselves richer through magic formulas and con games. But among these early magicians, frauds, and con artists were a few far-seeing "alchemists" who, through rigorous experimentation, transformed mysticism into science.

In this description is the second misconception about alchemy. Not only is it bad science and the way of charlatans, alchemy is also about cauldrons, sorcery, mysticism, and magic. Alchemy certainly was a secret science but not in the sense that its current reputation for being an occult practice would suggest. [Read Newman's *Promethean Ambitions: Alchemy and the Quest to Perfect Nature* (University of Chicago Press, 2004) or Brooke's *Science and Religion: Some Historical Perspectives* (Cambridge University Press, 1991) for more sympathetic and historically accurate views about the intersection of religion, magic, and science in alchemy.]

The third misconception comes to us via Carl Jung, one of the 20th century's most famous psychoanalysts, who devoted decades of his life to the study of alchemical texts, imagery, and the meaning of these archetypes in the collective consciousness of humanity and the dreams of individuals. Jung and his many followers certainly had a clearer appreciation of alchemy than do disdainful naturalists and those who live in fear of the occult – but their psychological understanding of alchemy and position that the alchemists were 'Gnostics' is a case of historical projection of one's own empiricist and anti-religious beliefs into the past. Or so the accepted authorities on alchemy now say (see Titus Burckhardt's discussion of Jung and alchemy in *Alchemy*, Penguin Books, 1972, pp. 8-9 and *Mirror of the Intellect: Essays on Traditional Science and Sacred Art*, Quinta Essentia, 1987, pp. 59-66 and 132-141).

If alchemy wasn't 'chemistry for idiots', witchcraft, or an initiatory path into the archetypes of our unconscious mind, what was it? It was a spiritual path to return fallen man to his Edenic perfection.

To understand how a science of metallurgy and physical bodies could cause the purification and perfection of the alchemist, body and soul, requires turning the modern world-view upside down. To the alchemist, as all traditional people or non-moderns understand, man is first and essentially spirit (as man is created by the Spirit), then soul, then physical body rather then the reverse. He believed the obvious, i.e., that the lesser thing comes from the greater thing and never greater from lesser.

His personhood or humanity he knew was a joining of soul and body without seam – and his tragedy was that he was 'fallen', i.e., that he had lost his spiritual capacity or 'intellectus' by means of which Adam walked and talked with God in the garden. Alchemy was the means, in conjunction with the Mysteries of the Church (or temple or mosque – there are alchemies in each of the revealed traditions, East and West), that he could regain this lost capacity; the substance changing from lead to gold was his soul and the riches he would glean were spiritual riches (i.e., immortality).

He was able to do this by effecting a similar change in metals. Because the traditional world view does not hold that there is a chasm between subject and object, that is, that objects do not have independent existence from their observers and vice versa, an alchemist understood the substances with which he worked as being related to him as night and day, male and female, sun and moon, and the other complementary antagonistic pairs which reflect the polarity of the Creative Principle or Word (think 'yin & yang'). This relationship amounted to a correspondence; as he purified himself in obedience to the work, the work would advance and his soul or bodily consciousness would go through correspondent changes. This was not magic or work independent of nature but an accelerating of the natural work by observance of supernatural, even contranatural Principle.

Titus Burckhardt, who with Mircea Eliade is the authority on the history and meaning of alchemy, wrote:

> Alchemy may be called the art of the transmutations of the soul. In saying this I am not seeking to deny that alchemists also knew and practiced metallurgical procedures such as the purification and alloying of metals; their real work, however, for which all these procedures were merely the outward supports or 'operational' symbols, was the transmutation of the soul. The testimony of the alchemists on this point is unanimous (*Alchemy*, Penguin, 1972, p. 23).

> 'To make of the body a spirit and of the spirit a body': this adage sums up the whole of alchemy. Gold itself, which outwardly represents the fruit of the work, appears as an opaque body become luminous, or as a light become solid. Transposed into the human and spiritual order, gold is bodily consciousness transmuted into spirit or spirit fixed in the body.... This transmutation of spirit into body and of body into spirit is to be found in a more or less direct and obvious manner in every method of spiritual realization; alchemy, however, has made of it its principal theme, in conformity

with the metallurgical symbolism that is based on the
possibility of changing the state of aggregation of a body
(*Mirror of the Intellect*, Quinta Essentia, 1987, p. 132).

As metals change from rough ores and solid states to more and
more pure conditions by change of states (to liquid and gas and re-
condensation) and combination with catalysts and purifying agents,
the alchemist effected changes in himself by correspondent changes in
his bodily consciousness while attempting the work.

> The Western alchemist by attempting to 'kill' the ingredients,
> to reduce them to the *materia prima*, provokes a sympatheia
> between the 'pathetic situations' of the substance and his
> innermost being. In other words, he realizes, as it were,
> some initiatory experiences which, as the course of the opus
> proceeds, forge for him a new personality, comparable to
> the one which is achieved after successfully undergoing
> the ordeals of initiation (Eliade, *The Forge and the Crucible*,
> University of Chicago Press, 1978, pp. 158-160).

[Eliade points out that Jung was right to have supposed that alchemy
had a soteriological role for the alchemist (*The Forge and the Crucible*,
p. 11) but in Jung's assumption that the alchemist was primarily a gold
seeker who experienced individuation (by contact with the archetypes of
change in the collective unconscious) the psychoanalyst was 180 degrees
off. Jung restricts the work to the psychic or animic sphere and to the
unconscious or subconscious part of this sphere; alchemy is essentially a
super conscious or spiritual work that happens through correspondence
with archetypes that are above, not below, individual consciousness (cf.,
Burckhardt, *Alchemy*, pp. 8-9).]

So what was alchemy? It was a traditional or sacred science, ancillary
to the work of the revealed tradition and its means of grace, for the
purification and perfection of the alchemist's soul in correspondence
with the metallurgical perfection of a base metal into gold. It requires
a view of man and of creation or cosmology that is opposite and
contradictory to that of the physical scientist and chemist of today, of
whom alchemists had only disdain; they thought men interested in
matter only for its manipulation were "charcoal burners" and anything

but wise. To an alchemist, the chemist neglects the greater thing in the lesser thing – and in himself.

Alchemy was not a reductive science focused on quantitative changes. It wasn't "stupid chemistry" but "accelerated transformation for salvation." The alchemist viewed nature's working as a rotation of the four elements, earth, air, fire, and water, and of the polar qualities, hot and cold, dry and moist. Seeing that change is everywhere a function of the action of the two tendencies found everywhere and in anything, expansion and contraction, the alchemist worked to simulate and accelerate this natural action in his alembic (alchemist's caldron).

Risking simplification, the base metal was reduced to *prima materia* by the repeated action of alchemical mercury and sulphur (not the same as the chemical substances with these names), in a process known as *solve et coagula*, "dissolve and congeal," "expand contract." By purifying this substance repeatedly in this way, the metal and alchemist are transformed in sympathy, as essential polarity is transcended and subject and object join, as in a mirror.

Two things are produced by this joined process. First and more famously, it yields a stone, the Philosopher's Stone, which can transform lead to gold and whose emitted elixir can make a man immortal. As important, though more important in terms of literature and *Harry Potter*, it creates a transformed person who is the conjunction of opposites, the resolution of contraries. Usually represented as a hermaphrodite or androgyne (a s/he), this alchemist is an incarnation of peace and love, words that mean "polarity resolved."

The creation of a spiritual androgyne, "neither male nor female, slave nor free, Jew nor Greek," prompted Martin Luther to say of alchemy:

> The science of alchemy I like very well, and indeed, 'tis the philosophy of the ancients. I like it not only for the profits it brings in melting metals, in decocting, preparing, extracting, and distilling herbs…; I like it also for the sake of the allegory and secret signification, which is exceedingly fine, touching the resurrection of the dead at the last day. (Brooke, p. 67)

The work of alchemy is about accelerating natural processes of expansion and contraction to resolve the great natural divisions of life and death and the supernatural divisions between God and man.

Alchemy requires a theocentric cosmology and quality-focused physics to comprehend. Though long ago a forgotten science and spiritual path, it lives on in the traditions of English literature, our next stop in "Alchemy 101."

Alchemy and English Literature

Alchemy as a sacred science was never an American adventure (with the exception of George Starkey). This science went into precipitous decline and corruption at the time of the Renaissance through the Enlightenment when it was eclipsed by the materialist view and priorities of modern chemistry. Though there was a glut of publication of alchemical treatises as it declined, this is evidence of its corruption. The "great work" was only passed in person from master to apprentice; books contain only the most arcane and hidden guides to the work, metallurgical and spiritual.

American readers, consequently, are unaware of alchemy except as the chemists, the illegitimate and disowned children of the alchemists, want us to remember them. This is perhaps no great loss, except for its reinforcement of our naturalist state religion, but it does have one consequence that touches on *Harry Potter* fans.

Alchemy is near the heart of great English fiction.

English Literature is rich in alchemical language, references, themes, and symbols from Chaucer to Rowling; to be ignorant of this language and imagery is to miss out on the depths and heights of Shakespeare, Blake, Donne, Milton, even C. S. Lewis and James Joyce. Ms. Rowling is not ignorant of literary alchemy. The *Harry Potter* books individually and as a series are built on alchemical structures, written in alchemical language, and have alchemical themes at their core.

Before touching on the use of alchemy in English Literature and why an arcane and sacred science plays such a big part in the history of English letters, here are three quick references so you can learn more about this on your own.

First, get yourself a copy of Stanton J. Linden's ***Darke Hieroglyphicks: Alchemy in English Literature from Chaucer to the Restoration*** (University of Kentucky Press, 1998). It is the academic review of all the treatments of alchemy in literature – to include the number of playwrights and writers who satirized and disliked the charcoal burners as well as the adepts – from the late Middle Ages to the 16th and 17th centuries.

[Though he does not discuss this, the writers of the twentieth century who revive alchemical usage, Joyce, the Inklings, Eliot, are the men who also revive interest in and appreciation of the writers of the 16th and 17th centuries. C. S. Lewis, for example, writes the '*Oxford History of the English Language*' volume for the 16th century, celebrates the world view and intention of its authors in his *Discarded Image*, and, after Charles Williams, writes explicitly alchemical novels in his *Space Trilogy*.]

Next, find Lyndy Abraham's *A Dictionary of Alchemical Imagery* (Cambridge University Press, 1998). There are seven or eight guides to and dictionaries of alchemy in print but Abraham's is the champion. In addition to first class entries on stages of the work and specific citations of alchemical references used by authors over many centuries, there is an index for the serious student of, say, Shakespeare or Blake, for easy access to this remarkable resource on alchemy in literature.

And, last, or almost last, ask at your local university library for a sample copy of the journal, *Cauda Pavonis* (Latin for 'the peacock's tail'). As they describe themselves, "*Cauda Pavonis* publishes scholarly material on all aspects of alchemy and Hermeticism and their influence on literature, philosophy, art, religion, and the history of science and medicine. Our approach to Hermeticism is, of necessity, interdisciplinary and not limited to any particular historical period, national emphasis, or methodology." For more information, contact the assistant editor, Roger Rouland, rrouland@mail.utexas.edu.

[Here's a web site for those of you who may want to learn more about alchemy, with or without literature. The site is a mixed bag but it is a very, very big bag! http://www.levity.com/alchemy/index.html.]

There is not space or time here to do justice to achemy in English Literature. If you're familiar with the topic, these resources are a great helps to a deeper appreciation, and, if this is all new to you, they are accessible introductions.

For just a taste, though, of how understanding alchemy opens certain writers, here is an entry from Abraham's *Dictionary of Alchemical Imagery* for 'red tincture'. The 'red tincture' is the red elixir of the philosopher's stone that, when thrown upon base metals, changes them into gold. As Abraham explains:

> It was thought that just one ounce of the tincture could transmute over a hundred or a thousand times its own weight of weight of base metals into pure gold. Shakespeare used 'tinct' in its alchemical sense in *Anthony and Cleopatra* when Cleopatra says to her 'base' attendant Alexas: 'How much unlike art thou Mark Anthony!/ Yet coming from him, that great Medicine hath/ With his tinct gilded thee' (1.5.34-36). Milton likewise used this metaphor when, in the creation scene in *Paradise Lost*, the stars multiply their light and Venus 'gilds her horns' from the sun's quintessential source, 'By tincture or reflection' (7.364-9) (*Dictionary*, p. 169).

William Blake, too, assumes his readers know their alchemy. As Alexander Roob explains in his *Mysticism and Alchemy: The Hermetic Museum* (Taschen, 2001), the two complementary and antagonistic principles of the alchemical work, the *solve et coagula* of alchemical mercury and sulphur, are where he begins his artistry:

> William Blake identified the male principle with time and the female with space. The interpenetration of the two results in diverse reverberations of individual events, all of which, taken as a whole – totality, the micro-macrocosmic body of Christ in the image of the "human and the divine imagination" – occur in a state of relative simultaneity. Each individual element opens up, in passing, into the permanent present of this fluctuating organism and in the process attains its "fourfold", complete form, which Blake calls "Jerusalem". This vision generated the kaleidoscopic, narrative structures of his late poems, which reveal themselves to the reader as a multi-layered structure of perspectival relations – aimed against the prevailing idea of a simple location of events in the absolutes of linear time and space (p. 25).

Alchemy is key to understanding Blake's last illuminated poem, *Jerusalem*, and his several paintings of Newton whom he singled out to deride for his mechanical and rational view. James Joyce in turn refers to both these works of Blake and other alchemical ideas and images in his *Ulysses* and *Finnegan's Wake* (*Alchemy & Mysticism*, pp. 482, 630). These are difficult writers and some of the best writers in our tradition; to understand them requires at least a grounding in alchemy. If I had all the pages I'd like here, you would be hearing about Shakespeare and C. S. Lewis as brothers in letters and in alchemy. Alas. No time here for *Taming of the Shrew, Romeo & Juliet, Perelandra* or *That Hideous Strength*!

Even if the alchemy-literature connection is all news to you and you go to the grave believing alchemy is just for New Age nits or Historians of Science, please play along with me. Pretend as if you accept it as gospel truth that English Literature from beginning to Rowling is front loaded with alchemical devices and images.

Why, if this is the case, should this be so? What is the connection between alchemy and literature that makes these images the preferred tools of the best writers for centuries?

I think the connection is probably most clear in drama. Eliade even suggests that the alchemical work grew out of initiatory dramas of the Greek Mystery religions (*Forge*, p. 149). Shakespeare doesn't just make asides to alchemy in his plays; many if not most of them are written on alchemical skeletons and themes. *The Tempest, Romeo and Juliet, Anthony and Cleopatra, Two Gentlemen of Verona, The Comedy of Errors, Love's Labours Lost,* and *The Merchant of Venice* come to mind; see Jean Paris' 'The Alchemistic Theatre' (*Shakespeare*, Grove Press, 1960, pp. 87-116), and Martin Lings, *The Secret of Shakespeare* (Aquarian Press, 1984). Frances Yates' *The Art of Memory* (University of Chicago Press, 1974, p. 365) argues persuasively that Shakespeare built the Globe Theatre on Hermetic principles for the proper staging of his alchemical dramas. Why?

If you recall your Aristotle on what happens in a proper tragedy, the audience identifies with the hero in his agony and shares in his passion. This identification and shared passion is effectively the same as the experience of the event; the audience experiences catharsis or 'purification' in correspondence. Shakespeare and Jonson among others use alchemical imagery and themes because they understood that the work of theatre in human transformation was parallel if not identical to the alchemical work. The alchemical work, of course, claimed to be greater than an imaginative experience, but the idea of purification by identification or correspondence with an object and its transformations is 'spot on' with the purpose of theatre.

Alchemical language and themes are the shorthand, consequently, of many great English novels, drama, poetry and prose. The success of an artist following this tradition is measured by the edification of their audience. By means of traditional methods and symbols, the alchemical artist provides delight and dramatic release for our souls through archetypal and purifying experiences.

Let me say that again slowly.

Alchemical language and themes are the shorthand of many great English novels, drama, poetry and prose. The success of an artist following this tradition is measured by the edification of his audience. By means of traditional methods and symbols, the alchemical artist provides delight and dramatic release for our souls through archetypal and purifying experiences.

That may be harder for some of us than the whole idea of alchemy as a sacred science. If you're like me, you grew up with the idea that entertainment was diversion and anything but life changing. It turns out this 'diversion' idea, really only in currency for the last seventy or eighty years, is a gross misconception. Anthropologists, historians of religion, and professors of literature will tell you that the rule in traditional as well as profane cultures such as ours is that Story, in whatever form, has an instructional or initiatory purpose.

Eliade in his *The Sacred and the Profane* is explicit in saying that, in a profane culture especially, entertainments such as reading fiction serve a religious function; they remove us from our ego-bound consciousness for an experience or immersion in another world or subcreation. C. S. Lewis in *Preface to Paradise Lost* asserts that this is the traditional understanding of the best writers, namely, that their role in culture is "to instruct while delighting."

Alchemy and literature are a match because they both endeavor in their undegenerate or orthodox state to transform the human person. Literary alchemy, the use of alchemical images and structures, has, consequently, been a constant in English poems, plays, and novels for six centuries.

Joanne Rowling, Alchemy, and Harry Potter

Hans Andrea, webmaster at the esoteric *Harry Potter* internet site "*Harry Potter* for Seekers," has made the case for several years that *The Alchymical Wedding of Christian Rosenkreutz* (1616) is an important source and model for the *Harry Potter* series. There are a remarkable number of correspondences between the "days" of this wedding and each of the six years we have read about in the *Harry Potter* books. Please see Andrea's article on the web for his explanation of the correspondences and how the works are linked at http://www.harrypotterforseekers. com/articles/crcinjeans.php

I cannot answer the question of whether *The Alchymical Wedding* is one of the inspirations of the *Harry Potter* series. Certainly it bears serious attention, because if she did use this model she won't have been the first to do so. Shakespeare, some have said, writes scenes almost direct from *The Alchymical Wedding* in his *Merchant of Venice* (Paris, op.cit, pp. 98-99). Whatever the answer to this specific alchemical question, other larger questions about Ms. Rowling and alchemy remain. Here are a few of them:

> • How can we tell if Ms. Rowling is intentionally using alchemical imagery?

> • What signs of the alchemical work are evident in the books individually and as a series?

> • How does understanding the alchemical themes and images of the series improve our understanding of the books and their power to charm and delight young and old around the world?

Here at last is the *Harry Potter* part of literary alchemy you came for! Let's jump right in.

How can we tell if Ms. Rowling is intentionally using alchemical imagery?

A question I am always asked when I say Ms. Rowling is writing alchemical literature in the tradition of English Literature is how I know she is. The implication, sometimes voiced, is that I have an agenda to show she is doing this in order both to support my thesis that she is writing within the traditions of the children's fantasy genre among others (rather than being an ex machina monster or goddess that fell from the sky) and to demonstrate a side-thesis, that, in being a traditional English writer she is almost certainly a Christian writer, whatever her orthodoxy. These questioners I have found will accept no proof as sufficient reason to accept my common sense observations and alchemical thesis other than Ms. Rowling's explicit testimony that she is an alchemist, the illegitimate daughter of C. S. Lewis, or a secret Bishop in the Church of Scotland.

In late February, 2007, an interview with Ms. Rowling from 1998 was posted on the encyclopedic Accio-Quote.org. She said in this interview, point blank, that, in fact, the books are suffused by alchemy, which sets both "the parameters of magic" and "internal logic of the series:"

> "I've never wanted to be a witch, but an alchemist, now that's a different matter. To invent this wizard world, I've learned a ridiculous amount about alchemy. Perhaps much of it I'll never use in the books, but I have to know in detail what magic can and cannot do in order to set the parameters and establish the stories' internal logic." Simpson, Anne. "Face to Face with J K Rowling: Casting a spell over young minds," The Herald, 7 December 1998;   www.accio-quote.org/articles/1998/1298-herald-simpson.htm

> "Most of the spells are invented, but some of them have a basis in what people used to believe worked. We owe a lot of our scientific knowledge to the alchemists!" http://www.accio-quote.org/articles/1999/0099-amazon-staff.htm

If the author herself had not said that alchemy is largely what the magic of Harry Potter is (and, searching Accio-Quote, she has not mentioned it again in her many interviews since 1998), how could we know or test the books to see if it is or isn't? I suggest the following tests for evidence in support of the alchemical thesis in addition to the author's 1998 testimony:

- First, the evidence should be fairly clear – we shouldn't have to be practicing alchemists ourselves to see the connections and the evidence shouldn't need to be tortured and twisted to fit the procrustean bed;

• Second, the books should show both a design akin and parallel to the stages of the alchemical work and a bevy of imagery and symbols that are taken from this same work; and

• Third, this evidence should not have another as likely or believable explanation from traditional or conventional literature.

These three tests take us to our second question!

What signs of alchemy are evident in the books individually and as a series?

The first test is one of clarity. Is the alchemy something an unprejudiced observer and non-specialist can see without squinting? Three pieces of evidence demonstrate that the alchemy connection screams from these books and is not tortured or even teased from them: book titles, alchemical characters, and Harry's turning into his opposite in each book.

The title of the first book in the *Harry Potter* series, as you all know, is *Harry Potter and the Philosopher's Stone.* Only Arthur Levine's brilliant marketing decision to change the title to *Sorcerer's Stone* obscures the alchemical title. If the man in the street knows anything about alchemy, it is that alchemists pursued the Philosopher's Stone to turn lead into gold. Even P. G. Wodehouse wrote a Jeeves novel based on the Philosopher's Stone!

The characters, too, point right at alchemy. Albus Dumbledore, we learn on the first train ride to Hogwarts by reading his Chocolate Frog card – which distinction we learn in *Order of the Phoenix* he treasures above all his titles – is an alchemist of some renown, even a partner of the famous Nicolas Flamel. This relationship, it turns out, is the key to unraveling the mystery of what is hidden at Hogwarts in Harry's first year.

Hermione Granger's name, as are several of the names in the books, has an especially obvious alchemical reference in it. 'Hermione' is the feminine form of 'Hermes', who, beside being the Greek messenger god (Mercury), was also the name of the great alchemist 'Hermes

Trismegistos' in whose name countless alchemical works were written through the centuries. Her initials (Hg) and her parents being dentists are also pointers to Mercury, which part Hermione plays in Harry's alchemical transformation.

Harry's Transformations from Lead to Gold

The alchemical work is about changing the soul from lead to gold, from sin and failing to virtue, in order to create a wo/man that is the union of opposites. We can see this in the title character's transformations in each *Harry Potter* book.

Philosopher's Stone: As the novel opens, Harry is an orphan child who lives in fear of his aunt and uncle and without any knowledge or delight in who he is. By book's end, he shows himself a champion of remarkable courage and daring – and reconciled to both his parents' death and destiny as a wizard.

Chamber of Secrets: Harry begins the book as a prisoner both of the Dursleys and of his own self-doubts and self-pity; at the heroic finish in the morality play acted out in the *Chamber*, he is the liberator of Ginny and vanquisher of Tom Riddle, who is an incarnation of selfishness and self-importance.

Prisoner of Azkaban: Harry blows up Aunt Marge on Privet Drive because he cannot overlook her slights of his parents; in the crucible of the Shrieking Shack, he rescues the man who betrayed his parents to Voldemort by offering his own life as a shield to him! Unforgiving judgment to Semi-divine Mercy in a year.

Goblet of Fire: Harry begins the book consumed by thoughts of what others think of him, his external person; by book's end, after trials with Ron, the Hogwarts student body, and a dragon, he is able to shrug off without a dent or tear a Daily Prophet hatchet job beaconed to all corners of the Wizarding World.

Order of the Phoenix: Harry is consumed by a desire of news at the beginning of the latest book. He struggles to listen to television reports, agonizes over the lack of reports from friends, and wanders his neighborhood in search of newspapers in trash cans. At the end, he is aware of his need to turn inward and discover and strengthen his inner life; his extroverted dependence on the outer world and events has become his point of vulnerability by which Voldemort manipulates him (and causes Sirius' death).

Half-Blood Prince: Having been broken down in the heat and drought of Phoenix, Harry is rebuilt and purified in the cold and damp of *Prince*'s ablutions for the revelations of the *Deathly Hallows*. Harry begins to reveal himself as the Gryffindor/Slytherin androgyne.

The titles of the books, the explicit and near-explicit references to alchemy in the names and lives of key characters and the transformations of the title character are all nearly transparent pointers to Rowling's use of literary alchemy.

Are both the design and predominant imagery of the books alchemical?

Our second test is about "depth." Do we see alchemy in the weave of this literary tapestry, beyond surface elements? Yes, we can.

This will require some knowledge and reference to details and to stages of the alchemical work the average reader cannot be expected to know, but the matrix and imagery of the *Potter* series are indeed from the alchemical work. The design, the predominant symbolism, and the themes of these books are derived from traditional literary alchemy

Let's start our look at "design" with a pretty straightforward alchemical image. The alchemical work is a series of purifications of a base metal from lead into gold that is accomplished by dissolving and recongealing the metal via the action of two principal reagents. These reagents reflect the masculine and feminine polarity of existence: 'alchemical sulfur' represents the masculine, impulsive and red pole and 'quicksilver' or 'alchemical mercury' the feminine and cool complementary antagonist. Together and separately these reagents and catalysts advance the work of purifying a base metal into "corporeal light" or gold.

Harry's two best friends are Ron Weasley and Hermione Granger. Ron, the red-head, passionate boy and Hermione, the brilliant, cool young woman are Harry's never fail companions. They are also living symbols of alchemical sulfur (Ron) and mercury (Hermione), being the feminine of the Greek name for Mercury. Together, and, more obviously, in their disagreements and separation, Harry's friendship with Ron and Hermione transform him from lead to gold in each book, as discussed above.

[For those involved in the "shipping" debate about whether Hermione was meant for Ron or Harry in the end, this point suggests the eventual love match of Ron and Hermione. "Medieval alchemists adopted from the Arabs the theory that all metals were a synthesis of mercury and sulphur, whose union might achieve various degrees of harmony. A perfectly harmonious marriage of the mother and father of metals might produce gold" (Mark Haeffner, *Dictionary of Alchemy*, Aquarian Press, 1994, p. 147). When Ron and Hermione stop quarreling and connect, as we saw in *Prince*, Harry's "perfection" is near.]

The Stages of Alchemy - The Cycle of the Series

Maybe you knew about the action of contraries in alchemy and about mercury and quicksilver, the *solve et coagula*; it is the background to all the twins in Shakespeare and the remarkable pairings of men and women in his better plays (think *Taming of the Shrew* or *Romeo and Juliet*). Probably fewer people know the stages of the alchemical 'Great Work' and what happens in each. What has often been described as Harry's annual hero journey is in fact the cycle of the alchemical transformation – and each stage of the work, in case you need a road sign, has a character named for it in the *Harry Potter* books.

The first stage of the alchemical work is dissolution, usually called the **nigredo** or the black stage. In the black, initial stage, "the body of the impure metal, the matter for the Stone, or the old, outmoded state of being is killed, putrefied, and dissolved into the original substance of creation, the *prima materia*, in order that it may be renovated and reborn in a new form" (Abraham, op. cit., p. 135). Sirius Black is named for this stage of the work; the book in which he died, *Phoenix*, was the nigredo novel of the series.

The second stage of alchemical transformation of lead into gold is the **albedo** or white work. It follows the ablution or washing of the calcified matter at the bottom of the alembic, the washing of which causes it to show the 'peacock's tail' (*cauda pavonis*) or the colors of the rainbow before turning a brilliant white. "When the matter reaches the albedo it has become pure and spotless" (Abraham, op. cit., p. 5). Albus Dumbledore is the character with the 'white' name; 'Albus' is Latin for 'white, resplendent.' Frequently used symbols of the albedo stage of the work in pictorial representations and descriptions of it are Luna (Latin for the moon) and a lily. ***Half-Blood Prince*** was Albus' book in many ways because it featured his tutorials with Harry to prepare him for Horcrux seek-and-destroy before combat with Lord Voldemort – and because of his fall from the Astronomy Tower, planned or unplanned, at book's end.

The third and last stage of the chemical work is the **rubedo** or the red stage.

> "When the matter of the stone has been purified and made spotless at the albedo it is then ready to be re-united with the spirit (or the already united spirit and soul). With the fixation, crystallization or embodiment of the eternal spirit, form is bestowed upon the pure, but as yet formless matter of the Stone. At this union, the supreme chemical wedding, the body is resurrected into eternal life. As the heat of the fire is increased, the divine red tincture flushes the white stone with its rich, red colour… The reddening of the white matter is also frequently likened to staining with blood."
>
> (Abraham, op.cit, p. 174).

Rubeus Hagrid has the red name; 'rubeus' is Latin for 'red' (the Latin for 'black', of course is 'niger' so Sirius' name is translated to English 'black' for obvious reasons). A common symbol of the red work and the Philosopher's Stone is the red lion, the house mascot for Gryffindor.

I offer for your consideration the possibility that the formula for each book thus far is a trip through these stages. Briefly, the black work or dissolution is the work done on Harry at Privet Drive by the Dursleys and in the dungeons by Snape at Hogwarts. The white work is Harry's study time or year at Hogwarts under the watchful eye of the white alchemist, Albus Dumbledore, in combination with and painful separation from Ron, Hermione, or both.

The red work is the crucible scene underground or in a graveyard in which Harry always dies a figurative death and is saved by love in the presence of a Christological symbol. The resurrection at story's end each year is the culmination of that year's cycle and transformation. The cycle then closes with congratulations and explanations from the master alchemist and a return to the Dursleys for another trip through the cycle. More on the three stages in a moment.

The Nigredo

Closer to my heart is the possibility that alchemy is the explanation for the structure and bizarre events of *Harry Potter and the Order of the Phoenix*. I went out on a limb in my first book and predicted that *Phoenix* would be the white stage of the alchemical work or albedo and that it would culminate in the death of Albus Dumbledore after he told all to Harry about his destiny. Need I say I was wrong? I thought that the Wizarding World couldn't get much blacker or Harry more burned down than he was in *Goblet of Fire* so that the nigredo or black work was over.

Again, how wrong I was… *Order of the Phoenix* from its hot and dry beginnings and sojourn in the House of Black to the police state of Dolores Umbridge ('grieving resentment' or 'grievous shadow' - 'a woman who blocks the sun'?) and the death of Sirius Black in the Department of Mysteries is the nigredo volume of the *Harry Potter* series.

Harry, literally and figuratively, is burnt up, broken down or dissolved, and bled until everything that he thought he was – Quidditch seeker, Ron and Hermione's superior, pet of Dumbledore, lover of Hogwarts, son and spitting image of a great man, victim of the Dursleys, valiant enemy of Snape, even his being the hero and man of action in time of crisis – are taken from him or revealed as falsehoods. The boundaries of his world collapse; the Dementors come to Little Whinging and Aunt Petunia knows about them. Privet Drive is no longer a sanctuary, however miserable, and Hogwarts is no longer edifying or any joy to him. The world is no longer separated into Good Guys, Muggles, and Death Eaters – and Harry has been reduced to his formless elements.

A kind friend and serious student of alchemy and literature in the United Kingdom, Alison Williams, wrote me at the time to say that she thought the predictions I made before *Phoenix* about Dumbledore's death were 'spot on' – only a book early. I, of course, think Alison is brilliant, especially because the events of *Half-Blood Prince* made us both seem like prophets. However you feel about *Half-Blood Prince* as albedo there is little doubt that *Order of the Phoenix* was Rowling's nigredo masterpiece. I felt shattered and undone and released from ideas of self and place throughout the book – and a new person at the end, as was our Harry.

We should note here two things that will be taken up in the alchemy practical exam at the end of this chapter. First, the importance of the play of contraries in *Phoenix*, that is, things turning into their opposites in the presence of heat, for the changes that take place in Harry. This is the heart of alchemy which is largely about the production of an alchemist who is the embodiment of these resolved contraries, what the sages called an alchemical hermaphrodite.

Second, that the nigredo stage ends before the very end of *Phoenix* with Harry cold and wet "shivering as if he lay on ice" (Chapter 36, p. 816; cf., p. 856) and sympathizing with Luna, all of which are signs of the beginning of the albedo. A similar set of changes at the end of *Half-Blood Prince* signal the beginning of the rubedo: the coupling of Ron and Hermione, the "marriage" battle over Bill Weasley's body, and the phoenix glimpsed rising from Dumbledore's tomb. The climax of the Great Work is upon us.

Imagery and Symbolism

We think of symbolism, after being trained by mechanical teachers and lifeless texts, as cardboard signs; 'this represents that.' "The white whale is a symbol for God, Mrs. Johnson," we all learned to say in 10th grade English. Alchemical and real literary symbolism, however, is a different beastie entirely than what we hated in school. An authentic symbol is a means of passage and of grace between what is real and the shadow world of time and space. As Martin Lings, author of *Symbol and Archetype*, wrote in his book on the mysticism and alchemy in Shakespeare's plays:

> Symbolism is not arbitrary, but is based on the very nature of things, on the make-up of the universe. According to all cosmological and metaphysical doctrines, whether Eastern or Western, earthly phenomena are nothing other than the shadows or reflections of spiritual realities. The symbolism of a thing is its power to recall its higher reality, in the same way that a reflection or shadow can give us a fleeting glimpse of the object that casts it; and the best symbols – the only ones worthy to be used in sacred art – are those things which are most perfect of their kind, for they are the clearest reflections,

the sharpest shadows, of the higher reality which is their archetype (*Secret of Shakespeare*, Aquarian Press, 1984).

The authors of this English tradition were no dummies. Shakespeare, Milton, Herbert, Donne, Blake, Joyce, Lewis, Charles Williams, Tolkien – the reason they write in alchemical symbols is because they are what Lings calls "the best symbols", "the clearest reflections… of the higher reality." These symbols do the job literature and drama set out to do.

Joanne Rowling is no dummy either. Her books are quite simply stuffed with alchemical images for our edification and transformation in the alchemy of reading. Here are three quick examples: the images in *Goblet of Fire*, in *Order of the Phoenix*, and the gang of doppelgangers in all the books.

Goblet of Fire Alchemical Images

The events of the Tri-Wizard Tournament and Harry's preparation for each trial by fire, water, or labyrinth are wonderfully engaging and fantastic in the root sense of that word. You should know, too, that each is from the alchemical work. A quick review of the tasks and search of guides to alchemical imagery in literature reveals the role in the Opus Alchymicum of dragons, the egg, the prefect's bath and water trial, the labyrinth and the graveyard resurrection and fight.

- **dragons**: symbols of matter at the beginning of the work being resolved into philosophical sulphur and mercury (Abraham, p. 59)

- **the egg**: "the alchemist's vessel of transmutation in which the birth of the philosopher's stone takes place…; also known as the griffin's egg" (Abraham, p. 66)

- **the bath**: "the secret, inner, invisible fire which dissolves and kills, cleanses and resurrects the matter of the Stone in the vessel" (Abraham, p. 17)

- **water immersion/flood**: "One of the alchemist's maxims was, 'Perform no operation until all be made water' (Eliade, *Forge*, p. 153). "A symbol of the dissolution and putrefaction of the matter of the Stone during the black nigredo stage" (Abraham, p. 78)

- **labyrinth**: "the dangerous journey of the alchemist through the opus alchymicum…. While in the labyrinth of the opus, illusion and confusion reign and the alchemist is in danger of losing all connection and clarity" (Abraham, p. 113)

- **grave**: "the alchemist's vessel during the nigredo" In alchemical lore, frequently a copulating couple are buried and die but, in their death, their spirits are joined and the Hermaphrodite body rises from the grave. This is the alchemical ending of *Romeo & Juliet* and why their deaths resolve their families feud (Abraham, p. 90)

All the alchemical images of Harry's four Tri-Wizard tasks are preparatory for the black stage of the great work or nigredo, to come in *Order of the Phoenix*. How did I miss it? (It was the reason I thought the nigredo was over!)

Order of the Phoenix Alchemical Images

Maybe you think these images and their sequence in *Goblet of Fire* was happenstance, a weird coincidence? Let's take a quick look at the alchemical symbols in *Order of the Phoenix*:

- **Nigredo:** As mentioned above, the real Black work happens in *Order of the Phoenix*. Harry has been undone by his experiences – he knows his parents aren't gods, he can't play quidditch, his own lack of self-awareness causes his godfather's death, he can't act at will, he can't get information, God/Dumbledore is strangely absent, the world hates him, he suffers privately for the truth ("I will not tell lies"), and his friends are honored before him. This dissolution (nigredo), though, is not his purification (albedo) and so we are left at book's end with only the formless dregs of Harry's character, which, frankly, aren't pretty.

- **The Black King:** Kingsley Shacklebolt is not a token black character but an alchemical reference to the "black king." The king of the alchemical work must die, usually by drowning, and "at this stage the matter is at its blackest black and is known as the black king" (Abraham, p. 111).

69

• **Dung**: Sirius and his friends call Mundungus Fletcher ('world-filth arrow maker') "Dung" as an affectionate nickname. Given the subject of this book, it is also a hoot that dung was the heat source for the first stage of the alchemical work and even "became a name for the matter from which the miraculous, rejuvenating elixir or Stone was made" (Abraham, p. 62). Expect big things from Dung.

• **Luna**: "Luna is the bride, the white queen, consort of King Sol. She is the moist, cold, receptive principle which must be united with Sol, the dry, hot, active principle in the chemical wedding" (Abraham, p. 120). A girl friend for hot and dry – burned to a cinder – Harry? Just in time: Luna "symbolizes the attainment of the perfect white stage, the albedo, where the matter of the Stone reaches absolute purity" (Abraham, pp. 119-120). No surprise that Harry and Luna were a couple in *Half-Blood Prince*, albeit only to one party…

• **Caput Mortuum**: One of the weirder images of *Order of the Phoenix* is the heads of dead house elves lining the stairway at the House of Black ('house' by the way is alchemical language for alembic or vessel). I first thought Ms. Rowling was pointing graphically to the sufferings of house elves and their disdainful treatment of these 'Kreachers' (which leads to horrible consequences for everyone). Which she may well be doing – but 'head of the dead' is also symbol for – what else? – "the initial stage of the opus, the black nigredo" (Abraham, p. 31). How appropriate for wall hangings in the House of Black!

• **James/Lily**: James Potter and Lily Evans at last become three dimensional in *Order of the Phoenix* and we get to see the reason or at least one experience that causes Snape to hate Harry so much. Harry gets to watch his 15 year old father, of whom we are told again he is almost a mirror image, and learns that his dad was something of a conceited bully whom his mother at that age despised. 'Lily' is synonymous in the alchemical work with 'Luna' (see above and Abraham,

p. 117-18). 'James', incidentally, is an alchemical name; St. James is the patron saint of alchemists (Roob, op. cit., p. 700).

• **Phoenix**: And how about the title of this book and the sacrificial bird of this title, the loyal hero that prevented my prediction of Dumbledore's death from coming true in *Phoenix*? Sure enough, the phoenix is an alchemical "symbol of renewal and resurrection signifying the philosopher's stone, especially the red stone attained at the rubedo, capable of transmuting base metals into pure gold" (Abraham, p. 152). The raven, in contrast, is symbol of the nigredo, as by now you might have guessed with the several Ravenclaw players featured in *Phoenix*.

And, believe me, there are more! A quick run through one Alchemical Imagery dictionary threw light on all the following subjects and symbols featured in the *Potter* series, each with an alchemical meaning that deepens Rowling's decision to use them in her story: bee (Dumbledore), blood, bolthead, castle, cervus fugitivus (stag), raven (raven's head), cupid, eagle, griffin, lazy Henry (Harry), house, melancholia, metamorphosis (Tonks), night, orphan, red man and white woman (quarreling couple – Ron and Hermione, Bill and Fleur), king, serpent, ship, Sol, skeleton, sulphur, quicksilver, tears, toad, unicorn, wolf, and worm.

Doppelgangers

Before leaving alchemical imagery I want to mention 'doppelgangers.' This staple of 19th century Gothic and romantic fiction is of a creature or pair of creatures that have complementary figures or shadows, which shadows reveal aspects of their otherwise invisible character. Think of Stevenson's *Jekyll & Hyde*, Stoker's *Count Dracula*, Shelley's *Dr. Frankenstein* and his monster, and the *Count of Monte Cristo*. Rowling points to these shadows in her principal characters in a variety of ways:

As **Animagi**: How many animagi do we know of in the books? James, Sirius, Peter, Minerva, Rita, for starters, and I'll add Albus who certainly as a former Master of Transfiguration at Hogwarts and alchemist has mastered this trick (I bet he's the tawny owl that appears in several places). Nymphadora Tonks as a shape changer (Metamorphmagus) deserves a special mention.

Half-breeds/mudbloods/monsters: Half-breeds and mudbloods as well as two natured monsters include Hagrid, Olympe, Fleur, Lily, Tom Riddle, Hermione, Remus, Tonks again and Severus (assuming he is a vampire). Harry, because he grew up as a Muggle, has an honorary membership here.

Threshhold characters (the 'Liminal'): these are the folks in Potterworld that live in two worlds or so far to the periphery of their own worlds that they cannot fit into the usual categories (good guy or Death Eater, for instance). Snape leads this group, Dobby is a close second, Firenze, Hagrid, Remus, Peter, Neville, squibs Argus and Arabella, Mundungus, and Percy – if he seems to have crossed the threshhold in *Phoenix* – fill out the set.

Twins, Pairs, and Brothers: George and Fred, the Weasley troop, Hagrid and Grawp, the Creevey brothers, Sirius and James, Crabbe and Goyle, Ron and Hermione, Slytherin and Gryffindor, Lily and Petunia, Lily and Narcissa (flowers of the same family), Peter and Neville (a cross-generational pair of look-alikes), Harry and Dudley, and Harry and Neville (joined by the prophecy). And those Parkinsons!

Harry/Voldemort: *Order of the Phoenix* begins with three mentions of Harry's feeling that his skull has been split in two and one has to imagine it must crack right down that jagged scar. It turns out that Harry's head really is divided and he has an unwelcome guest. He isn't carrying a passenger like Quirrell or possessed as was Ginny but Harry has a double nature or shadow in his link to Voldemort – and his inability to turn inward and confront this shadow is the cause of the tragedy at book's end. Like his dad at 15, he was willingly blind to the 'back' of his 'front.' Skip to Chapter 6 (pp. 267-275) for the Horcrux connection in this link.

Magical Creatures: Double-natured beasties featured in the Hogwarts Gallery include Centaurs, Griffins, Hippogriffs, and the Sphynx with a special mention due to the phoenix , thestral, and unicorn (because they are not what they seem, namely, bird or horse or even bird/horse/dragon).

That so many characters have a twin who is their likeness or antagonistic complement and so many others who live a double existence between worlds makes this aspect of Potterworld – itself divided between Magic and Muggle domains – oddly invisible to many. It's everywhere and consequently "nowhere." I suggest for your consideration that this pairing or unity in division is a central theme of the *Harry Potter* books – and that it has an alchemical meaning.

The activity of alchemy is the chemical marriage of the imbalance ("arguing couple") of masculine sulphur and feminine quicksilver. These antipodal qualities have to be reconciled and resolved, 'die' and be 'reborn' after conjunction before recongealing in a perfected golden unity. Certainly the similarity of this language to the Christian spiritual path is a remarkable one – and understandably. The symbols of the completion of the alchemical work are also traditional ciphers for Christ, the God/Man, in whose sinless two natures Christians are called to perfection in His mystical body, the Church.

But the end of alchemy is the creation of the Philosopher's Stone which is the transcendence of this imbalance, impurity, and polarity. It is also about the creation of the transcendent alchemist, the saintly God/Man often represented by a Hermaphrodite or "S/He," a person who is both male and female. Here polarity is not resolved as much as it is transcended and embodied in a harmonious unity, an incarnation of love and peace.

In your coming Practical Exam we'll see how the duality in every character that is not a pure-blood fascist highlights this androgynous goal of alchemy and points to the likely ending of the series, namely, the revelation of the Hogwarts Hermaphrodites. For now, let's leave these pairs with the surety that these liminal twins or doppelgangers are alchemical figures rather than accidental occurrences.

The Four Big Themes of *Harry Potter*

The four principal themes in the *Harry Potter* books are discussed in *Hidden Key to Harry Potter/Looking for God in Harry Potter*: prejudice, death, choice, and change. How do these themes appear in the light of alchemy? I think Rowling's meaning crystallizes around the alchemical perspective of these ideas.

Death is the necessary part of the alchemical work; only in the death of one thing, from the alchemical perspective, is the greater thing born. (Alchemists frequently cite John 12:24 and Christ's Crucifixion and Resurrection; Abraham, p. 28). But Love, the action of contraries and their resolution, transcends death; it is what brings life out of death, even eternal life and spiritual perfection. This is a direct match with Rowling's message about how to understand death and love.

Alchemy is about transformation from lead to gold, the spiritual work of human life. Each *Harry Potter* novel is a depiction of the process by which Harry is transformed – and each time we read and identify with his experience we as readers are changed by this alchemy of literature, too.

Harry's changes have always come as consequences of his heroic choices; Dumbledore has never failed to let us know in his farewell talks that it is one's choices that determine who we will be not just our birthright (if we have any). But the complement of choice or free will is fate and destiny – and this complement to choice appears in *Order of the Phoenix* via the Prophecy of which Harry is supposedly the fulfillment.

Rowling is resolving the traditional chestnut of fate and free will alchemically; Harry has a destiny in this prophecy, but he will only fulfill this destiny through his ability to make right choices. This again echoes the Christian/alchemical message that we are created as images of God, but, in order to become His likeness, we must die to the old, fallen man in us, and choose rightly the means to our perfection.

Looking for Better Explanations than Literary Alchemy

So we arrive at long last to the third and last question in our tests of the evidence for or against Joanne Rowling being an alchemical writer in the tradition of the English 'Greats'. Are there better or just simpler explanations than all this arcane imagery from a medieval sacred science? I can think of three contenders for an easier way to see it.

Ms. Rowling's imagination: This is the simplest alternative and one I hear often enough, namely, that Ms. Rowling's use of alchemical imagery is either a happy coincidence or a case of artists in different places and times being inspired by the same playful muse. Frankly, this perspective is borderline misogynist (can you imagine someone saying it about a man of Ms. Rowling's educational pedigree) and insulting to her genius as an author. Really, "it just happened"? Why not say she just "got lucky"?

Imaginative literature 'compost': Ms. Rowling has said in several interviews that her books' inspirations are drawn from the compost in her mind of all the books she has read. Certainly this includes all the imaginative literature and the Great books, poems, and plays of her native tradition. She did not say, however, that her inspirations went without careful sifting and plotting (years before the first book was written). Her characters, plots, themes, and imagery were not items that she picked from the top of her imaginative pile without discernment. Again, no accidents – and not simpler or better than the argument from alchemy and tradition.

Classical Literary 'compost': No different than the above compost except that this pile reflects Ms. Rowling's classical education. Yes, Homer and Virgil are in the pile, too, and other non-Englishmen, but the further back we go in time the more traditional and alchemical the view of the cosmos and the human person. Rowling definitely battles on the side of the Ancients in Swift's *Battle of the Books*.

There is no simpler or better explanation for the preponderance of alchemical references, themes, structures, images and symbols in the *Harry Potter* books than the common sense notion that she is writing brilliantly alchemical literature. Please note I am not saying alchemy is everything or the only thing you need to appreciate and understand what the books are about; it is one of five keys, after all. However, understanding alchemy and its usage in the tradition and in these books will take one a long way in appreciating the heights and depths of Ms. Rowling's genius.

Conclusion

The questions we should all be asking during this *Harry Potter* interlibrum period are these:

- Why are these books so popular?
- What need do they fill?
- What longing do they satisfy?

No book in our time or any other time (with the possible exception of Dickens' serials) has ever created such a following and diverse readership. We should be asking ourselves "Why?"

The alchemical connection helps answer this question. It points to the facts that:

• Joanne Rowling clearly understands both 'alchemy in literature' and the 'alchemy of literature.' Like Harry in Riddle's diary, we fall into her books and are carried through a Magic Mountain roller coaster experience of Harry's alchemical transformation and the kaleidoscope of symbols, themes, and imagery from centuries of literary usage.

• One reason the books are so popular is that they satisfy the need in us, born in a profane culture without heroes or avenues of transcendent experience – a materialist world in which such experience is not considered possible by "serious people" – of at least an imaginative experience of human transformation and perfection. We get this experience in our identification with Harry and we are better for it, more human even, for having been for a while at least in the alembic vessel changing from spiritual lead to gold, dying and rising from the dead.

• In brief, Joanne Rowling's novels are so popular because her works transform her readers via imaginative identification, experience, catharsis, and resurrection.

Please highlight *solve et coagula* in your notes, the aim of alchemy being the emergence of the Philosopher's Stone and Hermaphrodite, and the use of alchemical structures and themes in English literature for centuries. If we've won the beachheads that alchemy was not just stupid chemistry, that it's hard to read any survey of the better plays, poems, and novels in our language without some familiarity with literary alchemy, and that Ms. Rowling has built and stuffed her books with it, we're ready for some Arithmancy.

Alchemical Arithmancy (AP)

It's time to review what we learned in "Alchemy 101" and jump into the "Advanced Placement" alchemy course to get ready for our Practical Application final exam.

Alchemy 101 taught us that alchemy wasn't "quack chemistry" but an ancillary science with several revealed traditions for purification and a return to an Edenic state. We also learned that it was largely a science of correspondences in which repeated cycles of "expansion and contraction," *solve et coagula*, were used to reduce the subject to prime matter for recongealing as a unity of these contrary tendencies, the alchemical Androgyne.

Alchemy was pushed aside by materialist chemistry in the seventeenth century but lives on in the symbols and structures and even the language of English poems, plays, and novels. From Chaucer and Shakespeare to C. S. Lewis and James Joyce, much of the best English literature is laden with alchemy because the arts share the goal of transforming their subjects/readers through identification and catharsis. There is a host of guides and dictionaries to help the alchemical novice with obscure references and even an academic journal devoted just to this subject ("Cauda Pavonis").

We are interested in this because Joanne Rowling is the most recent and the most successful literary alchemist in the history of English letters. Her *Harry Potter* books feature alchemical themes, symbols, and characters in relatively transparent ways, from "Hermione Granger" being a stand-in for alchemical mercury or quicksilver (Hermes = Mercury, 'Hg' is the periodic table abbreviation for chemical mercury, her parents are dentists, the only profession that works with mercury, etc.) to her choice of titles. *Philosopher's Stone* is not especially subtle.

Now it's time to crunch some numbers. You've probably asked yourself what Hermione has been studying with Prof. Vector in Arithmancy all these years. Or maybe you've been struck by all the 7s, 4s, and 2s in the book and wanted to know if this was just a fetish or an arcane numerology peculiar to Hogwarts. The second level of studies, to get you from "recognition" to "knowing what to look for," is about these numbers as they work in *Harry Potter* and the traditional cosmology or worldview they reflect.

We'll start at the top: the number 7.

Why Seven is the "Most Powerfully Magic Number"

Let's start with why there are seven books and why Tom Riddle, Jr., thinks that seven Horcruxes are a sure pass to immortality. The answer to "the seven question" also explains why the Great Work of alchemy is often described as a seven stage process and even why there are seven days of the week, seven drawers in Moody's trunk, and seven players on a Hogwarts Quidditch team.

Seven is the number of transcendence or divinization.

Every *Harry Potter* book is an alchemical drama and the whole series is, too. The alchemical work, though often represented by three colors as beginning-middle-and-end "stages" (black followed by white followed by red), is a seven part cycle of transformation. This is why there are seven *Harry Potter* novels. Even Lord Voldemort understands that seven is more than a symbol for a quantity greater than six but less than eight. As he says to Professor Slughorn in their first discussion of Horcruxes:

> "Yes, sir," said Riddle. "What I don't understand, though – just out of curiosity – I mean, would one Horcrux be much use? Can you only split your soul once? Wouldn't it be better, make you stronger, to have your soul in more pieces, I mean, for instance, isn't seven the most powerfully magic number, wouldn't seven -?" (*Half-Blood Prince*, Chapter 23, p. 498)

Unfortunately, Professor Slughorn interrupts young Riddle at this point so we miss his lesson in demonically applied arithmancy. We can guess from context and traditional numerology, though, that Riddle's unfinished question would end "wouldn't seven Horcruxes effectively make you immortal and God-like?" I have read just enough fandom "New Age" alchemy speculations, nonsense about chakras, and even cut-and-paste layovers of western church sacraments to *Harry Potter* novels to realize that the meaning and symbolism of numbers fascinates people but largely escapes their understanding. They need a class with Professor Vector.

This misunderstanding is what we should expect in a historical period aptly described as "the reign of quantity," in which age numbers are only understood as ciphers for specific quantities. Traditionally, numbers represent qualities and relations primarily and quantities only incidentally. Here is a corrective "crash course" in traditional numerology as it relates to the number seven from an essay by Martin Lings, a tutorial student and friend of C. S. Lewis, as well as a brilliant poet, critic, and apologist for tradition in his own right. He explains why seven is the number representing the perfection of the human being as a microcosm of creation:

> In the series of seven figure numbers there are two that stand out from the rest as having an essentially Divine significance, namely, one and seven; between them, as between alpha and omega, is enacted the whole drama of existence. One is the Creator; two signifies the Spirit [in a footnote, Lings explains that "the Spirit, in Islamic doctrine, is the summit and synthesis of all creation, opening to the Uncreated and therefore possessing implicitly, if not explicitly, the Uncreated Aspect that is none other than the Third Person of the Christian Trinity"], three Heaven, four earth, and five man, whose place is as a quintessence at the centre of the four elements, the four points of the compass, and the four seasons of the year, which characterize the earthly state.
>
> But man cannot fulfill his function as mediator between Heaven and earth without the transcendent dimension of depth and of height, the vertical axis that passes through the centre of all degrees of existence and is none other than the Tree of Life. This superhuman dimension is implicit in the central point of the quintessence but does not become explicit until the number five is transcended. It is through six that the centre becomes the axis, that the seed becomes the tree, and six is the number of primordial man in the state in which he was created on the sixth day. As universal mediator he measures out, with his six directions, the whole of existence, and beyond six lies that from which existence proceeds and to which it returns. And God blessed the seventh day, and

sanctified it: because that in it He had rested from all his work (Genesis II:3).

Seven thus signifies repose in the Divine Center. From that point of view it is the symbol of Absolute Finality and Perfection, appearing in this world as a Divine Seal upon earthly things, as in the number of the days of the week, the planets, the sacraments of the [western] church, and many other septenaries, the mention of which would take us too far from our subject.

Martin Lings, 'The Seven Deadly Sins in the Light of the Symbolism of Number,' *Symbol and Archetype: A Study in the Meaning of Existence*, Quinta Essentia, pp. 98-99)

This is not "just a Christian thing," incidentally – Lings was a Sufi. Every religious tradition has its seven-based alchemy, and even Plato was consumed by the primacy of seven (the number of citizens in his ideal Republic? 5,040, which is "seven factorial," 7 x 6 x 5 x 4 x 3 x 2 x 1).

One of the septenaries echoing the Genesis creation account that Lings means here is the seven stage alchemical work. He quotes at length from Titus Burckhardt's *Alchemy* in his magisterial *The Secret of Shakespeare* to reveal the alchemical structures and meaning of *Anthony and Cleopatra*, *Romeo and Juliet*, and *The Tempest*, among others. Burchardt's exposition of the meaning of alchemy, too, largely depends on the correspondence of the seven planets and metals within the rotation of the elements (see *Alchemy*, Penguin books, 1972, Chapters 4 and 5).

Alchemy is a seven stage work because its aim is to restore the alchemist to the state of Adamic or primordial perfection (number 6) and transcend this for communion or apotheosis with God (number 7). This restorative labor in correspondence with the purification of metals requires seven turnings or stages in which all the imperfections and imbalances within the soul are resolved by reagents causing the psyche to expand contract (the *solve et coagula* of alchemical formula).

Magical education is a seven year process, not seven days, but like the alchemical work and the metaphysical week, it is about human transformation or "transfiguration." Ms. Rowling suggests this via the wizard game, Quidditch, where two teams each have seven players. A

Seeker, flying above the fray for the most part, seizes a Golden Snitch, an elusive golden ball with wings. This septenary of players is a pointer to alchemy both in the "seeking of gold" as its end and in the description of the Golden Snitch.

The popular edition of Burckhardt's ***Alchemy: Science of the Cosmos, Science of the Soul*** (Penguin Books, 1972) has a Golden Snitch on its cover in a reproduction of a 17th century alchemical drawing, produced on the cover of this book (the "winged sphere" represents *materia prima*, p. 194; the flying golden ball appears frequently in other alchemy texts). Hogwarts, the magical academy, is an alchemical seven year work in its games and studies – and to be sure we get this point, we know the School is directed by Albus Dumbledore, who, his chocolate frog card tells us, is "particularly famous... for his work in alchemy" (***Philosopher's Stone***, Chapter 6, pp. 102-103).

So why does the young Tom Riddle, Jr., who understands that seven is "the most powerfully magic number," want to create seven Horcruxes to achieve immortality?

Riddle's plan is to ape the "magic of transcendence" (by which immortality is rightly achieved) by creating a path of ego that is the inversion of the traditional way of communion. The alchemist's way is the path of resolving the contraries of hot and cold, dry and moist, that make up the four elements and four humors of the human person to become the Quintessence and then climb the Tree of Life to the Divine Center. Riddle prefers to "hold on" to his individual imbalances and imperfections. The Dark Lord wants his ego, the most ephemeral aspect of the human person with the closest ties to the body and the block to real immortality, to be eternal.

As the saying goes, if you want things to stay the same, everything will have to change. Riddle's seven-fold way to immortality through Horcruxes is the right way turned upside-down. Instead of peaceful resolution of "otherness" by love and seeking peace in balance, his Horcruxes are a satanic way that asserts his being personally above any principle; in short, his way is the way of murder, materialism, and idolatry. He pours his soul into material objects representing the four elements (represented by the mythic four founders of Hogwarts) after asserting his greater right to life than others by acts of murder. Riddle's seven-staged path is a return and repose only in himself rather than in

God – and, therefore, this materialistic atheism makes him less human as he proceeds down the path. Ms. Rowling represents this devolution via the changes in his physical appearance from something handsome and deiform to something demonic.

Harry, in contrast, at the end of six cycles of purification, is described by the Headmaster Alchemist as being "pure in heart" (cf., Matthew 5:8) and as having "a soul that is untarnished and whole" (*Half-Blood Prince*, Chapter 23, p. 511). Harry's job in defeating Voldemort now is to find and "destroy" the four founders' idols Lord Voldemort has created out of the pieces of his own soul, unite the four houses and the four magical brethren, and resolve at last the remaining imperfections within himself to complete the Alchemical Work's seventh stage and become the harmonious union of contraries.

Four = The World:
Four Ages, Four Elements, Four Humours, Four Cardinal Points

Four is the traditional number of "earth" or "the world of time and space." History is understood by the ancients and by modern Traditionalists as being a cycle of four ages (we live now in the last age, the "age of lead"). Matter is understood in terms of four qualities (hot, cold, wet, and dry) that combine in what are called the four elements: earth, air, fire, and water. Human beings have four humors, the balance or imbalance of which is the substance of our temperament, health, and vitality. Space is defined by the four cardinal points of the compass. Believe it or not, western buildings even have four walls because this was a representation of the world having descended from a circle (the meaning of domed buildings) or the polar Creative Word (pitched roofs).

This understanding of the world as "four" used to permeate Western culture and schooling. In the book mentioned in the introduction, *The Elizabethan World Picture*, by E. M. W. Tillyard, the author apologizes for repeating what he assumes the reader already knows about the four humors; he says this quaternary must be familiar to readers, "even to distress." I had never heard of the four humors before reading Tillyard's little book, though, and the situation hasn't improved since my high school days. My students think I'm trying to distinguish between types of comedy when I talk about the four humors. Most *Harry Potter* readers probably missed the alchemical "humor-ous" reference to Fleur as "Phlegm" beyond being a snot joke. An Elizabethan audience, in contrast, rich or poor, would have roared at the choleric women's discomfort with Bill's phlegmatic fiancée.

Seven is a number we can appreciate because of the Genesis account of Creation and the seven day week we observe (if we never think about it consciously). The rotation of the four elements and their resolution into a quintessence takes a little more work. Here's a quick introduction to the resolution of the four elements into a fifth element or quintessence.

Titus Burckhardt describes the quintessence as the hub of a four spoked wheel, the spokes being one of the four elements and the quadrants of the wheel being their respective natural qualities (e.g., the "fire" spoke bisects the "Heat" and "Dryness" quarters, the next spoke, "Earth," separates "Dryness" and "Cold," etc.). He explains the "fifth essence" at the center this way:

> Alchemically speaking, the hub of the wheel is the quinta essentia. By this is meant either the spiritual pole of all four elements or their common substantial ground, ether, in which they are all indivisibly contained. In order once again to attain to this centre, the disequilibrium of the differentiated elements must be repaired, water must become fiery, fire liquid, earth weightless, and air solid. Here, however, one leaves the plane of physical appearances and enters the realm of spiritual alchemy.
>
> Synesios writes: 'It is thus clear what the philosophers mean when they describe the production of our stone as the alteration of natures and the rotation of elements. You now see that by "incorporation" the wet becomes dry, the volatile stable, the spiritual embodied, the fluid solid, water fiery, and the air like earth. Thus all four elements renounce their own nature and, by rotation, transform themselves into one another.... Just as in the beginning there was One, so also in this work everything comes from One and returns to One. This is what is meant by the retransformation of the elements...'
>
> (Alchemy, Titus Burckhardt, Penguin, 1972, p. 96)

The seven stages return to the repose of One, the beginning of Creation, and the four elements are resolved in a single point where their qualities come to rest, the quintessence. Lyndy Abraham in *The Dictionary of Alchemical Imagery* explains how this is used in alchemical texts and literature:

> During the opus the matter for the Stone must be dissolved and returned to its primal state before it can be recreated or coagulated into the new pure form of the philosopher's stone. This cycle of *solve et coagula* or separation and union has to be reiterated many times throughout the opus. During this circulation, the elements earth, air, fire, and water are separated by distillation and converted into each other to form the perfect unity, the fifth element. This conversion takes place by unifying the qualities that each element has in common: earth which is cold and dry may be united with water through the common quality of coldness since water is cold and moist (or fluid), and air is united to fire through heat, since fire is hot and dry... In another alchemical metaphor, this process is described as the transformation of the square (four elements) into the circle (the united fifth element)....
>
> This process of transformation, of successfully converting the elements into each other, is often compared to the turning of a great wheel.... The contrary qualities of the four elements are likened to quarreling foes who must be reconciled or united in order for harmony to reign (see peace). The circulation of elements is identical with the process the alchemists describe as the conversion of body into spirit, and spirit into body, until each is able to mingle together, or unite in the chemical wedding to form a new perfect being, the philosopher's stone...
>
> (*Dictionary of Alchemical Imagery*, Lyndy Abraham, Cambridge University Press, 2001, pp. 137-138)

Ayurvedic and Taoist medicine have a conceptual framework almost identical to the Western four element theory. Acupuncture and shiatsu massage don't work except in resolving blockages or stagnation on yin and yang meridians that are kyo or jitsu, tendencies and qualities that are described in elemental terms much like those we have from the Ancient Mediterranean. Maybe this sounds laughably inane to you but this "rotation of the elements" and the "resolution of contraries" is both effective medicine and the heart of two movies you may have seen.

The two movies? "The Incredibles" and "The Fantastic Four." The cartoon "Incredibles" was a clear knock-off of the comic book "Fantastic Four," so let's look at the original foursome super group for a quintessence...

Storytellers like to use the four elements of fire, water, air, and earth to represent the power of harmony and peace and the madness of conflict and private understanding (*idios* in Greek). My favorite representation of this is *The Fantastic Four* comic books, first written by Stan Lee and drawn by Jack Kirby for Marvel Comics in the early 60s. I grew up reading these comic books and soon learned the formula (which is wonderfully preserved in the film). After the central conflict is identified, almost always against a super-powered baddie like Magneto or Dr. Doom, the team attacks him separately or disagrees about the best way to fight the baddie or offends one of the members of the team.

This disharmony proves to be a disaster. A clever villain works to encourage discord among the Four Elements team. The formula ending is when each of the Good Guys acts in harmony with the others to overcome impossible odds and defeat the enemy. Really, watching Mr. Fantastic (water), the Invisible Girl (air), the Thing (earth), and the Human Torch (duh) thrash baddies is always an alchemical morality play about the revealing and resolution of contraries.

In the remaining *Harry Potter* story, we have three sets of four that will have to be alchemically resolved and united – (1) the four principal species of magical creatures depicted in the Fountain of Magical Brethren, (2) the four Horcruxes, which objects, as possessions of the Four Founders, points to (3) the third set, the four Houses of Hogwarts. We know that these sets are story symbols for the Four Elements whose resolution in man are the quintessence of alchemy because Ms. Rowling has quite generously (and uncharacteristically) made a point of telling us this.

Not only does Harry read *Quintessence: A Quest* for Charms class in *Half-Blood Prince* (Chapter 15, p. 304) and is Fleur called "Phlegm," the bodily humor corresponding to the water element, but in interviews Ms. Rowling spells out the four elements backdrop to the four Hogwarts Houses:

> [In answer to a question about Death Eater children in the four Hogwarts Houses]
> JKR: Probably. I hear you. It is the tradition to have four houses, but in this case, I wanted them to correspond roughly to the four elements. So Gryffindor is fire, Ravenclaw is air, Hufflepuff is earth, and Slytherin is water, hence the fact that their common room is under the lake. So, again it was this idea of harmony and balance, that you had four necessary components and by integrating them you would make a very strong place. But they remain fragmented, as we know.
>
> [In answer to a question about why the Slytherins are allowed at Hogwarts]
> JKR: But [the Slytherins are] not all bad. They literally are not all bad. [Pause] Well, the deeper answer, the non-flippant answer, would be that you have to embrace all of a person, you have to take them with their flaws, and everyone's got them. It's the same way with the student body. If only they could achieve perfect unity and wholeness that means that they keep that quarter of the school that maybe does not encapsulate the most generous and noble qualities, in the hope, in the very Dumbledore-esque hope that they will achieve harmony. Harmony is the word.
> [MN/TLC interview 3, pp. 9-10]

The Headmaster we know from his chocolate frog card is an accomplished alchemist who succeeded with Nicholas Flamel in creating a Philosopher's Stone. It is as alchemist that "Dumbledore hopes" for a unification of the student body in its four houses and the purifications of its flaws rather than its dismemberment.

The Sorting Hat's "New Song" in *Order of the Phoenix* tells the story of the initial unity of the Four Founders and how they "like pillars four" had held up the school. This primordial unity, however, disintegrated into chaos like the formula failure of every Fantastic Four adventure:

The Houses, that like pillars four,
Had once held up our school,
Now turned upon each other and,
Divided, sought to rule.
And for a while it seemed the school
Must meet an early end,
What with dueling and with fighting
And the clash of friend on friend
And at last there came a morning
When old Slytherin departed
And though the fighting then died out
He left us quite downhearted.
And never since the founders four
Were whittled down to three
Have the Houses been united
As they once were meant to be.
(***Order of the Phoenix***, Chapter 11, p. 206)

The Sorting Hat ends the song with a plea for unity, as Nearly Headless Nick says it always does "when it detects great danger for the school. And always, of course, its advice is the same: Stand together, be strong from within" (***Phoenix***, Chapter 11, p. 209).

The discordant element in the four founders and their houses, if there is only one, is obviously Slytherin whose departure ages ago sealed the initial rupture. The Heir of Slytherin is known for his ability "for spreading discord and enmity" (***Goblet of Fire***, Chapter 37, p. 723) and for his inability to understand love, the power of harmony and union. The death throes of the greatest wizard-alchemist on the Astronomy Tower in his words to Draco Malfoy, offering him a life after death ("they cannot kill you if you are already dead") and sanctuary with a new identity are the last in a lifetime of alchemical efforts to reconcile Slytherin to its rightful quality within a harmonious Hogwarts.

However Christ-like these efforts, they fail – and the baton has been passed to Harry. He must find the four Horcruxes which Dumbledore believes in objects or relics belonging to each of the four Hogwarts founders. This symbolic effort may require another set of trials like the

Tri-Wizard Tournament and finding the Philosopher's Stone but this one linked to the four elements. Finding and destroying these four reservoirs of Voldemort's fragmented soul must transform Harry into the Quintessence that, like Dumbledore, can sacrifice himself for Slytherin's redemption and the return to the primordial unity.

Or something like that.

I suspect that Harry's success in destroying the Diary Horcrux in *Chamber of Secrets* and Dumbledore's spectacular difficulty in destroying the Ring Horcrux before the opening of action in *Half-Blood Prince* (assuming for a moment the latter wasn't both a staged event and effect) points to Harry's being uniquely qualified and capable in this task. Dumbledore learned the hard way that Harry has a special gift for Horcrux destruction which makes him "more valuable" than Dumbledore in the war against Voldemort. I suspect Harry has this ability for any one or all of the following three reasons:

(1) His sevenfold path of purification and spiritual perfection is antithetical and correspondingly many times more powerful in comparison to the dark magic of Lord Thingy's egotism (see above);

(2) Harry's way is dependent on his love for others and specifically on the sacrificial love of his mother, which power is one of resolution rather than destruction (love resolves contraries rather than destroy one aspect of a polarity) . As Dumbledore repeatedly tells Harry, this is Voldemort's undoing because he cannot understand or resist this power (witness his inability to possess Harry in the Ministry of Magic, Phoenix, Chapter 36); and

(3) Harry is (a) the Heir of Gryffindor or just a Gryffindor champion and, *mirabile dictu*, (b) his scar is a Horcrux that Lord Voldemort accidentally created in Godric Hollow the night of the Potter murders. Harry being himself, then, the combination and resolution of the Gryffindor-Slytherin polarity, a Hogwarts Hermaphrodite, is able to destroy or resolve the dark magic of the Horcruxes by absorbing the fragment of Voldemort's soul which each contains.

His Gryffindor courage and impetus to loving sacrifice for others combined with his acquired Slytherin nature, his realized double nature or hermaphroditism, makes Horcrux destruction possible without harm. In fact, as one writer claims, it explains his ability to outbattle the risen Voldemort at the end of *Goblet of Fire* (http://news.bbc.co.uk/go/em/fr/-/cbbcnews/hi/newsid_4690000/newsid_4697000/4697049.stm). How Harry's scar became a Horcrux is discussed in Chapter 6.

Beyond Horcrux' destruction or absorption, Harry will also have to complete the alchemical work of uniting the four Hogwarts' houses and the four species of magical creatures depicted in the Fountain of Magical Brethren. The four Houses will, I think, fall into line when the Gryffindor-Slytherin antipathy is loosened (about which more in a second). The harmony of elves, goblins, centaurs, and magical folk, on the other hand, seems a noble ambition that might take generations to realize.

The Fountain of Magical Brethren in the Ministry of Magic shows a token elf, goblin, and centaur in fawning submission to a grand wizard and witch. Though Harry drops a bag of money into the Fountain in thanksgiving for his acquittal at the Wizangamot hearing, he recognizes the statues are risible misrepresentations (*Phoenix*, Chapter 9, p. 156). This statue set is destroyed in the battle between Dumbledore and Voldemort (in which battle the centaur, elf, and goblin do Dumbledore heroic service – and the elf and goblin applaud him later). Dumbledore explains to Harry later that this destruction was a good thing because there is no harmony among the Magical Brethren due to wizard "indifference and neglect."

> "Indifference and neglect often do more damage than outright dislike....The fountain we destroyed tonight told a lie. We wizards have mistreated and abused our fellows for too long, and we are now reaping our reward" (*Phoenix*, Chapter 37, p. 834).

We know that the goblins are in a state of semi-revolt, that the house-elves are largely treated as disposable slaves, and that the centaurs are treated contemptuously by the Ministry (at least as represented by Dolores Umbridge), if the horse-men in turn have only disdain for witches and wizards. The obedience and affection shown by the statue's elf and goblin figures for Dumbledore (*Phoenix*, Chapter 36, p. 817), however, and the centaurs' tribute to Dumbledore at his funeral give us reason to hope that the Magical Brethren are capable of supporting and uniting behind a loving wizard free of prejudice.

But, as you're no doubt noticing, alchemy isn't just about four elements being reconciled. Its action, the *solve et coagula* ("dissolve and rejoin") of alchemical purification and perfection, is about the reconciliation of contraries that are pairs. Let's take a look at the number two.

Answering the Twin Enigma:
Revealing and Resolving the Remaining Contrary Pairs

Tom Riddle's name, because "Thomas" is Aramaic for "twin," is cryptonomic shorthand for "twin enigma" or "the problem with contrary pairs." As the Heir of Slytherin, the cause of division and the father of lies, Tom Riddle, Jr., is aptly named. The last book in this seven part alchemical drama will have to answer the "double trouble" in general and specifically the Harry-Lord Voldemort doppelganger.

As I explain in Chapter 2 of *Looking for God in Harry Potter*, the crossgenerational rivalry that echoes through the years from Godric and Salazar to Harry and Draco is the Gryffindor/Slytherin enmity. We see the dueling and fighting between the champions of these houses and descendants of the feuding founders in "Snape's Worst Memory" (*Phoenix*, Chapter 28) and in almost every exchange between Harry and Draco (see *Chamber of Secrets*, Chapter 11, for an actual Potter/Malfoy duel).

But Gryffindor/Slytherin hostility isn't the only hostile pairing in the books, if it is the most important. The whole world is a have/have not polarity between the Magic/Muggle peoples. As you've seen, almost every individual (except the Pure Blooded family members), has a twin aspect within him. We have Half-Bloods, a Half-Veela, a Half-Giant, a Werewolf, a Metamorphagus, and a host of magical folk that can transform themselves into animal, even insect alter egos called Animagi. The others create psychic ciphers from happy thoughts that are a signature of their character. These Patronuses are the best defense against the demon-like dementors that Rowling has said are the story symbols of depression and despair.

There are also pairs of folk akin to Frankenstein and his monster, whose conflict will have to be resolved in the last book. Harry and Draco as the representatives of traditional Gryffindor/Slytherin conflict are obvious doppelgangers. Harry as the spitting image of his late father, James, is paired again with Professor Severus Snape, whose hatred for James seems to have been extended to the look-alike son with more than a hint of sadism. These relationship nightmares are where the great divide in the Magical World, the Grand Myth with "constitutive 'other'," (postmodernist terms – see chapter 4) between Gryffindor and Slytherin are played out – and this is the polarity the alchemy of the books must resolve.

Pride and Prejudice: the Last and Greatest Polarities

If the hatred Harry feels for Draco and Severus is resolved, the Gryffindor-Slytherin gorge is more than half-bridged. We have a hint this is possible, despite Harry's denials he will ever forgive Snape. He has pitied both Severus and Draco, if only fleetingly (pitying Severus after seeing Snape's humiliating fifth year memory, Draco after the Tower breakdown). But will Harry be able to see past his Pride and Prejudice and love them? That's a stretch – but it does point out the final polarity to be revealed and resolved.

For Harry to be perfected, the "pure heart" and "whole soul" that Dumbledore says he is (at least in comparison with Lord Voldemort), which is to say, for Harry to be the Quintessence that harmonizes the various quaternaries in the story and defeat the Dark Lord, his own internal doppelganger will have to be revealed and resolved. Harry's problem is his prejudice.

Austen's novel *Pride and Prejudice* was originally titled *First Impressions* (see Rodney Delasanta's "Hume, Austen, and First Impressions" in the June/July 2003 issue of *First Things* magazine). The novel, believe it or not, is largely an argument with philosopher David Hume contra empiricism or the trusting of judgment exclusively derived from sensory impressions and physical measurement. Ms. Rowling, a devout Austen reader and admirer, is writing her books in the same vein. Her arguments against personal judgments based on anything but love and discernment of character, in brief, against pride and prejudice, are a large part of the moral virtues these books are teaching.

Harry, alas, is not immune to the failings of pride and prejudice. The revelation of how jaundiced his view is will be a very important moment in the last book. If he realizes that he is not a Dumbledore man, "through and through," because his "age-old prejudice" against Slytherins Snape and Malfoy disables his judgment and ability to love, then he will be able to love them as they are and as a Dumbledore man would.

His pride, however, is the chief obstacle to this realization and the key support of his prejudice. Harry believes to his core that hating Slytherins is not a blinding prejudice that incapacitates his love but that it is evidence of his righteousness and virtue. Short of a miraculous vision of Fawkes at home in the apartment on Spinner's End, the only way I can see Harry's pride as a Serpent Slayer being broken is for his own Slytherin nature to be revealed.

Harry is a snake pit internally, if the narrative is to be trusted. Harry speaks easily to serpents as a Parselmouth, and was even in the snake that attacked Mr. Weasley in the Department of Mysteries, courtesy of his mind-link with Lord Voldemort. Beyond speaking with and co-habitating with snakes, though, Harry also has a snake that in *Phoenix* rises up from within him to attack the Headmaster. If you dismiss that as a Voldemort-inspired nasty, then should we credit the Dark Lord for the serpent that rears his head within Harry as love for Ginny (*Half-Blood Prince*, Chapter 14, p. 286)?

Harry will probably be forced to come to terms with his resemblance to his serpentine enemies, the object of his disdain and prejudice, when he realizes his Orestian scar is a Horcrux. When Harry is forced into seeing that the serpent within him and the powers he enjoys courtesy of the Horcrux make him at least as Slytherin-esque as those he hates self-righteously and from prejudice, his Gryffindor-firster pride may break. In humility, he may be able to transcend his prejudice and embrace his enemies because he will understand how his pride and prejudice have, in large part, made them his enemies.

Why will humility break this six year old mental habit? Because pride and prejudice are, alchemically speaking, isolating and separations of the world into "self" and "other" with the elevation of self over others. Even if the prejudice is only against those who are prejudiced, the poison of pride creates a polarity – not to mention the self-contradiction (as you see every day in your friends who brag about their inability to tolerate the intolerant, only hating hatred, etc.)! Only discernment of prejudice from love, as we see from Dumbledore, love for both the prejudiced and the object of prejudice, is a liberating discernment.

This, alas, is a consciousness rarely achieved except through suffering and humility (cf., Dostoevski's maxim that suffering is the origin of consciousness). Look for a change in Harry when he realizes that he is a Horcrux himself and that the part of him which is Voldemort is what threatens all his friends. He is a Hermaphrodite now, but when he becomes aware of his duality, perhaps this self-understanding will humble him sufficiently to understand Severus and Draco differently. This Harry will be able to unite the Four Houses, rally the four groups of the Magical Brethren, and absorb or neutralize the Four Horcruxes before defeating Tom Riddle, Jr., a seventh of the man he once was, with love. This Harry will be the Quintessence, conscious alchemical androgyne, and maybe even the Philosopher's Stone himself.

Conclusion

Harry, unknowingly, may already have united the poles of Hogwarts partisanship and duality. He may have reached the point of being the Hogwarts Hermaphrodite who has joined opposites harmoniously – and Harry may not be the only or even the most important Hermaphrodite or Philosopher's Stone at Hogwarts.

To get at that, we need to look at the last stage in the alchemical work, namely, the Rubedo, or "red" stage. ***Deathly Hallows*** will almost certainly be the red stage the way ***Phoenix*** was the Black stage and ***Prince*** the White. The next chapter is a practical application of how the literary alchemy pattern may play out in the seventh book.

Alchemical Keys to the Rubedo

You have taken Alchemy 101 (chapter 2, part 1) to get an idea of what literary alchemy is about and how it permeates the *Harry Potter* novels. In AP Alchemy, you got a bucket full of arithmancy, or the symbolism of number as it relates to how Ms. Rowling puts together her books. In the practical applications test at the end of your studies, we're going to use what is rightly a text interpretation tool and turn this tool to the work of speculation.

This is only possible or desirable because we're waiting on *Deathly Hallows*. If the books are written according to alchemical formula as they seem to be, we should be able to guess some of the things that "have to" happen in the last stage of the Great Work. Let's explore what the qualities of the climax of this final alchemical process might look like in the last book of the *Harry Potter* series.

The Rubedo: The Last Stage's Signs, Characteristics, and Meaning in English Literature

Although the Great Work of alchemy is a seven step process largely about the rotation and resolution of the contrary qualities of the four elements, it is frequently described as a three phase work, with each phase assigned a color (think beginning-middle-end spread out over seven turnings of a wheel). The first stage is the nigredo or "black" phase in which the leaden material or "lead character" is loosed of all his formal characteristics and reduced by fire into prime matter or his essence. The second stage is the albedo or "white' phase in which the prime matter recongeals from the shattering and burning and is purified by washings (ablutions) for perfection. The third and last stage is the rubedo or "red" phase in which the Philosopher's Stone, blood red, emerges from within the white stone accomplished in the albedo, and the work is completed.

When I noticed that there are three characters named for the stages of alchemy – Sirius Black, Albus Dumbledore, and Rubeus Hagrid – and that the Black work seemed (to me!) to have been accomplished in *Prisoner* and *Goblet*, I predicted that Albus Dumbledore would die in the fifth book. I assumed *Phoenix* would be the albedo, that Albus would die in it, and Harry would have two books in which to lose a few battles to Voldemort and make an astonishing come-from-behind win in the last book (featuring heroic Hagrid the Red, of course).

So much for mechanical predictions made according to formula. *Phoenix* turned out to be the nigredo climax in which Sirius Black died and Harry was broken down to nothing but the essential prophecy. The nigredo begins in the fifth book – laden with nigredo imagery from the tradition of literary alchemy – because the great drama of the stories does not take part in earnest until Voldemort returns incarnate at the end of *Goblet*.

Because the book after *Phoenix* had to be the albedo, I predicted in 2003 the next book would open in a cold rain and that Dumbledore would certainly die in *Half-Blood Prince*, which I said would be as "white" and "phlegmatic" (cold/wet) as Phoenix had been "black" and "choleric" (hot/dry). Fortunately, Ms. Rowling this time made me look smart, if a few wags were heard to say that a broken clock is right twice a day, too.

Deathly Hallows will almost certainly be the rubedo of the alchemical work in the *Harry Potter* series because, after a black stage novel and a white stage book, the red stage is all that's left. What do the various dictionaries and guides to alchemy, literary and traditional, say we can expect from the final stage in this work? The nine alchemy books, historical and literary, I have looked at describe the rubedo as the stage in which:

(1) all contraries are revealed and resolved;

(2) the chemical wedding is celebrated; and

(3) the Philosopher's Stone is produced.

Let's take a look at what these three things could mean in the *Harry Potter* finale after making an important point about what the rubedo is not.

Immanence and Revelation, not Transcendence

Titus Burckhardt, Swiss Art historian and expert on traditional science and sacred art, described the three stages and colors of the alchemical Great Work in terms of the three cosmological tendencies or gunas of Hinduism:

> It is to be noticed that the three principal colours, black, white, and red (which are also to be found in Hermetically influenced heraldry) designate in Hindu cosmology the three fundamental tendencies (gunas) of the primordial materia (Prakriti).
>
> Here black is the symbolically 'down-ward' movement (tamas), which flees the luminous Origin; white is the 'upward' aspiration towards the Origin, towards the Light (sattva); and red is the tendency towards expansion on the plane of manifestation itself (rajas). With these interpretations in mind, one may be surprised to find that in alchemy it is not white, but red, that represents the final result of the work.
>
> According to the Hindu doctrine the cosmos is so constructed that firstly tamas, the down-ward striving force, throws down the anchor into darkness, then rajas, expanding in breadth, develops multiplicity, and finally sattva, like an upward-striving luminous flame, brings everything back to the Origin.
>
> The mere comparison of the three alchemical colourings with Hindu cosmology is already a clear indication of the point of view of alchemy and the precise limits of its symbolisms. After the 'spiritualization of the body' – which in a certain sense corresponds to bleaching, and supersedes the initial blackness or corruption, comes as the completion, the 'embodying of the spirit' with its royal purple-red colour.
>
> The same rhythm can also be transposed to other modes of spiritual realization. The significant point here is that the emphasis lies on the manifestation of the Spirit and not on the transcending – or the extinction laden with nigredo imagery from the tradition of literary alchemy of limit bound existence. (Burckhardt, *Alchemy*, Penguin, 1972, pp. 182-183)

Alchemy is about the resolution of contraries, the polarity of existence, but not to leave the world or become something superhuman. It is a return to the Origin or point of nonduality, and a manifestation of that point's peace, stillness, love, and timelessness to the world. Alchemy is about returning to the Garden and living with God as designed.

This is important to remember for the seventh book in two respects. First, it isn't a story of Harry's perfection in the sense of his becoming Godlike in order to defeat the Dark Lord. Harry will or won't defeat the Dark Lord because he will or will not manifest or suddenly show himself as the resolution of contraries, what you could call "love on legs."

The *Philosopher's Stone* shows itself as white in the albedo (producing silver in its lunar stage) and only becomes red and gold-producing during the rubedo from this white stone. Abraham defines the rubedo as the "reddening of the white matter of the Stone at the final stage of the opus alchymicum" (*Dictionary of Alchemical Imagery*, CUP, 1998, p. 174). The rubedo is about transformation or transcendence as much as it is simply an appearance of what already is. The last part of the work unveils the change that has happened before and has not been seen.

Second, what will be appearing will almost certainly not be a red Philosopher's Stone. We need to be looking for the human equivalent of the Stone, what the alchemists called the Androgyne, Hermaphrodite, or the *Rebis* ("Rebis" is Latin, *Res bis*, "thing twice" or "matter doubly"). A Hermaphrodite, of course, is a person who is simultaneously a man and woman, and the alchemical texts often picture the alchemist at the end of the work as a man/woman symbol of the "perfect integration of male and female energies," the yin and yang or inherent polarity in the created world. There is a Rebis pictured on the cover of this book.

I'm pretty sure we won't be seeing any transsexuals or cross-dressers in *Deathly Hallows* or literal androgynes in the grand finale (though Neville's successful defeat of his boggart in *Chamber* by feminizing Snape and the Headmaster's joke with Severus that year at the Christmas feast are meaningful). There will be characters, however, who demonstrate that they embody contrary tendencies and partisanship, who cross boundaries and bridge groups in opposition. One or more of these characters is the figurative Philosopher's Stone and rightful successor to Albus Dumbledore, master alchemist.

Now that we know what the end game is, let's look at the characteristics of this third stage.

All Contraries are Revealed and Resolved

The alchemical dictionaries describe the detailed stages of the rubedo as an imbibation (a bird drinking its bath water or final distillation of the stone's purity), a cibation or cohobation ("the nourishment of the philosopher's stone born from the union of Sol and Luna at the chemical wedding," Abraham, p. 40), a multiplication or augmentation, and a projection ("where the tincture is thrown over a base metal to transmute it into gold," Abraham, p. 132). I cannot imagine Ms. Rowling using these steps literally.

Can you see Harry taking a bath with Myrtle the night before his great battle with Voldemort, being careful to drink the bath water for good luck, having a breakfast of meat and milk with a baby bird he picked up at Bill and Fleur's wedding (born there, really), growing to hundreds of times his normal size, and then spewing magical gold-making elixir? If you can, I suggest you lie down and put some cold towels on your head. You've had too much literary alchemy in too short a time.

We're more likely to be successful looking in general terms for characteristics of the rubedo, rather than a blow-by-blow, lock-step allegory. The weather is a good place to start because it is always a display of the contraries hot and cold, dry and moist. The weather and everything "red."

The sun was beating down on Privet Drive in *Phoenix*; the nigredo's sun, as you'd expect, was a blistering hot agent of drought. The sun will return to the magical world in the rubedo final chapter, I'm sure, but a sun less of burning away formal attachments than of the sun in "sunshine" laws. The sun in the seventh year of Harry's education will be the light of dawn that reveals what has been hidden in darkness and makes the world seem golden. The close of *Half-Blood Prince* is a hint of the weather ahead. "Harry felt his heart lift at the thought that there was still one last golden day of peace left to enjoy with Ron and Hermione" (*Half-Blood Prince*, Chapter 30, p. 652).

But the heat will be like the Bunsen burner under the crucible of events in what promises to be a story that is anything but meditative.

VoldeWar II will be in full swing and the red-hot action here promises to burn away the many conflicts needing resolution by battle and revelation.

There were a host of symbols and signs of the black and white stages employed in literary alchemy. The red stage has its markers and metaphors as well. The Philosopher's Stone that the rubedo produces, for example, is known by a variety of other names:

> The Stone is endowed with many names, some of which are: elixir, tincture, medicine, panacea, balsam, arcanum, quintessence, tree, rose, lily, hyacinth, east, morning, living fountain, white stone, red stone, ruby, crystal, diamond, sapphire, Adam, paradise, Sophia, hermaphrodite, man, red king, red lion, microcosm, salvator, servator, filius macrocosmi, homunculus, sun, son, daughter, orphan, bird, Hermes bird and phoenix (***Dictionary of Alchemical Imagery***, Lyndy Abraham, p. 147).

Of these, Ms. Rowling has already cued us to look for quintessence, red king, red lion, the orphan, and the phoenix. And we have quite a few "reds" on hand to make things interesting in the red stage.

First, we have the red-headed Weasleys. These "Burrow" residents (outside the village of Ottery St. Catchpole) are not pest weasels but the heroic vermin killers famous for their loyalty to the death and for their courage in attacking beasties many times their size to protect or avenge their loved ones. Weasels have even been considered symbols of Christ because they are in legend the only animals able to kill the dreaded Basilisk/cockatrice – and to defeat this satanic animal they must sacrifice themselves (go to the Internet and see http://ww2.netnitco. net/users/legend01/weasel.htm if you think I'm making this up). Ms. Rowling is said to be a great admirer of weasels. Go figure.

The Weasleys are a large part of the Arthurian romance in *Harry Potter*, too, especially now that Merlin/Dumbledore is dead and departed. All the boys have the names of kings and knights, Arthur, Percy, and Ron being direct connections to Camelot (Ron was the name of Arthur's lance), and Ginny's real name is Ginevra (an alternate spelling of "Guinevere").

Harry Potter readers should be surprised if Bill is the last combat casualty from this clan of warriors; between Molly's vision before the boggart in 12 Grimmauld Place and the choleric passion to mix it up even Arthur displays, few of us will be surprised if Fred and George die heroically and fewer will weep if Percy falls (unless, of course, he returns to the fold before dying or, as I think likely, is revealed to have been a double agent, spying for the Order on the Ministry). We have hints of the twins' death or mourning others' deaths as early as Stone, Chapter 7, in which they sing the school song as a dirge; the figurative death or unification of twins is an alchemical topos or cliché for the end of the work (cf. Abraham, p. 206). Don't sell Fred and George any life insurance.

Next we have Rufus Scrimgeour whose first name means "red man" and whose last name is an antiquated spelling for "scrimmager" or "battler." He seems to have more steel in his spine than Fudge, but so does the average lap dog. His only actions in **Half-Blood Prince** were to arrest the innocent (Stan Shunpike – Death Eater!) and put up posters about how best to protect yourselves, posters people are too frightened to stand read. Perhaps in the rubedo his fiery nature and combative spirit will show itself to be more than the superficial concerns of a law and order politician.

Most important of the Reds, of course, and nearest to Harry's heart is Rubeus Hagrid. Hagrid is the first magical person Harry meets in his conscious life, the savior that rescued him from the Dursleys and revealed to him the magical world in which he belonged. Rubeus is a Dumbledore man, through and through, by confession (remember his outrage in the Hut on the Rock when Vernon Dursley says an unkind word about the Headmaster?) and in deed (his inability to believe ill of Severus in several books and even at the end of *Prince* because Dumbledore trusted him).

Hagrid Rubeus' sacrificial love for unlovable brother Grawp, a giant even their mother couldn't love, and for the most horrible of magical creatures (dragons are one thing, but Acromantulas and Blast-ended Skrewts? Sheesh) makes him an oversized Dumbledore who sees the inner good in everyone. As a half-giant, the beloved Keeper of Keys, I'm afraid, is also like Dumbledore, another double-natured stand-in for the God-Man who sacrificed Himself for us. This and his roguishly rouge name suggest that Hagrid won't survive the last book. Ms. Rowling in a July 2006 interview said she granted a reprieve to one character she thought would die. I'm hoping she meant Hagrid.

He doesn't have to die, after all. Unlike Black and Albus, whose stages had to end to get through the alchemical work, Rubeus as the physical embodiment of the third and last stage is the destination. And, on top of that, Ms. Rowling is anything but mechanical in her use of alchemical imagery and is not bound to kill off characters because of their names. With the death of Albus Dumbledore, we're all left thinking anybody and everybody could die in the last book. "If Dumby's dead, nobody's safe…" That doesn't mean Ms. Rowling has all the beloved characters on a "hit list," though, just that we'd believe anything is possible.

Hagrid's child-like innocence, his unconditional, sacrificial love for those despised by the world, and the possible symmetry of his death ending Tom Riddle's nightmare existence (by destroying the trophy Horcrux Riddle was given for "saving" Hogwarts from Hagrid's pet, the lie that caused Hagrid to be expelled from Hogwarts?)… these things, as much as his name, make me worry for poor Hagrid. If you're looking for positive signs, reflect on the near consonance of "Rubeus" and "Rebis," the alchemical androgyne.

More signs? Well, look for septenary deadlines – seven months, seven days, or seven hours counting down as the seven year Great Work comes to a conclusion. We might see a snake like Nagini eating its tail (the uroboros is a symbol of the rotation of the elements), a man or a man and woman suspended on a wheel as a four spoke axis (the turning of the great wheel), and a square resolved into a circle (the preferred image for this four element into quintessence formula being a house described in these geometric terms – a domed building?).

These are rather esoteric possibilities of seven counting down to one, four being reduced to quintessential unity, and black and white becoming red and ending. The more to be expected possibilities of contraries being revealed and resolved and couples joining for death and birth are plot points we read about in *Half-Blood Prince*.

In addition to the several revelations I've discussed above of secret Jekyll-Hyde-like doppelgangers, the rubedo must resolve the contraries of the central Gryffindor/Slytherin conflict in three generational rounds: Harry/Draco, Harry/Severus, and Harry/Tom Riddle, Jr. Harry must also either overcome his internal "otherness" or prejudice before or during this work so he can absorb or destroy the soul fragments in the four remaining Horcruxes, rally the four groups comprising the Magical Brethren, and unite the four Hogwarts Houses for the battle with Voldemort and the Death Eaters. If Harry successfully resolves these quaternaries, he will have become the quintessence himself, a synonym in many alchemical texts for the Philosopher's Stone.

If he hasn't already resolved and incarnated those contraries, albeit unconsciously, by the end of *Prince*.

Remember, the Philosopher's Stone is supposed to emerge during the rubedo from the white stone that appears at the end of the white work. The alchemical androgyne, a human stand-in for the Stone in alchemical texts and literary alchemy, should not be created in the action of the last book but step out from behind the white curtain. I think we can be reasonably certain the last book's S/He won't be a sexual resolution of contraries but the personification of both Gryffindor and Slytherin qualities in dynamic balance and at peace.

More on the Hogwarts Hermaphrodite in a second. First we've got to get to the wedding on time.

The Chemical Wedding is Celebrated

Harry Potter fandom is a spectrum of opinions, all, in my experience, passionately defended or disparaged (as a rule, consequently, I run from fan website and engagement with fandom controversies). As you would expect, then, the idea of literary alchemy as a skeleton for these books has been met with derision and dismissive contempt and it has been praised as important for having a full appreciation of the artistry of the books.

Those who think it a lark or silly are usually unaware of the depth of the literary alchemy tradition in English fiction – poems, plays, and novels – or are ignorant of images other than the Philosopher's Stone. I cannot say I enjoy or appreciate their scorn – but that's fandom!

I have to wonder, though, if even the alchemy naysayers will be able to ignore and neglect the Chemical Wedding announcements we were all sent in *Half-Blood Prince*. Remember the wedding mentioned in Chapter 3 in connection with the rotation and resolution of the four elements?

> The contrary qualities of the four elements are likened to
> quarreling foes who must be reconciled or united in order for
> harmony to reign (see 'peace'). The circulation of elements
> is identical with the process the alchemists describe as the
> conversion of body into spirit, and spirit into body, until each
> is able to mingle together, or *unite in the chemical wedding*
> to form a new perfect being, the philosopher's stone…
> (*Dictionary of Alchemical Imagery*, Lyndy Abraham, Cambridge
> University Press, 2001, pg.138, emphasis added)

The rubedo as the final stage of the Great Work features the wedding of the Red King and White Woman, their copulation and death, and the birth of the orphan ("the Philosophical Child"). Burckhardt calls the chemical marriage the "central symbol of alchemy" (Alchemy, p. 149) and it has been the subject of literature from Shakespeare's *Romeo and Juliet* (1595), John Donne's *Extasie* (1607?) and *The Chemical Wedding of Christian Rosenkreutz* (1616) to Blake's *Jerusalem* (1804-1820),C. S. Lewis' *Perelandra* (1944) and *That Hideous Strength* (1946), and Lindsay Clarke's *The Chemical Wedding* (1990). You will forgive me, then, if I spell out how Bill Weasley and Fleur Delacour conform to the Red Man and White Woman of alchemy and what their wedding may mean in the ultimate *Harry Potter* novel.

Let's review the unfolding of the Bill-Fleur romance before tracing their likenesses as Sol and Luna, the betrothed couple for the alchemical wedding.

Fleur's first sighting of Bill is before the third Tri-Wizard task (the labyrinth, which image is, yes, used in alchemical texts as a symbol of the Great Work: *Dictionary of Alchemical Imagery*, p. 113) when Bill and Mrs. Weasley stand in for Harry's family at 'the morning greeting.' Fleur, the Beauxbaton's champion, is immediately smitten with the handsome Bill.

Fleur Delacour, Harry noticed, was eyeing Bill with great interest over her mother's shoulder. Harry could tell she had no objection whatsoever to long hair or earrings with fangs on them (*Goblet of Fire*, Chapter 31, p. 616).

Her interest in the dashing Gringotts Curse Breaker grows in the next year when we learn that Bill, too, is smitten. When Harry arrives at 12 Grimmauld Place, the House of Black, he asks about Bill.

"Is Bill here?" he asked. "I thought he was working in Egypt."

"He applied for a desk job so he could come home and work for the Order," said Fred. "He says he misses the tombs, but," he smirked, "there are compensations...."

"What d'you mean?"

"Remember old Fleur Delacour?" said George. "She's got a job at Gringotts to eemprove 'er Eeenglish – "

"– and Bill's been giving her a lot of private lessons," sniggered Fred. (*Phoenix*, Chapter 4, p. 70)

These lessons have led to an engagement Fleur tells Harry about at the Burrow in Chapter 5 of *Half-Blood Prince*. Alas, it seems that Mrs. Weasley, Hermione, and Ginny all despise her and hope very much that the wedding, planned for the next summer, falls through.

At book's end, however, Bill is mauled by Fenrir Greyback in the battle between the Order of the Phoenix and the Death Eaters at the stairs below the Astronomy Tower. Greyback was not a transformed Werewolf at the time, so, though the cursed wounds are incurable and largely untreatable, there was some question in the hospital wing about what would happen to him.

It turns out he will only be the long-haired man with fang earrings instead of the longhaired man with fangs. But in the moment of shock over the extent of his wounds, Mrs. Weasley suggests, not too delicately, that the wedding is off (she says he "was going to be married") in front of Fleur. Fleur erupts in anger, Mrs. Weasley yields in respect and repentance, and both women collapse in each other's arms in tears. The wedding is on. (*Half-Blood Prince*, Chapter 29, p. 623)

So what?

Well, the alchemy here is not unlike that of the Ron/Hermione couple acting as the alchemical reagents sulphur and quicksilver (mercury) on Harry throughout the books. This explains, I think, Ron's fascination with Fleur and in watching Fleur and Bill to pick up "snogging" pointers (*Half-Blood Prince*, Chapter 16, p. 330). In terms of the four humors, the Weasleys are all choleric, which is to say, "hot and dry" like fire. Fleur, as you'd guess from Ginny's nickname for her, is phlegmatic or "cold and moist" like water.

Both Bill and Fleur are cartoons or caricatures of the archetypal studly man and drop-dead beautiful woman. When Bill is bit by a werewolf, he risks becoming in fact only the macho image he has projected to the world for some time (I mean, fang earrings?). Fleur's hypnotic beauty and her enchanting kisses both are signs that she is almost an allegorical figure for feminine allure and magic. Bill is a machismo kind of guy with a werewolf lurking below the surface (one step up from the already fiery weasel!) and Fleur is the fashion model, wild white woman whose Veela talons, cruel beak, and scaly wings are just below the horizon.

Ginny is right on, too, when she says that Bill is interested in Fleur because he "likes a bit of adventure" (*Half-Blood Prince*, Chapter 5, p. 93). Fire and water are opposites that attract, if they are a combination that resolves the qualities of both. Fleur, the silver-haired, super-feminine, and Gaullic beauty featured in *Half-Blood Prince*, is a cold and wet sign of the white work that features the water element and coagulation after the torching experience of *Phoenix*.

When we see Fleur become angry and aggressive over the passive body of Bill who was bested by Greyback, however, at the end of *Half-Blood Prince*, we know that she has become sufficiently masculine or choleric to move the choleric Mrs. Weasley to a more feminine and passive state. The chemical wedding at the end of the rotation of the elements, when water becomes fiery and fire liquid or passive, is in full progress.

As any student of *Romeo and Juliet* (or *West Side Story*) will tell you, however, while the Chemical Wedding of opposites may mean great things for the citizens of Verona because the Capulets and Montague reconcile over the dead bodies of the honeymooners, it's not a wedding or marriage that parents hope for their children. Why the new king and queen or at least corresponding archetypes of masculine fire and feminine water die soon after their marriage reflects the end and goal of the alchemical work. Lyndy Abraham explains:

> Alchemy is based on the Hermetic view that man had become divided within himself, separated into two sexes, at the fall in the Garden of Eden and could only regain his integral Adamic state when the opposing forces within him were reconciled. The union of these universal male and

female forces produced that third substance or effect which could heal not only the diseases of the physical world but also the affliction of the separated soul.

Metaphysically, the chemical wedding is the perfect union of creative will or power (male) with wisdom (female) to produce pure love (the child, the Stone). The creation of this Stone always involves some kind of sacrifice or death. Thus emblems of the chemical wedding almost always include emblems of death which overshadow the *conjunctio*....

The death at the wedding symbolizes the extinction of the earlier differentiated state before union, and also powerfully conveys the alacrity with which the festive moment of the coagula or wedding is transformed into the lamentation of the *solve* or death. Many texts say that the *solve* and *coagula* are simultaneous.

Alchemical theory stated that generation could not take place unless there had first been a death. In Christian mysticism the same idea occurs with the parable of the grain of wheat which must first die in the earth before it can bring forth fruit (John 12:24-25), a parable which the alchemists often cite. The philosopher's stone cannot be generated until the lovers have died and their bodies putrefied in the mercurial waters....

The bodies of the lovers (the red man and the white woman) lying dead in the grave symbolize the death which frees the soul to be released and rise to the top of the alembic. (***Dictionary of Alchemical Imagery***, pp. 36-37, emphasis added)

I imagine this sounds perfectly dreadful to you, especially if you're thinking it means Bill and Fleur's wedding day will be a blood bath. It needn't be (I'll explain why in a minute), but, even if it is, these deaths – be they literal or figurative experiences – bring forth life.

Closely related to the symbolism of marriage is that of death. According to some representations of the 'chemical marriage' the king and queen, on marriage, are killed and buried together, only to rise again rejuvenated. That this connection between marriage and death is in the nature of things, is indicated by the fact that, according to ancient experience, a marriage in a dream means a death, and a death in a dream means a marriage.

This correspondence is explained by the fact that any given union presupposes an extinction of the earlier, still differentiated, state. In the marriage of man and woman, each gives up part of his or her independence, whereas the other way round, death (which is in the first instance a separation) is followed by the union of the body with the earth and of soul with its original essence.

On 'chemical marriage' Quicksilver takes unto itself Sulphur, and Sulphur, Quicksilver. Both forces 'die,' as foes and lovers. Then the changing and reflective moon of the soul unites with the immutable sun of the spirit so that it is extinguished, and yet illumined, at one and the same time. (Burckhardt, *Alchemy*, pp. 155-156)

The child born of the coition of this death to self and opening to the spirit is the "philosophical child" or "philosopher's stone," also known, for obvious reasons, I guess, as "the orphan." Ms. Rowling, by making mom here a mercurial birdwoman, paints a detailed alchemical picture, because, as Abraham tells us, "the birth of the philosopher's stone from the union of male and female substances at the chemical wedding is frequently compared to the birth of a bird," specifically, the "Bird of Hermes" (cf., *Dictionary of Alchemical Imagery*, p. 25).

The Philosopher's Stone is Produced: The Hogwarts' Hermaphrodite

I have to think the first question I'll be asked by readers after they read this is, "So, you're saying Bill and Fleur will die at their wedding or soon after and that a child will be born miraculously from their brief marriage and that this bird-child will be the answer to Death or at least Lord Voldemort? What do you take me for?" At least that's what I would be asking.

Let me say again that literary alchemy doesn't force plot turns. The real master alchemist here, Ms. Rowling, is obeying the rules of alchemical drama certainly, but she does so in conformity to the tradition of telling the tale as it needs to be told. As I said, I don't expect to see an imbibation, a cohobation, an augmentation, or a projection forced in sequence into the story line. We could recognize it if she plays with any of these ideas but they aren't necessary.

What I mean by this is that Bill and Fleur don't have to die physical deaths. The couples joined by chemical marriages in Lewis' *Ransom Trilogy*, for instance, don't die except in the Elizabethan usage of that term for sexual congress. The death Bill and Fleur die is in the "extinction of their earlier, still differentiated state" of fire and water. This rotation of the elements can be a physical death, of course, but it is the death to self, in Fleur's case phlegmatic excess and selfishness (seen in righteous anger with her mother-in-law to be) and in the Weasley's case to choleric British pride and machismo (seen in Bill's passivity in the hospital bed and Molly's surrender to and embracing her daughter-in-law with the offer of a family heirloom to highlight her silver hair).

This death has already happened and is the accomplishment of the alchemical wedding – which death and wedding promises a new life to celebrate at book's end. Ms. Rowling said as an aside in a July 2006 interview that, while she was giving one character something of a reprieve from what she thought was a death sentence, two others died she'd thought would survive. I worry for the Weasley boys but especially for the new Mr. and Mrs. Weasley. Their death at book's end, especially if Fleur has had a child, brings an end that echoes the Potters' death at the beginning of this series, something we should expect in a book largely made up of alchemical cycles and circles of purification and transformation.

The production of the Philosopher's Stone, then, is well under way by the end of *Half-Blood Prince*. To repeat what Ms. Rowling said in December 2005:

> JKR: So much that happens in six relates to what happens in seven. And you really sort of skid off the end of six straight into seven. You know, it's not the discreet adventure that the others have all been, even though you have the underlying theme of Harry faces Voldemort, in each case, and [....] there has been an adventure that has resolved itself.
> SF: Yes, exactly.

> JKR: Whereas in six, although there is an ending that could
> be seen as definitive in one sense, you very strongly feel the
> plot is not over this time and it will continue.
> www.accio-quote.org/articles/2005/1205-bbc-fry.html

We know the Stone exists in its white form at Dumbledore's tomb; the seventh book will be the revelation or rubification of the Stone. Similarly, we have seen the preface to the Chemical Wedding and we have been shown the various quaternaries and contraries that need to be revealed and resolved in this finale to the seven stage alchemical work. The seven will become One, the various fours will become or unite behind the Quintessence, and the twos – especially the Gryffindor-Slytherin split between Harry and Draco, Harry and Severus, and Harry and Lord Voldemort but also all the doppelgangers, the contrary pairs, even the twins, if Fred and George die heroically as I suspect – will come into the light of day and find resolution and peace. The house-elf slaves will be freed literally and the Magical World figuratively speaking.

We can look at the appearance of the Stone as something progressive on which the story will depend or something that will appear in the storyline naturally without seeming to cause mission success or failure.

The progressive line says either Harry will transcend his prejudices and blindspots to become the Philosopher's Stone/Quintessence/Hermaphrodite he is destined to be and transform into a vehicle of love (destined from his beginnings as "the orphan" and "philosophical child" as much as by prophecy) or the Bad Guys will triumph. The victory of the Bad Guys doesn't seem likely, so the alchemical progressivists expect Harry to clear the big hurdle at story's beginning or at the very end, namely, his understanding of Snape.

Ms. Rowling has prepared us for his reconciliation with Severus Snape in the several times Harry has said he will never forgive him. As Joyce Odell writes in her magisterial essay in *Who Killed Albus Dumbledore?* (Zossima Press, 2006), this is such a strong repetition of his statements about Sirius Black in *Prisoner* that we can almost consider his make-up with Professor Snape a done event. It won't be easy, of course. As we're told about Percy and his continued distance from his family, "Dumbledore says people find it easier to forgive others for being wrong than being right" (*Prince*, Chapter 5, p. 96).

Frankly, I doubt the progressivists' "alchemy first" ideas. It seems at least as likely to me that the alchemical androgynes or "S/Hes" I am calling Hogwart Hermaphrodites will show their paired natures and resolution of partisan spirit. We know one such wizard; I think there are at least three others.

I think there is more to the alchemical idea of androgynes I am calling Hogwart Hermaphrodites than this "love or defeat" ending. There are several of these Hermaphrodites who represent alchemical resolution of contraries or love who can be the great revelations and deliverers of **Deathly Hallows**.

The only master alchemist we have met is Albus Dumbledore, and the Headmaster is the grand Hermaphrodite. He is no respecter of persons or privilege and shows no favorites on either side of the Slytherin/Gryffindor axis or divide. Review his conversations with the nasty villains in the books: Lucius Malfoy, Fenrir Greyback, even Lord Voldemort. He is always cordial, courteous, and respectful. Dumbledore is not patronizing them. He loves them. He certainly isn't pigeon holing them as a Gryffindor partisan would.

Love, "more wonderful and more terrible than death, than human intelligence, than forces of nature" (**Phoenix**, Chapter 37, p. 843), is the resolution of contraries and the rising above ego. Love is also the signature victory and sign of the alchemical androgyne. S/He doesn't take sides because, resting at the center and Origin, S/He can take all sides, even while resisting those who imagine their ego-selves to be the center and Origin of all things.

And to whom does Dumbledore show special attention? The freaks, the dangerous, and the disaffected. He does this because he has transcended the partisan perspectives of his peers and has taken a much larger view, what one could call the ontological or metaphysical view. We're not surprised he invited a boy wizard who happened to be a werewolf to school or a half-giant because we know from his love of lemon sorbets ("Zots") that he values the interior, the "surprise inside" rather than the exterior man or woman. Subject/object, inner/outer are the great polarities of human thought and the Headmaster has transcended them.

Lord Voldemort is the inversion or carnival mirror image of Dumbledore, this incarnation of love or Rebis. Incapable of the self-transformation by humility and love to create a Philosopher's Stone himself and become this androgyne, the Dark Lord celebrates his ego, passions, and desires as the Center and Origin of all things and despises everything and everyone that is not stronger than himself.

But Lord Voldemort, despite himself, is still a Hogwart Hermaphrodite, an embodiment of the Gryffindor/Slytherin polarity. As the Heir of Slytherin, he prides himself as the reservoir and fountain of this extreme quality in the Hogwarts quaternary. Dumbledore's "gleam of triumph" at the end of *Goblet* while interviewing Harry, however, revealed the Dark Lord had fallen into Dumbledore's trap (explained at length in Chapter 6. By using Harry's blood for his macabre rebirthing, blood from a Gryffindor family and tinctured with the sacrificial love of Lily Evans Potter, Harry's Gryffindor nature is now part of his substance, the material of his physical body. Voldemort, unknowingly, is now a Gryffindor/Slytherin androgyne, though only as an incarnation of the love of self.

And, as Harry has known since the Sorting Ceremony in his first year at Hogwarts, the Potter boy, though in Gryffindor, Captain of the Gryffindor Quidditch team, best friends of the Gryffindor Prefects, and sworn enemy of everything Slytherin, has a little Slytherin genie inside his bottle.

> "You can speak Parseltongue, Harry," said Dumbledore calmly, "because Lord Voldemort – who is the last remaining ancestor of Salazar Slytherin – can speak Parseltongue. Unless I'm much mistaken, he transferred some of his own powers to you the night he gave you that scar. Not something he intended to do, I'm sure..."
>
> "Voldemort put a bit of himself in me?" Harry said, thunderstruck.
>
> "It certainly seems so."
>
> "So I should be in Slytherin," Harry said, looking desperately into Dumbledore's face. "The Sorting Hat could see Slytherin's power in me, and it –"
>
> "Put you in Gryffindor," said Dumbledore calmly. "Listen to me, Harry. You happen to have many qualities Salazar Slytherin prized in his hand-picked students. His own very

rare gift, Parseltongue – resourcefulness – determination – a
certain disregard for rules," he added, his mustache quivering
again. (*Chamber*, Chapter 18, pp. 332-333)

This genie has grown right along with Harry so that he can often know Lord Voldemort's moods, even to the point of being able to see what the Dark Lord sees. And, unlike the Tom Riddle ("twin enigma") monster, Harry has a pure heart and the power of love.

Both Voldemort and Harry have grown from homunculus or "philosophical orphan" into the alchemical androgyne or Philosopher's Stone. Harry was the baby left on the Dursley's doorstep who was forced into the role of the Chosen One because of the scar Horcrux. The Dark Lord forcefully as a baby in *Goblet*'s rebirthing scene, even if a baby with an adult mind, took on his double nature; his rebirth was not possible because of sacrificial love but sprang from egotism and hatred. This contrast means all the difference in how the two Hermaphrodites experience love.

If you imagine the Gryffindor and Slytherin poles of existence as opposite electrical podes on a battery, Harry is a clean connection and conduit of the powerful current resulting from the meeting and resolution of contraries. Dumbledore's triumph was realizing that the reconstituted Voldemort would always feel this current most strongly when fully engaged with Harry because Voldemort, too, is a "conductor," however unwilling and unconscious.

Love is the union of opposites, again, like the positive and negative podes on a battery. Both Harry, because of his Gryffindor nature and Slytherin Horcrux, and Voldemort, because of his being the Heir of Slytherin and being bodily a Gryffindor because of the blood used at his rebirthing, are powerful conductors of love, full and open connections between the electrical podes. Harry, however, has a pure heart and experiences this connection as love and light. The Dark Lord, with a heart of darkness, experiences this same power as hell.

When these two Hermaphrodites do battle, look for an echo of both the *Phoenix* climax in which Lord Voldemort could not possess Harry and the battle before the Mirror of Erised in *Stone*. It is Eastern Orthodox Christian belief that heaven and hell are the same "place," namely, God's Glory or love that all people experience at death according to the capacity of their hearts for love. We'll almost certainly see Harry attempt to "close the circuit" to test Voldemort's tolerance for love. We know as a Gryffindor/Slytherin conduit that he'll feel every bit of current Harry transmits.

The surprise Hogwarts Hermaphrodite, the big twist we discussed in the chapter on narrative misdirection, is Severus Snape. Like Harry the true Gryffindor, Severus seems to define, with Lord Voldemort and the Death Eaters, the Slytherin aspect of existence, in a perversely sadistic and cruel rendition. But there's the matter of his calling himself the "Half-Blood Prince." What sort of nut-case student living in Slytherin calls attention to his Mudblood ancestry?

How about a man who is all Slytherin on the outside and all Gryffindor on the inside? Joyce Odell argues cogently on her Red Hen Publications website and in the essay published in **Who Killed Albus Dumbledore?** (Zossima Press, 2006) that Snape has been a Dumbledore man at least since his graduation from Hogwarts. He is a wizard brave and accomplished enough to know his own value despite his not being born to wealth or power ("Prince," in addition to being a family name, speaks to a certain self-importance). Snape seems to have a little bit of Gryffindor in him, as well as his heroic service to the Order in Lord Voldemort's inner circle reflects. The real world Coat-of-Arms for the Prince family is colored red and gold, the colors of Gryffindor. Put Snape down as the Dark Horse candidate for "Heir of Gryffindor."

In fact, the inability to place Snape on either side of the Gryffindor/ Slytherin divide certainly is what has made him the most fascinating character in the series. Lord Voldemort seems to have staged both his attacks of the past two years in such a way as to trap Severus and reveal his true loyalties because of his preoccupation with this fence straddler.

But Snape isn't fence-straddling.

He's living as a conscious conduit between the electrical poles that define the Wizarding World. Unlike Harry, who doubts the power he is able to transmit, Snape survives because of this conductivity and the infinite wattage of love. Severus Snape is the alchemist's apprentice and great-souled man, if he cannot feel anything but disdain for Harry, his master's favorite. He isn't an artificial or accidental Hermaphrodite like Voldemort and Harry but a man who has deliberately and sacrificially bridged the Gryffindor/Slytherin fault line.

Professor Severus Snape, quite simply, is the giant and tragic hero of these books, and, if he isn't Heir of Gryffindor, he is the successor to Dumbledore and one of the only men capable of "playing his part" via Polyjuice as discussed in Chapter 1 and playing the part of a sadist, too, in convincing fashion.

Rubeus the Rebis?

But there's another figurative giant in these books, I think, who also happens to be a literal half-giant. It wouldn't be a complete list of Hogwarts Hermaphrodites without Hagrid. He's a poster child for the rubeo, certainly, because his first name is a strong pointer to rubification (could he be any more of a red-necked rube?). Like Dumbledore, his de facto daddy and mentor, he sees what nobody else sees in monstrous creatures and people, their lovable and needy side. Never an unkind word about Severus from the half-giant on campus.

As part killer-giant, part-wizard do you think he embodies the poles of existence, the human and the inhuman? Do you doubt that he's pure of heart? The reason the Headmaster told MacGonagall in *Stone* that he would trust Hagrid with his life (and probably did in *Prince*) and certainly did trust him with Harry's life the night the Potters were murdered is that Rubeus is a Rebis. The illustration on the cover is of the alchemical, androgynous Rebis, straddling a dragon atop a Golden Snitch. Who else could be a Rebis atop a dragon than Rubeus, the half-giant?

Firenze the Centaur tells Hagrid to give up his attempts to help his brother Grawp, efforts that seem fruitless and are certainly nearly killing the Keeper of the Keys. But this Dumbledore man persists in loving his brother sacrificially. We see the result at the end of *Prince* as Grawp consoles his older brother at the funeral. The power of love writ very large, in giant letters. Considering the payback he owes Riddle, Jr., I think the last-in-standing may very well be first in the battle-line in the face-off to come with Voldemort.

Dr. Daniela Teodorescu, French professor and Mugglenet writer, maintains that Hagrid is also a hermaphrodite in the sexual sense of the word. Dr. Teo isn't saying Hagrid isn't manly enough or that he doesn't like women. Just the opposite. He's a mommy. She writes:

> I am rereading SS/PS and ran into the image of Hagrid

> knitting. And Hagrid says Norbert knows his mommy; he mothers creatures, Monsters, his own brother. Hagrid can also be spotted cooking in a flowery apron. Goes with your double gender theory very, very well. (Correspondence, 23 July 06, "Mommy Hagrid')

The alchemical Rebis is a man/woman or figurative hermaphrodite. Ms. Rowling goes out of her way to point to Hagrid as a comic "Mr. Mom" to his pet monsters, to his brother, and to Norbert. Only Severus Snape is also seen in women's clothing, again, seemingly just for laughs. Knowing that the true heroes of these books will be those characters who unite opposites in harmony, Hagrid's flowery apron and Snape's "witch's hat topped with a stuffed vulture" (*Prisoner*, Chapter 11, p. 227) are appropriate and powerful dress.

Predictions

There is a whole chapter of predictions at the end of this book but the alchemical ones can go here for neatness' sake. A quick review, then:

Ms. Rowling has said there will be deaths in the last book and there's not much of a surprise there. I assumed Hagrid would be first to take a wand bullet, but she said in a June 2006 interview that she gave a character a reprieve she had thought would die. I've never prayed for a literary figure (and won't begin here), but let's hope that the love Harry fans feel for Hagrid will help him more than the prayers of millions helped the late Little Nell in Dickens' *The Old Curiosity Shop*.

Ms. Rowling said a pair of characters died instead. I assume this was Bill and Fleur because an alchemical pair almost has to die in the rubedo. Ron and Hermione played this part for the first six books; I shudder at the reaction of fandom if the younger quarrelling couple, Harry's best friends, buy the farm.

The rubedo is characterized by an unveiling or rubification of the *Stone*, which in story form will almost certainly be the unveiling of the Hermaphrodite or Rebis. We'll discover how Harry's scar is a Horcrux and the Chosen One is a living Gryffindor-outside/ Slytherine-inside love conductor.

Snape will also be outed at last as a Slytherin-outside/Gryffindor-inside conductive bridge, perhaps even the Heir of Gryffindor and

Dumbledore stand-in. Because Voldemort's rebirthing rewired him so he, too, is a superconductive wire across these electrical poles, despite his inability to endure a closed circuit and love at high amperage, look for Harry and Severus, willingly or unwillingly, to destroy the Dark Lord together.

And Rubeus? He'll be in the thick of it and, possibly, it is the big rube's destiny to deliver the death blow to the Chief Death Eater. As you'll see in Chapter 4, it is important that the first be last and the last first in Ms. Rowling's postmodern epic – and no one except a house-elf is lower than Hagrid in the Wizarding World, thanks to the young Tom Riddle, Jr.'s framing the boy half-giant.

A Live Journal writer named Swythyv wrote in her predictions of what will happen in the seventh **Harry Potter** novel that a "fifth house" will appear among wizards. "In Book 7 we will be shown a 'fifth element': a sector of Wizarding society that discards House affiliation and rises above blood status. It is the merit path in this closed society. Those who rise to the top in it may change their names, and become their own tradition" (**Who Killed Albus Dumbledore?** Chapter 7, Zossima Press, 2006). I doubt we'll see this meritocracy, though, in the formal sense of a closed club or Unspeakables status.

But I think we will recognize at rubedo's end those magical people who resolve the contraries of their every day life. The magic-people who bridge the seemingly infinite ego-chasm and delusion of self-importance and pride that separates "self" and "other," between our Gryffindor and Slytherin natures, will become conduits of the love and grace that is the most powerful magic and contranatural force in time and space. We'll recognize these Rebises in the story line as they reveal themselves – and we'll be challenged to try to close that canyon between us and others, subject and object, in imitation.

Conclusion

Later chapters will argue that Ms Rowling uses the traditional patterns of literary alchemy as a means of sharing her postmodern themes. Together these patterns, postmodernism and alchemy, especially when combined with a knowledge of her hero's journey pattern and the use of narrative misdirection, seems more useful than a divining rod in the discernment of the last book's possibilities. It is the radical and traditional worldview of strength, even supernatural power, coming from a self-denying harmony, from a sacrificial love that conquers death, that informs and drives these stories.

Alchemy, as a metaphor for our resolution to transcend ourselves and our egos, opening ourselves to spirit and love and life, is the language and heart of *Harry Potter*. Pottermania is what it is because this language speaks to the human heart, a heart whose life-giving contraction and expansion in rhythm seems designed and longing for this message of powerful love and true peace. Ms. Rowling's rubedo will be the final experiment in the Great Work that has transfixed if not yet transformed her millions of readers.

Because the keys that unlock *Harry Potter* work together, it's important as we finish the discussion of our second key, literary alchemy, to ask if alchemy tells us anything about the first key, narrative misdirection. Narrative misdirection suggests that *Deathly Hallows* will have to be about everything in *Half-Blood Prince* that Harry didn't see or understand. There was no Dumbledore denouement to reveal, as there were in the other five books, much of what Harry missed. With *Half-Blood Prince* sliding into *Deathly Hallows*, as Ms. Rowling says it does, we're left waiting on the big twist and surprises in the last book about what we missed in *Prince* because we were suckered again into accepting the third-person, limited omniscient view and believing Harry has a clue.

Literary alchemy tells us that (as crazy as the Polyjuicing Dumbledore theory may be, with the idea that Severus, Horace, and Hagrid stage a drama for Voldemort using Harry's scar Horcrux mind connection as a minicamera), we should be looking to learn in the rubedo (*Hallows*) what already happened in the albedo (*Prince*). There should be nothing but revelations of transformations that have already taken place in previous stages.

The Hero's Journey

Before we get to postmodernism and the themes of our age that permeate *Harry Potter* at least as much as literary alchemy, we deserve a break. The third key is not as mentally challenging. No Rebis or arithmancy, not even a little deceptive narrative misdirection here to trip us up. If you've read one *Harry Potter* novel, you've seen the pattern of Harry's adventures that Ms. Rowling follows almost slavishly in all six books. It's Harry's annual Hero's journey.

The reason I say "almost slavishly" is that the small twists she makes every year in the formula makes the repetition delightful and fresh. The few serious readers I've met who don't like the books have been those that try to read them one after the other in rapid sequence. They tell me the formula journey becomes rather annoying on the fourth or fifth ride on the coaster over the same tracks, however clever the variations.

The *Harry Potter* Hero's Journey magic formula, in brief, is a ten-step trip with a large helping of detective fiction, bildungsroman, satire, and even Christian fantasy thrown in. Let's look at the ten steps in the first five books, and then see how *Half Blood Prince* conforms to and departs from the pattern Ms. Rowling has used with some thoughts at the end about how she may adapt the formula in the finale.

1. The Privet Drive Opening

The first five *Harry Potter* novels, with the exception of the first book's first chapter, begin during Harry's summer vacation from Hogwarts – if life with the Dursleys can be called a "vacation." As troubling as Harry's life here is, the opening events always provide clues as to what will be happening at book's end.

Phoenix, for example, starts out with Harry "hot and dry" in the drought both figurative and literal that he experiences away from his friends and feeling his head "split" in his fight with Uncle Vernon. Every *Potter* novel is about Harry's transformation into his opposite; the hot and dry clue in Chapter 1 points to his change in Phoenix via alchemical transformation to "cold and moist" (see Harry by the lake in *Phoenix*, Chapter 38).

Key Three: The Hero's Journey

His run-in with the Dursley's window and with Dudley's fist that both "cleave" and "split" his head foreshadow the "two minds" Harry has in this book, both in respect to his shared nature with Voldemort and his forced (and painful) separation from his old understanding and relationships. It pays to read these opening chapters carefully.

Prince, however, starts out with a bang and a surprise because we do not see the Dursleys or Harry until the third chapter of the new book. This is and is not a departure from formula.

It is an obvious departure in that first we visit 10 Downing Street and Ms. Rowling's hilarious caricature of Tony Blair with the new and old Ministers of Magic. Then we eavesdrop on a chilling conversation and oath in Severus Snape's off-campus rooms before coming to Privet Drive. But this is a departure in form, not content or intent.

In each of the previous books we have learned from Harry's behavior at home (and from the events that take place with the Dursleys) what the rest of the story will be about, at least in terms of how Harry will have to change and what mystery there is for him and his friends to solve at school. We rarely leave for Hogwarts without a pretty clear picture of (a) what problem Harry has personally – say, "anger" or "self-importance" – that he will transcend in the course of the book and (b) what mystery he, Ron, and Hermione will have to solve in the coming year.

In *Half-Blood Prince*, we don't learn these things on Privet Drive. By the time we meet Harry in this book, he is waiting on Albus Dumbledore to come and pick him up. We learn the circumstances of the story to come – Lord Voldemort and the Death Eaters at war with the magical community – in the first chapter's visit with the Prime Minister (as well as that Ms. Rowling is perhaps a little frustrated that few people are commenting on her gifts as a satirist in the tradition of Swift, Dickens, Cruickshank, and Blair/Orwell).

We learn the central mystery to be solved in this book – what has Draco Malfoy been told to do by Lord Voldemort? – in the chapter where Malfoy's mother extracts an Unbreakable vow from Snape. In the third chapter, the first with Harry, he is asleep waiting for Dumbledore; we should know by now that this means he will be vigilant at book's end having said goodbye to the Headmaster. Mary Ailes, a Barnes and Noble University.com Discussion Room member, pointed out that Harry's sleeping posture at his bedroom window, "glasses askew and his mouth wide open," as he waits is what Harry finds at book's end. At the base of the Astronomy Tower when finding Dumbledore, "Harry reached out, straightened the half-moon spectacles upon the crooked nose, and wiped a trickle of blood from the mouth with his own sleeve" (*Prince*, Chapters 3 and 28, pp. 38 and 608).

The first chapters in the first five books and *Prince* look a little different, then, but achieve the same effect. Not to mention that Harry's story in *Prince* does begin at Privet Drive, albeit not until Chapter 3.

2.   Escape to Hogwarts

Every *Potter* novel, again with the understandable exception of *Philosopher's Stone*, includes something of a magical escape from the mundane world of the Dursleys to Harry's magical life at Hogwarts. The flying Ford Anglia, the Knight Bus, the Quidditch World Cup, and the Escape to the House of Black are all markers of the beginning of Harry's annual "hero's journey" and "alchemical work." Harry's split existence with Muggles and magical folk has so far been two radically separated lives, which great divide required a significant leap to overcome.

Harry's worlds, however, began to collapse and intersect in *Phoenix* and this trend is continued in *Half Blood Prince*. In *Prince*, Harry's escape is brought about by a wizard seeming to be Albus Dumbledore who appears again on the doorstep of Privet Drive after some fifteen years, this time to take Harry away. They disapparate after a short talk with the Dursleys for a visit with Horace Slughorn. The second step conforms to the pattern of magical escape or departure and continues the breakdown of Harry's bipolar lifestyle. The picture of Albus Dumbledore doing his best to sit and have drinks with the Dursleys speaks to his, "break down the barriers of prejudice" agenda. His banging the Dursleys heads with drinks and chastising them for being horrible parents should raise a red flag about whether this is the Headmaster or a more "severe" stand-in.

3.   The Mystery to Solve

Each *Potter* book in itself is a mystery or detective novel with Harry, Ron, and Hermione starring as The Hardy Boys meet Nancy Drew. From the mystery of the Gringotts bag in *Stone* to the bizarre appearance of Dementors in Little Whining in *Phoenix*, each book is shaped by an overarching riddle that the three detectives strive to unravel without breaking too many Hogwarts rules. What the riddle of each book will be, of course, is impossible to predict; the only thing we can know for sure is that there will be one. The story is narrated in the third person, limited omniscient perspective; the narrative drive comes from our wanting to know the solution to the mystery each year.

Half-Blood Prince's mystery is revealed in Severus Snape's library apartment in Chapter 2 and given a big push forward in Hogsmeade at Borgin and Burkes and on the Hogwart's Express where Harry eavesdrops on Malfoy and friends. "What is Malfoy's mission from Voldemort?" Mystery present, right on schedule and according to formula and pattern; onto Hero's Journey, step four.

4.   The Problem with Snape

It wouldn't be a satisfying *Harry Potter* novel without at least one mano-a-mano confrontation with the Potions Master become teacher of Defense Against the Dark Arts. Professor Snape – and his astonishing hatred of Harry – is the never-ending mystery of the series, a mystery that has in several ways made Snape the most interesting and important character of the books. We learn something new about him in every novel.

The confrontation (or two or three) with Severus Snape insures we touch base with the central mysteries of the whole series of books, which are (1) the nature of Harry's relationship with the Dark Lord and (2) whose side Professor Snape is on. *Half-Blood Prince* did not disappoint in this regard, with Severus bullying and badgering Harry from the moment he steps off the Hogwarts Express and continues without a break every time they meet or speak until they actually fight it out after Severus seems to murder Albus Dumbledore. This has only served to heighten the mystery, alas, but the requirements of story formula have certainly been satisfied. Step five?

5.   Life with Ron and Hermione

The Terrible Trio of Harry, Ron, and Hermione is in one sense a cliché of great literature and storytelling that stretches from Dostoevsky's *Brothers Karamazov* to the Star Trek and Star Wars adventures. On the other hand, Ms. Rowling gives this mind-body-spirit tryptich such a convincing and central place in each year's adventure that our experience when reading rides the roller-coaster of the changes in this key relationship from novel to novel.

From the birth of their friendship in the battle with the troll in *Stone* to Ron and Hermione's elevation to Prefect status apart from Harry in *Phoenix* (and the agonizing divisions in *Chamber*, *Prisoner*, and *Goblet*), we have learned to expect that Harry's life with the alchemical pair or "quarrelling couple" of Ron and Hermione, alchemical sulphur and mercury respectively, will be the frame in which every *Harry Potter* adventure takes place.

Ron and Hermione, both in their differences and working together, are the water on a rock that most change Harry for the better over the course of a year. *Half-Blood Prince* was no exception as we get to see Ron and Hermione try to show the other that they can date other people – with predictably painful emotional results for all three – and eventually they come to be boyfriend and girlfriend in a Junior Varsity alchemical wedding. Check off this step...

6.   Crunch Time Decision

Every adventure story has its decision-making crisis and the *Harry Potter* novels are no exception. This has become so much a matter of routine in these stories that Lord Voldemort wrote the script for Harry's choice to rescue Sirius in *Phoenix*, to take advantage of his formulaic "people saving thing." How predictable is that?

Every year's mystery comes to a crisis, at which time Harry has to decide whether to risk his life to save the world or not. Not much of a choice for Harry the Lionhearted, of course, and his only struggle in *Half-Blood Prince* was that when the crisis came, it arrived as twins. Harry learns simultaneously from Professor Trelawney that Malfoy has achieved his furniture-fixing objective in the Room of Requirement and that Severus Snape told the Prophecy to Lord Voldemort which doomed Harry's parents.

He learns these twin news bombshells on his way to Dumbledore's office to go searching for a Voldemort Horcrux – what is Harry to do? Crisis step, multiple checks.

7.   Underground Battle

Every great hero's journey from Homer's *Odyssey* and Virgil's *Aeneid* to Dante's *Comedia* features a trip to the underworld or to the dead. Ms. Rowling tips her hat to this tradition by having the climactic battle between Harry and the forces of evil take place underground (*Stone*, *Chamber*, and *Phoenix*), after a brief trip underground (*Prisoner*), and in a graveyard (*Goblet*).

Every year recounted in the first five books, then, has featured an underground battle with the Dark Lord or his Death Eaters. Not in *Half-Blood Prince*, though – or at least not at first look. There is nothing like the trips "miles and miles" below Hogwarts we had in the first two books or the trip under the Whomping Willow or the fight far beneath the streets of London in the basement of the Ministry of Magic. We don't even portkey to a graveyard where most of the people present are underground as Harry did in *Goblet*.

But there are two underground scenes of importance – or "one and a half" underground scenes, let's say.

The first is the trip with Dumbledore to the seaside cave (Chapter 26) in search of a Voldemort Horcrux. They fight with the challenges and traps set by Voldemort at Lake Inferi, which include a host of dead bodies that live underwater. Shades of Styx? You betcha.

The "half" underground scene is Harry's fight with Severus at the gates of Hogwarts. I say this battle scene is "half" underground though obviously it is not beneath the surface of the earth because it follows two dramatic descents: Dumbledore's drop as a seeming corpse from the astronomy tower and the flight of Snape and Malfoy from the same tower down the stairs with Harry in heated pursuit. Dropping the many flights of stairs from tower to ground level for the final one-on-one satisfies the "underground" setting for the climactic battle.

8.   "Death" and Return to Life

One of Ms. Rowling's departures from classical "hero's journey" formula is the way each battle in the books is resolved. In every one of her books Harry dies a figurative or near death – and rises from the dead in the presence of a traditional literary symbol of Christ (a Philosopher's Stone in *Stone*, a Phoenix in *Chamber*, *Goblet*, and *Order of the Phoenix*, and a White Stag in *Prisoner*). This is a strong pointer to the theme of "love's victory over death" that shapes the meaning and the power of these magical "mystery plays" as well as to how Harry will ultimately overcome Tom Riddle, Jr.

In *Half-Blood Prince* we have a choice of symbols, believe it or not, depending on what you think of Severus Snape.

The obvious choice for the symbol of Christ? Buckbeak/Witherwing (BB/WW) the Hippogriff. A hippogriff is a flying combination of steed and griffin. The griffin part, half lion, half eagle, is a traditional symbol of Christ because it represents in animal form "the King of Heaven and Earth" as the eagles are king of heavenly animals or birds and the lion of terrestrial beasts. A hippogriff (after Orlando Furioso) is sometimes said to be a symbol of love, and, inasmuch as God is love, of Christ. BB/WW rescues Harry from a seemingly murderous Snape in Chapter 28, the 'Flight of the Prince' (*Prince*, pp. 604-605).

The problem is that in each of the five previous books Harry signals this moment by saying something about dying or being near death before his rescue or recovery near this symbol. Harry doesn't say anything like this when Severus seems to be about to kill him. Buckbeak appears after Harry is knocked down by Snape's "white-hot, whip-like something" that "hit him across the face." He has the wind knocked out of him, but he doesn't think "so this is death" like we'd expect because of his performances in previous books before the Christ symbol saves him.

Harry does speak of death, though, on the page before this confrontation. Having been hit with an Unforgivable Cruciatus Curse, Harry thinks, "… he would surely die of this agony, Snape was going to torture him to death or madness –" (p. 603). But it isn't Snape cursing Harry. Severus is, in fact, saving Harry from the other Death Eaters (by reminding them that "Potter belongs to the Dark Lord – we are to leave him! Go! Go!").

But, hey, c'mon…. Does that make Severus Snape a Christ symbol?

Well, yes, he is.

Most obviously in his name, The Half-Blood Prince. You don't have to be very clever to see in that name "a double-natured King." As all of Rowling's book titles are cryptonyms for Christ, this is an easy leap.

Severus is the double-natured man who transcends the Gryffindor/ Slytherin divide as we just learned in the literary alchemy chapter.

But that means that Dumbledore's murderer is a symbol of Christ?

There are at least three possibilities to explain what happens on the Tower in *Prince*: the storyline as presented is true and Professor Snape kills Dumbledore, Dumbledore has planned the event ever since his death was "stoppered" by Severus early the previous summer and takes the hit on the Tower, and the man on the Tower who seems to be Dumbledore is not Dumbledore and Snape doesn't kill him. Even if you assume that possibilities one and two are true, though, Severus is a decent symbol of Christ.

Assume that Dumbledore had demanded from Snape that Severus blast him should the situation require it (if his hand injury was a mortal wound or he knew drinking the Horcrux draught or Stygian waters would kill him, this makes sense). The fight between Snape and Dumbledore reported by Hagrid to Harry may very well have been only Snape's resistance to this horrible obedience to a friend and mentor.

It is a horrible obedience because it would mean giving up or sacrificing his life for a friend (Dumbledore) and an enemy (Harry Potter). Snape, as Dumbledore's killer, will never be safe again from the Order of the Phoenix – or from the Dark Lord if he learns it was less the Unbreakable Vow that made him do it than obeying Dumbledore's instructions. Professor Snape's sacrifice of his own life, in this light, is the ultimate act of love for the world. One could even say that it was Christ-like.

I wouldn't be so sure, even though we have been assured that "Dumbledore is definitely dead," that Severus murdered Dumbledore, or that he murdered anybody for that matter, on the Astronomy Tower. Severus' dual nature, long-suffering, and salvific sacrifices will have to speak for themselves at story's end. More on this in the coming chapters.

9.   Dumbledore Denouement

It wouldn't be a *Harry Potter* novel, we thought, without the meeting with Dumbledore at the end of the book to explain what has happened and why it happened. The moral of the story – and the introduction to the action of the next book! The ending of *Phoenix* in Dumbledore's office was no exception to this rule, however different (and violent) the fifth year's meeting between student and headmaster turned out to be. As Harry slides into his Slytherin half-nature as alchemical Rebis, it really could have been a lot worse. The nigredo is an ugly business.

It is to be noted here, too, that each story's ending is the explanation of the incredible surprise that took place in that book. More often than not (in every one of the first five books except *Phoenix*, unless you count the revelation of Umbridge's sending the dementors to Little Whining) we learn how we were taken in by a good guy who is really a bad guy or vice versa. This is, as we'll discuss in Chapter 4, Ms. Rowling's postmodern lesson to us about prejudice, in that we are exposed as having mistaken and misjudged a character entirely in our rush to pigeonhole the white and black hats.

I half expected, consequently, to learn at the end of *Half-Blood Prince* that Arabella Figg was a turncoat or that Rubeus Hagrid was the Half-Blood Prince and Heir of Gryffindor. We have to expect the world to be turned upside down at story's end if we are to learn what JKR is teaching. (Arabella, incidentally, is the name of a very frightening woman in Bram Stoker's *Lair of the White Worm* – and please don't doubt that Ms. Rowling has read this book).

The end-of-year conference in *Half-Blood Prince*, of course, was a little lopsided as Dumbledore had died or at least left the stage of active players. The White Tomb and Harry's reflections about the Headmaster there are the neat summary of what has happened in the book behind us and a pointer to the book ahead – which is what we looked for each year when Harry was debriefed by the big, white bumblebee. Please recall from Chapter 1 how Dumbledore's absence at book's end creates a train-sized passage for wholesale narrative misdirection. Without Dumbledore there to explain how mistaken and narrow Harry's view of events is, we're left believing he knows what he is talking about.

Check off step nine (and check out the tomb scene at the end of Hughes' *Tom Brown's School Days* for the "tip of the hat" to the first British schoolboy novel in the last chapter of *Half-Blood Prince*).

10. King's Cross Finish

Every year's journey ends at King's Cross Station, Platform 9 and ¾, at the London intersection of the magical and Muggle worlds (and, if memory serves, where Ms. Rowling's parents first met). King's Cross Station after a trip on the Hogwarts Express. "Last stop! King's Cross!"

Every year until *Half-Blood Prince* Harry has been picked up by the Dursleys and we prepare for another trip to Hogwarts in the coming year. But this year Harry decides to skip the trip home after the funeral and begin his next adventure right after stopping for just a moment at the Dursleys to recharge his magical protection.

That there is no visit to King's Cross this year came as something of a relief to me because of the suicide terrorist bombing at that exact underground station just weeks before *Prince* was published. Harry is on his way to the Dursleys' home, though, so even though we do not match up quite perfectly with the "yellow footprints" painted on the ground to mark Rowling's repeated tale-trail, we do have conformity to purpose. Step ten, check.

With the exception of the first and last steps of Harry's annual journey, then, every one of Ms. Rowling's Hero's Journey Ten Points was in place for *Half-Blood Prince* – and even the two exceptions perform the function of what we expected to happen at King's Cross and Privet Drive.

Should we expect the same formula in the last novel?

Yes and no.

No, we shouldn't because Harry's plans, as he shared them with Ron and Hermione at the end of *Prince* are anything but formulaic. He said in response to Ron's hopeful assertion that Hogwarts remain open next year (because it would be safer there than anywhere else):

> "I'm not coming back even if it does re-open," said Harry.
>
> Ron gaped at him, but Hermione said sadly, "I knew you were going to say that. But then what will you do?"
>
> "I'm going back to the Dursleys' once more, because Dumbledore wanted me to," said Harry. "But it'll be a short

visit, and then I'll be gone for good."

"But where will you be if you don't come back to school?"

"I thought I might go to Godric's Hollow," Harry muttered. He had had the idea in his head ever since the night of Dumbledore's death. "For me, it started there, all of it. I've just got a feeling I need to go there. And I can visit my parents' graves, I'd like that."

"And then what?" said Ron.

"Then I've got to track down the rest of the Horcruxes, haven't I?" said Harry, his eyes upon Dumbledore's white tomb, reflected in the water on the other side of the lake. "That's what he wanted me to do, that's why he told me about them. If Dumbledore was right – and I'm sure he was – there are still four of them out there. I've got to find them and destroy them, and then I've got to go after the seventh bit of Voldemort's soul, the bit that's still in his body, and I'm the one who's going to kill him. And if I meet Severus Snape along the way," he added, "so much the better for me, so much the worse for him." (**Prince**, Chapter 30, pp. 650-651)

Ron and Hermione then tell Harry they're joining him for this last crusade. Ron reminds him, too, that they all are obliged to attend Bill and Fleur's alchemical wedding.

Harry's itinerary, at first glance, seems a definite departure from the first six years of his magical education. For starters, it seems certain he won't be coming back to Hogwarts.

But, as a point of fact, oddly enough, none of Ms. Rowling's Hero Journey steps require a trip to Hogwarts. Harry can blast away from the Dursleys' and just go somewhere else (as he has several times, especially to the Burrow, where Ron says he is obliged to go). As long as Ron and Hermione are along for the ride (and they've bought a ticket) and we meet up with Severus Snape, as we are bound to, Ms. Rowling can bring her alchemical Great Work to a finish outside the usual cauldron of Hogwarts School of Witchcraft and Wizardry.

Having said that, I'm fairly confident Harry will be going back to Hogwarts, perhaps not as a full-time student, but certainly for his remaining school year. The school is too much a part of the formula and stage setting of these stories for Ms. Rowling to abandon it completely or make it a side element.

Harry can come back and be faithful to his Horcrux/Voldemort/ Snape seek-and-destroy mission in three or four different ways. The most obvious is his learning at the Dursleys,' at the Burrow wedding, or more likely, at Godric's Hollow that the Horcrux secrets he needs to learn are back at his alma mater. Be it Founders' artifacts, Riddle trinkets, the Hogwarts graveyard (Deathly Hallows?), or his own scar that he needs help removing or disarming, Harry will need to return to Hogwarts.

Perhaps the Order of the Phoenix will set up Headquarters at Hogwarts. Or it will come under attack and Harry will feel obliged to be in the thick of its defenses. Or Ron and Hermione will be made Head Boy and Head Girl – and they set him up in a nice room in the Room of Requirement. Or any combination of these things.

Ms. Rowling thinks in terms of patterns. To understand her books and thinking, it behooves us to be looking for the patterns in her books she uses so effectively. If we want to guess or speculate about where she is going, the same rule applies. Look for her adherence to the formulas we see in every one of the first six books. Literary alchemy and the Hero's Journey's Ten Steps are your best places to start.

Repeated Elements

After the literary formula of a Hero's Journey, the next pattern we should look at are the story elements that Ms. Rowling uses repeatedly in the stories, especially if any of these signature qualities of her books do not appear in one or both of the last books. The things she does repeatedly, like her choice to use alchemical symbolism throughout the books and to frame them on a Hero's Journey skeleton, are good signs that she will use them again. If she has given these elements a rest in *Half-Blood Prince* or in both ***Order of the Phoenix*** and ***Half-Blood Prince***, give those elements special attention. She's saving them for the "big twist" at story's end.

There are six especially important repeated elements to unlock the upcoming ***Deathly Hallows*** and the meaning of these books. I'm not going to talk about the repeated elements that may or may not be foreshadowing of future events. We'll pass over Trevor the Toad, Goblin Revolts, the Draught of Living Death, and references to and instances of beheading, even the sock sub-theme. The six repeated elements, in the first five books at least, were provided by Dumbledore in the debriefing at story's end.

The six elements are:

- Harry's cluelessness;
- Lord Voldemort's plans;
- Harry's peculiar scar;
- The New Guy's secret,
- Faked Deaths, and
- Mistaken identities.

Harry's Cluelessness

As discussed in the first chapter's exposition of narrative misdirection, the only thing we know for certain in the *Harry Potter* novels is that Harry won't get the mystery right. He's heroic, he's virtuous, but he believes that whatever he sees, thinks, or feels is pretty much the way things are. And, in this, Harry is just plain dopey. Looking over his shoulder and into his thoughts, we never know even half of what's going on, but the poor lad believes he has a grip on the big picture. His track record, though, says otherwise.

In *Stone*, he thinks Snape is the agent of Lord Voldemort in hot pursuit of the Philosopher's Stone. Wrong. Severus Snape is doing everything he can to keep Harry safe and keep the Stone from Quirrelldemort.

In *Chamber*, he thinks the Diary is a truth-teller. Wrong. The Diary is a Horcrux of Riddledemort and is a lying, murderous vehicle of the Dark Lord. Whoops.

In *Prisoner*, he believes that Sirius Black is the man who betrayed his parents to Voldemort – and that his godfather is out to get him. Really wrong. Black is trying to save Harry from the rat who did betray his parents, who is disguised as Ron's pet, Scabbers.

In *Goblet*, Harry trusts 'Mad-Eye' Moody. Again, big mistake. Moody turns out to be Barty Crouch, Jr., a Death Eater doing everything possible to smooth Harry's portkey trip to the Dark Lord's rebirthing party.

Key Three: The Hero's Journey

In *Phoenix*, Harry disregards the advice of his elders and tries as hard as he can to open himself to the dream about the Department of Mysteries and the long passageway. Dumb, dumb, dumb. If he had worked on his Occlumency instead, he wouldn't have been sucked into Lord Voldemort's trap – and Sirius wouldn't have died.

And in *Half-Blood Prince*, Harry is convinced that Draco Malfoy is a full-fledged, tattoo-bearing Death Eater on a secret mission from the Dark Lord. He also thinks that Severus Snape is a Black Hat and that Dumbledore is a fool to trust him.

In *Prince*, he is, of course, exactly right.

Or so the story line would have us believe.

I'm saying you've got to be borderline blind and silly if you'll believe this. The no-twist, "Harry was 'spot-on'" ending of *Half-Blood Prince* is the necessary table setting for the series conclusion, in which story we'll almost certainly learn what Dumbledore couldn't tell us at *Prince*'s finish. Narrative misdirection is what Ms. Rowling does best and it requires Harry's being woefully mistaken about what's going on in the book. Thinking that Harry is right is like believing that the Brooklyn Bridge is for sale. If you're thinking, "Everyone's got to get lucky once, right?" I'm telling you, "Not in this game."

The questions to ask are not whether Harry missed something but "how much did he miss?" and "what particular things?" After *Phoenix*, we should be wondering if anyone is taking advantage of his gullibility and "people-saving thing." The first thing he certainly missed was what Lord Voldemort was up to off-stage in *Half-Blood Prince*.

Lord Voldemort's Plans

Every *Harry Potter* novel has at least three stories, the second of which we only learn about at the end. The first story, the one we watch over Harry's shoulder, is about what he's doing, experiencing, and thinking. The second story is what Lord Voldemort and his servants are doing. (The third story, which we've never been told, is what Dumbledore and/or Snape are up to.) Joyce Odell, the Red Hen, says that it always pays to recall that "the Villain is the Story." The books confirm that the real story is the Voldemort action taking place off-screen.

In *Stone*, we learn at story's end that Voldemort, residing beneath

131

Quirrell's turban, is doing everything possible to survive and to get his paws on the Philosopher's Stone. There are hints that something evil is going on at Hogwarts, but the Dark Lord piggybacking a faculty member? Total surprise both to Harry and to us readers.

In *Chamber*, Voldemort again comes to Hogwarts, this time inside his Diary Horcrux. Harry suspects this-and-that wizard mistakenly but is shocked at the climactic scene in the *Chamber of Secrets* to learn that his good buddy Tom Riddle is the young Lord Voldemort doing everything he can to learn all about Harry and to kill him.

In *Prisoner*, we learn in the crucible of the Shrieking Shack that Black is not a Death Eater or a blackguard and that Pettigrew/Scabbers was and is the Dark Lord's servant. Knock us over with a feather.

In *Goblet*, Harry learns in the graveyard, that while he was doing everything possible to survive and thrive in the Tri-Wizard Tournament, Voldemort was working his plan to get Harry ready for his victory trip to the Re-Birthing Party. And a real surprise party for Harry that was.

In the climax of *Phoenix*, of course, he finds out that the "dreams" he's been having are planted images of the Dark Lord, again getting him to come to a private party he really doesn't want to go to. The Death Eaters have a good laugh at how Harry has, once again, neglected to think about what Lord Voldemort could be doing off-stage.

And in *Half-Blood Prince*, Harry figures out in the very beginning of the book, well before they get to Hogwarts, that Draco is a Death Eater on a secret mission from Voldemort. Events and the Dumbledore-Draco dialogue on the Astronomy Tower show that Harry was exactly right; the only thing he hadn't figured out about the mission was that it was an Albus-assassination-attempt.

This, of course, is what we're supposed to believe.

If you believe it, I suggest you reconsider.

First, Harry has always been shocked at story's end to find that he hadn't considered what the Dark Lord had been planning all through the book. In *Prince*, he's only surprised at what the mission was about and that it seemed to succeed. This is an obvious and radical departure from formula.

Big red flag. Do you feel the rug coming out from underneath you? It should be pulled in the next book now that you're standing right where the author wants and you're leaning the way she hopes.

Second, all we learn on the Astronomy Tower is that Draco was given a semi-suicidal assignment by Voldemort to kill Dumbledore. What we don't learn includes:

- Who was helping him (the great help he told Severus he was getting);
- Why only second string and physically violent Death Eaters are sent to Hogwarts and the Tower to help him;
- What Dumbledore and Snape are doing throughout the book; and
- Why Voldemort believed that an underage wizard was ever going to be able to kill the greatest wizard then living.

As Dumbledore says to Draco on the Tower, "Nobody would be surprised that you had died in your attempt to kill me – forgive me, but Lord Voldemort probably expects it" (*Half-Blood Prince*, Chapter 27, p. 592). So Dumbledore, or whoever is playing his part, doesn't believe that Draco's assassination assignment was the heart of Lord Voldemort's scheming for the year. Given that Harry believes it was and Harry is always wrong about or oblivious to Lord Voldemort's plans, why should we agree with him?

Look to find out in the final chapters of *Deathly Hallows* what Lord Voldemort's real mission was backstage during the action of *Half-Blood Prince* as well as his big plans for the takeover of the Wizarding and Muggle worlds (breeding dementors, right?). Draco is nothing but a stand-in and a distraction, almost certainly. Or so the patterns suggest.

Harry's Scar

Here's a good litmus strip question for how obsessed a *Harry Potter* reader is. Just ask "how many times does Harry's scar hurt and Ms. Rowling describe the ordeal as 'pain beyond anything Harry had ever experienced'?" The true believers can give you three or four instances without straining. Checking my books, I found Harry in agony about his scar in *Stone*, Chapter 17, p. 294, *Chamber*, Chapter 17, p. 320, *Goblet*, Chapter 33, p. 657, and *Phoenix*, Chapter 36, pp. 815-816. I'm confident there are more.

In every book, Harry has his scar moments. Dreams and the presence or high emotions of Voldemort seem to set it off with remarkable regularity. In *Phoenix* especially, Harry's scar is going off consistently and painfully like the "alarm bell" curse scar that Cornelius Fudge dismisses it as at the end of *Goblet* (Chapter 36, p. 706). It seems throughout this entire year, the scar is "hurting" him, "blinding" him with pain, and seeming to split his head in two.

And in *Half-Blood Prince*, the scar pain and mention of the scar just stop. All gone.

Why?

As you'll recall, Dumbledore gave this explanation to Harry in Chapter 4, 'Horace Slughorn:'

> "Lord Voldemort has finally realized the dangerous access to his thoughts and feelings you have been enjoying. It appears that he is now employing Occlumency against you."
>
> "Well, I'm not complaining," said Harry, who missed neither the disturbing dreams nor the startling insights into Voldemort's mind. (*Prince*, p. 59)

There are several things that are wrong with this explanation, which problems, taken together, make the explanation less than credible.

Voldemort's great success in *Phoenix* was invading Harry's mind and planting suggestions, images, and feelings there. No doubt a large part of Harry's adolescent madness and ALL CAPS "conversations" with his friends are due to Voldemort's influence (and his becoming part-Slytherin in the nigredo), even Voldemort's presence..

Lord Voldemort gives all that up because he thinks Harry has "dangerous access" to his thoughts and feelings? Isn't that a bit of a stretch? As we'll explore in Chapter 6, it seems more likely that this accomplished wizard would only practice Occlumency to shield his intrusions into Harry's head so he can look through Harry's eyeballs without setting off Harry's scar-alarm.

If we do buy Dumbledore's explanation to Harry, though, Harry shouldn't feel relieved. The only reason the Dark Lord would be frightened or even concerned about Harry being able to deliberately plumb Voldemort's head would be if he's planning something horrific. Lord Thingy is not looking out for Harry's long-term health and safety.

Harry should be instantly on guard and concerned.

Nope. Not Harry. "Scar not hurting? Whew," he thinks, "Onto other things."

In addition to being another pointer to the repeated elements of Harry's cluelessness and of Lord Voldemort's off-stage planning about which Harry is ignorant, the absence of scar pain throughout *Half-Blood Prince* highlights the departure from formula this represents. In the first five books, the scar is with us. In *Phoenix*, especially, the scar's tingling or pain is a constant element. In *Prince*, it vanishes.

You still standing on that carpet? Can't feel it moving at all? The scar becomes invisible in *Prince* in order to position us properly for the "big twist" coming. Just like Harry, we're delighted to forget about it. Look for it at the heart of the revelations in the last chapters of *Deathly Hallows* or, as mentioned above, as one of the reasons Harry learns early in the book that compel him to return to Hogwarts for his last school year. It seems plausible, even probable, that (1) Harry's scar is a Horcrux (see Chapter 7), (2) which Voldemort is using as a window into Harry's world, and that (3) the action of *Half-Blood Prince* is staged to deceive him.

The New Guy's Secret

We learn in one of Dumbledore's Voldemort Defense Training sessions with Harry in *Half-Blood Prince* that the Dark Lord had cursed the Defense Against the Dark Arts position when Dumbledore turned down Voldemort's job application. "You see, we have never been able to keep a Defense Against the Dark Arts teacher for more than a year since I refused the post to Lord Voldemort" (Chapter 20, p. 446).

This is the explanation for one of the more interesting repeated elements in these stories. The "new guy" on the faculty, always the Defense Against the Dark Arts teacher, turns out to have a fairly astonishing secret. (Rubeus and Firenze join the faculty, too, but they aren't strangers to us when they appear as teachers.)

Professor Quirrell? Servant and vehicle of Lord Voldemort at Hogwarts. Gilderoy Lockhart? Fraudulent hero whose adventures (and consequent book royalties) have been stolen from the memories of brave witches and wizards around the world. Remus Lupin? Werewolf! Mad-Eye Moody? Death Eater setting up Harry for a trip to a graveyard.

Dolores Umbridge? Over-the-top bureaucrat who sicced Dementors on Harry over the summer break in Little Whining.

The pattern is obvious and dramatic. The New Guy or Gal has a secret – and it's a whopper.

In *Half-Blood Prince*, the New Guy is the emeritus chemistry teacher, Horace Slughorn. His secret? An affection for crystallized pineapple? Cloying social parasite's disease? Likes to dress up as living room furniture?

Horace Slughorn isn't what he appears to be. He's holding onto a big secret. At the Dumbledore requiem/faculty meeting at the end of *Prince*, Horace is sweating it out, literally and figuratively, as he argues for the closing of the school and his chance to leave with his secret undiscovered.

That's how the pattern works. At least, the way it worked until *Phoenix*.

Umbridge's secret in *Phoenix* was pretty lame. We knew she was crazy and a sadist by book's end; discovering she sent the Attack Dementors to get Harry was not an earth-turning shocker. Slughorn, though, while not as unpleasant as Dolores (ugh), seems transparent in character. Nobody's hero, certainly.

The patterns suggest this anomaly alone should raise another red flag.

Again, patterns don't lie and every Defense Against the Dark Arts teacher has had a secret. Expect to find out Sluggo's secret is one of the whopper twists of the whole series. Could he be EVIL Slughorn, a theory I championed in the first chapter of *Who Killed Albus Dumbledore?* Maybe. I suspect, though, that Horace is in on the "Deceive Voldemort Scar-O-Scope Broadcast" that Dumbledore's friends are producing at Hogwarts. I'm willing to bet, in fact, if the stakes aren't too demanding, that his secret is that neither of the Potions Masters are who they appear to be at least at one point or two in *Half-Blood Prince*.

Read Sally March Gallo's essay on Horace – and stage magic, believe it or not – in the third chapter of *Who Killed Albus Dumbledore?* for an education about Sluggo's real world, historical model. Be forewarned, though; if you really want to believe it's Dumbledore on the Astronomy Tower, don't read Ms. Gallo's exposition of who Horace Slughorn is and what he is capable of doing. Hold on to your beliefs.

Key Three: The Hero's Journey

Faked Deaths

Another of the most important repeated events and inexplicable allusions in the *Harry Potter* series is to a faked or staged death. The event that we know took place is Peter Pettigrew's "demise" after the Potters were murdered, a death that he orchestrated both to escape Sirius Black's revenge and to lay the blame for betraying the Potters on our favorite big, black dog of an Animagus. The "big twist" in the hottest end-of-book crucible we have seen thus far is the revelation of Peter's staged death that Sirius and Remus reveal to Harry, Ron, and Hermione in *Prisoner's* Shrieking Shack finale.

Peter, of course, wasn't one to let a good trick go without repetition. When he discovers that Black is inside Hogwarts and out for blood earlier in *Prisoner*, Scabbers again fakes his death and pins the blame on Hermione's pet cat/kneazle, Crookshanks.

The inexplicable allusion to a staged death comes from Dumbledore himself on the Astronomy Tower in his appeal to Draco.

> "I can help you, Draco."
>
> "No, you can't," said Malfoy, his wand shaking very badly indeed. "Nobody can. He told me to do it or he'd kill me. I've got no choice."
>
> "He cannot kill you if you are already dead. Come over to the right side, Draco, and we can hide you more completely than you can possibly imagine. What is more, I can send members of the Order to your mother tonight to hide her likewise. Nobody would be surprised that you had died in your attempt to kill me – forgive me, but Lord Voldemort probably expects it. Nor would the Death Eaters be surprised that we had captured and killed your mother – it is what they would do themselves, after all. Your father is safe at the moment in Azkaban…. When the time comes, we can protect him, too. Come over to the right side, Draco…you are not a killer…." (*Prince*, Chapter 27, pp. 591-592)

Dumbledore simultaneously suggests that the Order will stage two deaths to throw the Death Eaters off their scent and that this is almost a matter of routine to them. Perhaps Pettigrew as a former member of the Order learned this gem of a stratagem from the Good Guys the way Draco learned about communicating at a distance via enchanted coins from Dumbledore's Army (*Prince*, Chapter 27, p. 589). Fandom scratches its collective head in thinking whom they could have hidden before by a staged death – Snape's parents? Regulus Black?

Ms. Rowling has made it very clear that "dead is dead" in her magical universe and that "Dumbledore is definitely dead." There won't be any Aslan resurrections or Gandalf-landing-on-the-Balrog-just-right in her stories. But, she also has shown that both the white and black hats in her stories are not above faking a death or two if it suits their purpose.

Look for a Shrieking Shack-like revelation in the grand finale about whose death was faked either at the end of *Prince* or in the last battle with Voldemort in *Deathly Hallows* – or both. Somebody has to have been sipping at the Draught of Living Death we've been reading about for six books....

Mistaken Identities

The last repeated pattern I want to share with you of the set of things we see in every book and usually find out about in the battle scene or Dumbledore denouement is the number of mistaken identities we see in this series. There's a little overlap with the "New Guy's Secret," of course, because as often as not, their secret is that he isn't what or who we think he is. That's why I'm wagering that Horace turns out to be someone else, even if only for one prolonged adventure.

The objection I hear most often to any theory about Horace Slughorn's secret is that it is unlikely he is very bad or very good because everything we know about him in *Half-Blood Prince* tells us he is neither very bad nor very good. Just a slug, and a self-important slug at that.

Of the mistaken identities in these books involving the New Guy, though, you tell me in which ones Ms. Rowling tipped her hand so that we knew this character wasn't what he seemed:

- Professor Quirrell;
- Professor Lupin; and
- Professor Moody.

The revelations of their duplicity in each case arrived like a lightning bolt. In each case, it appeared that Dumbledore was deceived as well as Harry and we readers. There were few if any clues to speak of. Ms. Rowling barely plays fair here – except we should know enough by now to look hardest at the New Guy to see if he is somebody whose identity is hidden from us.

How about all those Ministry warnings not to trust that everyone you meet is who they say they are? Dumbledore's asking Harry how he knows he isn't a Death Eater in disguise? Molly and Arthur Weasley's precautions before Molly is to let Arthur into the Burrow? It's not as if Ms. Rowling isn't pointing to what she's doing.

There is a subtheme of people appearing as something other than what they appear, especially involving the liberal use of Polyjuice Potion, the difficult-to-brew goodie that allows a person to become another person for a period of time. Crouch, Jr., uses it to good effect in *Goblet*, but Harry, Ron, and Hermione use it in Chamber and Draco, Crabbe, and Goyle are into it regularly as well in *Half-Blood Prince*. The two most interesting characters in *Prince*, of course, are potions making geniuses, Severus and Horace, and Slughorn has a cauldron full of Polyjuice Potion brewing in his first N.E.W.T. level class with Harry's classmates.

As important, really, is the entire subject devoted to shape-changing at Hogwarts, Transfiguration. The masters of this magical art are able to become Animagi, animals retaining human consciousness. The Marauders, Professor McGonagall, Rita Skeeter, and we assume, Dumbledore, a former transfigurations teacher and alchemist, are all able to pull off the feat – and those not able to transform themselves can be transformed by adepts, as Crouch/Moody demonstrated with Draco the Bouncing Ferret.

Not to mention our friend, Tonks, the Auror and Metamorphmagus.

But in *Prince*, as with Harry's scar, we have none of this. Even Tonks stops changing the shape of her nose and the color of her hair. There isn't a single mistaken identity, everybody is who they seem to be (besides Crabbe and Goyle), and, well, that's that.

I have discussed this absence with a few friends on my private boards and several theories of who might be somebody else in Polyjuice disguise. What is remarkable about their reaction is that it is uniformly dismissive. One maven assures me that Polyjuice switches are impossible because changes by potion have been "used so many times" that it must be stale and tired for her to trot it out again. Others say that Ms. Rowling doesn't give us any signs of anyone being someone else and surely there would be something pointing us to a character's having been switched out.

These are thoughtful readers, nice people, and good friends with whom I have to disagree. They are missing a huge chunk of what these stories are about. They don't get the patterns game we're playing, for one thing. Or the larger meaning, the theme in these books that the repeated mistaken identities reinforce.

There will almost certainly be *Deathly Hallows* revelations of the several concealed persons in *Half-Blood Prince*. It is part of the weave and woof of the stories. And it is an essential part of the postmodern myth that Ms. Rowling is writing.

The One as Sum: The Six Foreshadowed Endings

I'd like to end each of these chapters by trying the key we've just learned about in the lock of the door separating us from what happens in *Harry Potter and the Deathly Hallows*. As noted above, we should expect to see most if not all of the ten steps in Ms. Rowling's version of the classical hero's odyssey.

The cyclical nature of this adventure gives us more clues.

A Hero's Journey, after all, is a circle. The hero is obliged to return, much transformed by his adventures, to the point of this adventure's origin. Harry comes back every year to the Dursleys' home on Privet Drive where the next cycle of his seven year alchemical transformation will begin in the next book. In this chapter on the Hero's Journey key to unlock *Harry Potter*, we've reviewed the ten steps Ms. Rowling has given Harry's odyssey each year and noted six of the more important repeated elements.

The importance of "closing the circle" or the unity of the Hero's Journey is the help it gives us in seeing the end of the series in previous endings. It is a classical topos or cliché that the telos or "end, purpose" of everything – to include stories - can be found in its arche or beginning. Each *Harry Potter* book begins with the problem that Harry must overcome in that year's alchemical catharsis (See *Looking for God in Harry Potter* for more on this subject). Each of Harry's first six years has been a full alchemical cycle in itself as well as a part of the seven stage Great Work.

Just as every year in this series describes a circle, the various endings will probably be joined in *Deathly Hallows.* The summary ending of the last cycle and adventure should reflect the ending of each of the previous six books. As lines of possibilities in our game of literary Sodoku, then, we can look for an element from each of the first six books' endings in the seventh.

Here is a quick list of obvious points from the endings of the six books we have in hand, listed in reverse order with stray thoughts about what we might look for in *Deathly Hallows*:

• Look for either a sacrificial death or a staged death a la Dumbledore's dive in *Half-Blood Prince.* My first thought, because it is the rubedo, is that it will be Rubeus Hagrid. My gut feeling (and fear) is that it will be Severus Snape, having been cut down by Peter Pettigrew.

• Don't be surprised if there is a secret, too, from the Department of Mysteries (the light behind the door, the Veil, the golden Fountain of Magical Brethren…) and a "Voldemort within Harry" moment straight out of the battle royale in *Phoenix.* Harry's only hope, perhaps, is embracing Voldemort again, literally and figuratively this time, thereby defeating him with love. Linda McCabe has written that this is the end we might expect from a story with so many Arthurian references: Arthur and Mordred in a death embrace. As we'll see, this jibes with the idea of the Hermaphrodites as conductors of love.

• Several books have ended with revelations of hidden identities that we've swallowed because of narrative misdirection – most importantly, Quirrell in *Stone,* Sirius Black in *Prisoner,* Barty Crouch, Jr., in *Goblet* – so the end of *Deathly Hallows,* will probably feature the goodness of an apparent bad guy revealed – and the badness of a seeming good guy brought to life. For reasons I'll explain in Chapter 6, Lupin may not be who he seems to be, Severus is a Dumbledore man, Horace Slughorn is not the callow, shallow boob he seems, and even how and when Dumbledore "died" will surprise us.

• *Chamber of Secrets* and two other books ended with a Harry-Tom Riddle subterranean battle, so expect another in their final confrontation. Where? Unless he returns to a battle scene or an echo of one (say another graveyard?), Harry may be headed to King's Cross Station for the climax of **Deathly Hallows**. It isn't "miles beneath Hogwarts," certainly, but because of the meaningful name and it being an intersection with the Muggle world, it has a familiar resonance. Harry having to rescue the Dursleys? Sounds cathartic to me.

• And, first and last, expect the ending of all the books to reflect the beginnings and endings of the first book with (1) a surprising Slytherin defeat caused by the courage of Neville Longbottom in confronting his friends and (2) the helplessness of Harry Potter, infant-like in his innocence, after surviving inexplicably and against all odds a confrontation with the Dark Lord.

As noted above, the first time you reread **Half-Blood Prince** you are struck by all the perumbration or foreshadowing in the first chapters. It's hard to miss the second time through **Prince** all the telescopes folks are carrying, pointers to the climax of the book on the Astronomy Tower. Remember, also, Dumbledore's position in the cavern and on the ground beneath the Astronomy Tower (glasses askew, mouth open) is the way Harry is described at the beginning of Chapter 3, Will and Won't.

Foreshadowing in picture and theme is a favorite Rowling tool, then, one she pulls from her classical training in which "the beginning is half the end." We can expect to be startled, nonetheless, even when looking for a finish with all the previous endings included, at how deftly she manages it (and how she invites us to go back and find all the pointers to the story's resolution in the first six books).

Segue to Postmodern Themes

Fully rested? Okay, then, time for the most challenging and perhaps the most important key of the five – the postmodern themes of the **Harry Potter** books. These themes and the resonance they have with 21st century readers are probably, if you could choose only one reason, the cause of Pottermania.

Disney Does Derrida:
Postmodern Ideas in Pop Culture

"Bigotry is probably the thing I detest most. All forms of intolerance, the whole idea of "that which is different from me is necessary evil." I really like to explore the idea that difference is equal and good. But there's another idea that I like to explore, too. Oppressed groups are not, generally speaking, people who stand firmly together — no, sadly, they kind of subdivide among themselves and fight like hell. That's human nature, so that's what you see here. This world of wizards and witches, they're already ostracized, and then within themselves, they've formed a loathsome pecking order." – J. K. Rowling

http://www.accio-quote.org/articles/2000/0900-ew-jensen.htm

Thoughtful people, insecure folks, and your just plain neurotic man-on-the-street (is that all of us?) spend quite a bit of time, albeit for different reasons, thinking about what other people think about them. Call it the "Bobby Burns Syndrome" (a la his 'To a Louse:' "O wad some Power the giftie gie us/ To see oursels as ithers see us!"). As someone who writes and talks about *Harry Potter* in my free time, I don't have to work at finding out what others think of me. *Harry* fans who have read anything I've written feel free to tell me and the world online what an idiot or genius I am on their Live Journal site.

The off-the-wall and unedited criticism can be a little galling, as you can imagine, but, by and large, it's good to know how you're being pigeonholed. The two big mental categories most of *Harry* fandom has stuffed me in (so they can safely disregard anything I say contrary to their opinions) are "deluded Christian" and "the Alchemy Guy." If you graduated from the literary alchemy sequence here in Chapter 2, you understand the alchemy tag I wear. The reputation I have as a reader forcing Ms. Rowling into a Christian straitjacket is more interesting.

The resistance to the possibilities that Ms. Rowling is what she says she is, namely, a Christian, and that she is writing edifying books that draw heavily from a literary tradition that is almost exclusively Christian is not restricted to fundamentalist *Harry* Haters from every Christian community. The chief resistance to these ideas comes from the "unchurched" parts of fandom who don't want Harry to be something as "white bread" as a Christian hero. The "fundies" are, as a rule, more fun than these folks.

What has challenged me for the last few months has been realizing that those readers who think I have exaggerated the specifically Christian message of Ms. Rowling in her books, what could be called her "Inkling likeness" or "evangelical intent," may be on the right track, albeit traveling in the wrong direction. Comments Ms. Rowling made in her interviews at the release of *Half-Blood Prince* and a lecture by Houston Baptist University's Andrew Lazo about C. S. Lewis and J. R. R. Tolkien, have made it clear to me that, as important as the Christian elements are in the *Harry Potter* stories, they aren't the only reason they are so popular.

Transcendent or timeless qualities alone aren't enough to sell millions of books or we'd all be reading the *Paradisio* and *Paradise Lost*. For books to sell well they need to resonate with the spirit of the times in which they are written first if there is to be any chance of their readers sticking around for the more edifying alchemical drama.

Duh.

While listening to Lazo's lecture on the remarkably modern qualities of J.R.R. Tolkien's and C. S. Lewis' writing at the *Past Watchful Dragons* C. S. Lewis Conference at Belmont University, it occurred to me that I needed to take a long look at Joanne Rowling's *Harry Potter* books in a similar light. Is Ms. Rowling a writer very much of our times; is she, in the parlance of university literature professors, a "Postmodern Writer"? The question struck me as at once self-evident and at least as fantastic as most postmodern literature and criticism fancies itself.

The common sense of the idea is, of course, what else could she be? A time traveler? Ms. Rowling lives in the here and now of the 21st century, breathing the air and shaped by the ideas of our postmodern times. For her to be anything else or to believe that she is more of a different age or period than her own, perhaps, as, say, an Inkling or a second Jane Austen. These are possibilities, prima facie, that should make us skeptical – and I say that as one that has said both these things. Her unprecedented success alone shows Ms. Rowling is speaking to the hearts of the readers of her times effectively and profoundly, not as an anachronism or a dinosaur throwback.

This idea – Rowling as postmodern – struck me as bizarre, too, however obvious or undeniable it may be, because it is something like what several of the more ardent Harry Hating Christian critics say she is. My favorite is the inimitable and unsatirisable Brjit Kjos, the internet goddess and fundamentalist culture warrior, who has said that Ms. Rowling AND her Christian admirers are horrid "PoMos" and bound for hell for their relativism and amorality. Michael O'Brien and Richard Abanes, though more carefully packaged (and coherent) than Ms. Kjos, have made similar noises vis-a-vis Harry's postmodernism.

This struck me as odd – that an idea could be simultaneously "necessarily true" and something voiced by writers and thinkers who have proven themselves again and again to be incapable of reading *Harry Potter* except in a risible sociopolitical context. Looking at Ms. Rowling in light of the times in which we live, though, does throw light on several topics of controversy and curiosity about her books. Not only does the idea of Ms. Rowling as a postmodern writer illumine her use of magic in the books, which deconstruction of Levitical teaching still ignites criticism in some culture war enclaves, it also explains the academic and literary prize communities' disregard for *Harry Potter* and her recent flip-flop flap about whether she thinks C. S. Lewis is a "genius" or a transparent pedant.

Let's look first, then, at what postmodern literature is, and then at Ms. Rowling as a postmodern writer to see how she fits and does not fit this pigeonhole from a literature textbook. Pardon the necessarily extended departure here from *Harry Potter* to lay the groundwork for an appreciation of Ms. Rowling as a writer of our times and her books as the postmodern epic.

Postmodern Literature

To get your head around postmodernism and the sub-category of postmodern literature ("PoMo Lit"), you need more than a literature textbook. A survey of Western Civilization text is a good start, but you'll also want anthologies of Comparative Religion, Epistemology, Linguistics, and any texts dealing specifically with Modernism and Postmodernism. The task is getting a grip on how we think today, which, beyond the trick of looking at your own vision or eyeballs, requires a perspective on how we came to think this way.

If you haven't already done this work with your University backhoe, I'm going to assume that has been your conscious choice. I won't drag you, consequently, through the four signature criticisms made by postmodernists and this school of thought's distinctive method. In case you are interested, though, they are

- presence or presentation (versus representation and construction),

- origin (versus phenomenon),
- unity (versus plurality), and

- transcendence of norms (versus their immanence). It typically offers an analysis of phenomenon through constitutive otherness. *From Postmodernism to Modernism: An Anthology* (Cahoone, ed., Blackwell, 2001), pg.14

In fact, I'm going to skip over even defining what postmodern literature is except as much as we need to discuss relevant characteristics to decide whether Ms. Rowling is or isn't fairly criticized or applauded as a postmodern. The best way I can think of to share these characteristics, that is, without boring you to tears with stuff undergraduate English majors at University study, is to talk about a movie I watched with my children, Disney's Sky High.

Disney Does Derrida

I'm not a big fan of movies but I like sitting with the family in the living room to watch a fun film on the DVD player the local librarian gave us (the guy determined to bring us out of what he imagines is a quasi-Amish existence, two steps and a Cuisineart removed from the Mennonites). The kids live for these nights, if the younger boys always ask afterward if I'll read to them before they go to bed.

I'd never heard of *Sky High* but that's par for the course and my wife, Mary, told me it was about superheroes. I grew up on a binge diet of comic books, *Lay's*™ Potato Chips, and television, so I thought this would be a great flashback for me. You'll recall how much I enjoyed the Fantastic Four flick.

It turns out *Sky High* is not really about superheroes fighting Bad Guys like Superman and Spiderman do. It's a movie about the children of superheroes and their top secret high school on a floating island in the sky (hence "Sky High"). What's great about it, for me at least, is that it serves as a great example of postmodern storytelling.

There was nothing revolutionary or ground-breaking in the story. Almost any popular movie or book of the last ten years, from *The Matrix* to *Artemis Fowl*, could be reviewed for the same purpose. Last Christmas at www.HogwartsProfessor.com, I used the Rankin-Bass Christmas special Rudolph the Red-Nosed Reindeer (1964), the most popular television show in history, to illustrate postmodern themes.

I use *Sky High* here, though, to encourage you to go and rent it if you haven't seen it yet or even if you have. The movie illustrates ten key points about the way we see things today that storytellers of our times incorporate into their stories to make us feel at home. After seeing how it works with *Sky High*, watch *Happy Feet* and *Apocalypto* – or any of the *Harry Potter* flicks – with your PoMo score-card. They're all making the same postmodern points.

We'll use these points as gauges for *Harry Potter* and Rowling's postmodern qualities in a moment. If you haven't seen Sky High, don't worry. You can rent it at any big-box movie store, you haven't missed much if you decide not to see it, and, if you do, you'll like it more after reading here what it's really about…

Sky High: The Movie

Sky High is a story about the son of America's greatest superheroes, essentially Captain America and Wonder Woman (though they're given different names). Mom and dad have secret identities as Real Estate agents – and a Bat Cave beneath their suburban home in California complete with bat poles. The story opens on the boy's first day of Superhero High School and the son is under a lot of pressure from parental expectations. Distracted as they are by real estate deals and saving the world, the parents haven't noticed the boy isn't superstrong like dad and can't fly like mom. Kirk Russell, frankly, is brilliant as the voice of the super-powered, clueless dad.

The freshman class at Sky High, all sons and daughters of one or more superheroes, has to be sorted into the two tracks of study at the school, "Heroes" and "Hero Support." "Hero Support" is for children with second-rate superpowers like glowing neon or melting like a popsicle or shape changing into a purple gerbil. These losers are called "Sidekicks" and are either abused by the kids on the "Heroes" track or neglected. Mostly they get stuffed into lockers.

The lead character, powerless Will Stronghold, has a best friend, Lola, a girl with powers like Batman's nemesis "Poison Ivy," namely, the ability to control the growth and tendrile strength of plants. Incredibly, she refuses on principle to show her substantial powers at test time when her class is divided into tracks. She winds up alongside Will with the Sidekick losers. Will discovers, too, he has a superpowered enemy at school, a boy named Warren Peace (ouch), whose dad is a superbaddie put in jail by Will's mom and dad.

Will has to come out of the closet as a Super Dud one night at home with dad. "The Commander" thinks his boy is being charitable in hanging out with Sidekicks. Will lets him know that he isn't the son they thought he was. The parents have a small identity crisis, but Will's acceptance of himself as "more than okay" even though not what his parents wanted or expected is a liberating experience for him. And for his Sidekick friends as well, all of whom overhear the exchange. When Will is forced into a cafeteria fight with Warren Peace later that week, his superstrength emerges.

Which isn't without consequent problems. First, he has to leave his Sidekick friends for Hero track training. This leads to his being caught up, of course, in the popularity schtick of high school. He neglects his Sidekick buddies, especially Lola, to hang with the "In-Crowd."

Long story short, at the big Homecoming Dance, the leader of the "In-Crowd" reveals herself to be a supervillainess who can turn everyone into babies, which she does. All the important "big power" heroes get hit with her infantalysis ray gun (egad, she calls it her "Pacifier"). The Sidekicks and Warren Peace are overlooked and manage to escape from the locked auditorium. Will had decided not to come to the dance, but his parents are there as special guests and are the first heroes to get babied. Whah.

Will figures out in the Bat Cave at home who the baddie really is and catches the bus to Sky High, a school bus driven by the ultimate Sidekick (two superhero parents, no powers). Together with Warren Peace and the Sidekicks, whose collective marginalized powers turn out to be just the ones needed to save the day, Will and Lola kick butt and restore everyone to his or her rightful place.

Rightful places? Mom and dad grow up, literally and figuratively – with the Commander even acknowledging that the Sidekicks are the real Heroes – and the baddies, all Hero-track "In-Crowd" students who oppressed and belittled the Sidekicks, wind up in a prison that robs them of their powers. Will's best friend becomes his girlfriend, his worst enemy becomes his best friend, and his one date girlfriend (the super villianess) became his arch enemy. As he says at the finale, "all in a day's work at High School." Fade from Sky High. Credits. Curtain.

Sky High as PoMo Cliché Track

You couldn't ask for a better snapshot of postmodern literature. Here are the ten most characteristic postmodern elements and themes with illustrations taken from *Sky High*. Please make a mental note of the fact that I am not saying any of these qualities is unique to postmodernism or begins with literary postmodernism. I am saying that they are qualities of literary postmodernism consequent to their reflecting the postmodern view and outlook as it has been described by the folks who track and tag "historical periods" and "Ages."

1. *Constitutive Otherness*

Jean-Francois Lyotard, Philosophy Professor and leading exponent of postmodernism, defined it in his *The Postmodern Condition: A Report on Knowledge* as "incredulity towards metanarratives." The defining myths of a culture, their "metanarratives" or "Grand Narratives," impose a rational order and hierarchy on those who live within it. This order is necessarily oppressive, exclusive, and incomplete because of the groups that are marginalized by this myth of origins, worth, and ends. Those in power use every social structure to perpetuate the metanarrative of their value and the relative worthlessness of those not in power, structures including law and language, art and literature, even movies. "Truth" according to the more radical postmoderns is also a social construction and necessarily incomplete and not Truth in fact but a lie because of the exclusion of the perspectives of the disenfranchised.

Fostering our "incredulity in metanarrative" is the whole point of *Sky High*. The "Grand Narrative" of the superhero children's high school, in fact, the whole superhero culture, is that, on the one hand, there are real heroes, and on the other those who don't measure up to this standard. The non-heroes, the "Hero Support" citizens, are the kids whose powers are not big enough or flashy enough to pass the entirely subjective, fate-determining exam their first day at school (given by the gym teacher. . .).

We identify with these Sidekicks, of course, and learn by movie's end, along with Will's dad, the super Superhero, that as Cahoone says about the postmoderns, "the margins constitute the text" (*Anthology*, p. 16). The Sidekicks define the superhero culture from the margins and outside; they are the missing, necessary pieces of truth that will save the culture in crisis.

The postmodern enemy is always the pervasive cultural belief in the Foundation story, the metanarrative, that defines and divides the world into good people and marginal "others."

2. *Linguistic support of Marginalization*

If you grew up when I did (the 70s and 80s), you remember the first time the guy you used to call the "mailman" became the "mail carrier," when the school janitor became a "sanitation engineer," and when "God the Father" became politically incorrect except for Bible-believing "cave people," so inclusive-language Bibles and prayer books were rushed into print. I didn't make much of it, I confess, but it represented an important victory for the postmoderns. Language is a primary vehicle of the oppressive metanarrative, and the first step to liberating those diminished by a culture's racist, sexist, and homophobic myths is to strip the language of its nuanced poisons.

Sky High's second class citizens and pariahs are those whose powers are deemed inadequate for whatever reason (in the movie, the test in the gym is laughably arbitrary). They are put in a learning track with the euphemistic but demeaning name, "Hero Support," but everyone calls them (they call themselves) the Sidekicks. The great victory in consciousness-raising is won when Kirk Russell's character realizes and acknowledges that both names for the lesser powered are lies; the Sidekicks are Heroes. Enlightenment!

3. *Self-Actualization*

Postmodernism suggests that "liberation" and "freedom" are not possible solely by legislation and social change. Our real powers as individuals lie in the choices we make independent of the mores and defining metanarratives of the culture in which we live. In so much as we refuse to accept categories and being categorized, we self-actualize and empower ourselves.

Sky High teaches us this in several ways. First, the lead male character, Will Stronghold, has no superpowers until he has his self-acceptance talk with superdad, comes out of the closet as a Sidekick, and arrives at some peace about who he is. Then, as circumstances require (the need to protect his friends and later to save the school), his powers show themselves. Constricted by the expectations of others, Will Stronghold was defined by others and is a nobody. Self-actualizing, he is more powerful than either of his parents or anyone at Sky High.

The lead female character, Will's best friend and wanna-be girlfriend, Lola, really understands this. She refuses on principle to take part in the powers test her first day at school in the gym and sides with the oppressed by choice. What "The Commander" only realizes after being babified and growing up (being "born again"?), Lola gets from the git-go. Artificial divisions in metanarrative, however necessary in any foundational myth, diminish the marginalized and present a misrepresentation of the whole truth. The really smart people understand this and do not participate in the process to elevate themselves or to diminish others.

4. *Political subtext*

Postmodernism may have been born in French universities of the 1960s, but it was always a political football as much as an academic point. It is the intellectual backbone of feminism, affirmative action programs, gay rights, and requests for payouts to the descendants of African slaves. The selling point of a political party's "Rainbow Coalition" isn't so much in numbers amounting to electoral majorities as it is to redressing the wrongs done to marginalized, minority voices in the name of cultural Grand Narratives of the past and present.

Sky High is wonderfully subtle on this point. The only oppressed characters in this story are superhero children whose powers aren't accepted by the power mavens of the imaginary world in which they live. Remarkably, there is no racism, sexism, homophobia, age discrimination, or class tension in this school (which, of course, makes the fact that the school floats undetected several thousand feet in the air over California seem realistic). All we have is this artificial, discriminatory, and oppressive distinction among students between Power Haves and Power Have-Nots.

The homosexual conflict, though, actually is in there and is very funny, wrapped up and disguised as it is in the superpower wrapping. Will's conversation with dad about being a Sidekick rather than a Hero is a hilarious "coming out" scene that, without the subtext of dad's fears that his son doesn't like girls, isn't very funny at all. The parents' great relief when a buxom girl shows up who is obviously smitten by their son – and he with her! – underlines this tension.

The lesson Disney wants us to take away isn't about superheroes. But they aren't about preaching tolerance of alternative lifestyles from the roof tops, either, not after the Southern Baptist Convention just lifted the boycott on Disney World. When Disney Does Derrida, the subtext is everything – and the celebration of the minority, oppressed view in *Sky High* is just subtle enough to delight the Hollywood mandarins while simultaneously flying under the radar of the Focus on the Family culture warriors.

Note in *Sky High* that the marginalized characters are all deemed to be Sidekicks because they were born with powers or qualities that don't measure up to their culture's unexamined, subjective standards. It is not a measure of justice, objective measures, or choices they have made that have forced them to the edge of the Public Square but accidents of birth. This reflects the prevalent belief, unfortunately substantiated by experience, among women, ethnic minorities, and homosexuals that they are second class citizens because of what they were born as rather than because of their choices.

5· *Deconstruction of Superheroes*

"Deconstruction" is a fifty-cent piece word but, to risk over simplification, it means "breaking down." In stories, if I write in a character that acts out of step with how the surrounding culture expects this sort of person to act, my story is "deconstructing the metanarrative" on this point. Hollywood's annual story about a preacher who is, egad, also a sinner is deconstruction tantamount to breaking down a dead horse. The happy black family on "The Cosby Show" was, in contrast, remarkably effective deconstruction.

Marvel Comics broke down the myth of godlike superheroes in the early 60s with its angst-ridden 'Spiderman' and 'Fantastic Four' comic books. Sky High, consequently, isn't about challenging our understanding of its superpowered characters, if any of us harbored the notion that being able to fly or punch out Godzilla would solve all our personal issues.

The very funny portrayal of the Stronghold family as ***Ozzie and Harriet*** on steroids, however, is effective deconstruction. We see powerful people who are clueless about their child – they don't know Will doesn't have superpowers and he's 14? – and we learn through this example that the power holders are missing out on the whole picture. The skeleton holding up every metanarrative is that the Grand Myth actually describes the world as it is and that the power holders are in the position they are in because they are better, smarter people than the alienated others. ***Sky High*** isn't heavy-handed with its message – but the postmodern message is delivered. The Sidekicks have the larger picture and are better people than the anointed ones. More on this in a second.

6. *Genre blurring, High art/popular entertainment mix*

One of the postmodern movements that doesn't receive the criticism given to its philosophical, linguistic, and literary off-shoots is postmodern architecture. This architecture, representing an undeniable and visible break with modern Bauhaus glass-and-steel-box buildings, is known for what is called "double coding." The buildings are still largely the glass, concrete, and steel monsters of the modern era but with a second "coating" or coding, if you will, of one or more architectural styles to soften the edges of its appearance and even to poke fun at itself.

We see something like this layered approach in postmodern literature with the blurring of genres in stories and with the mix of tone and theme ranging from high art and ideas to popular entertainment. The effect of this blurring and mixing is, first, to deconstruct the reader's preconceived notions of what he or she is reading. "Hey, this isn't just a National Geographic special on Antarctica – it's a burlesque musical comedy and Wagnerian opera about penguins, too!" This creates an opening through which writers can drive home larger messages about the oppressive cultural myths that have us in a literal headlock.

Sky High delivers on this point. It's a seamless combination of three Hollywood cliches: superhero films and television shows, from the camp Batman serial to the recent CGI heavy Marvel Comics movies, suburban high school flicks, from *Beach Blanket Bingo* to *Fast Times at Ridgemont High*, and teenage-angst B-movies like *I Was a Teenage Werewolf*. *Sky High* is laughing at all three models and at itself with a perfectly straight face so the formulas of each are transparent and fun, even engaging and, mirabile dictu, believable.

While we're laughing and engaged, of course, we purchase and devour without thinking critically the postmodern message about oppressed minorities and the need to be on the lookout for divisive, discriminatory ideas we accept as truth. The Gospel of Lyotard, Jencks, and Irigaray is smuggled into our hearts – and we love it.

The high art stuffed in with this genre slurry? It's the Freudian mythology of our relationship with our parents. Will is just like us when we were children as the film begins – a nobody who thinks of his parents as the two most powerful people on the planet, terrified he'll never measure up to their expectations. The rest of the story is just his coming to accept himself, which conscious choice liberates him from the comic book burdens of his parents, and eventually makes him more powerful than mom and dad (and without the hilarious costume).

7. *Self mocking*

When you're selling the message that all message bearers and truth tellers are liars and oppressors, it pays not to be making too hard a sales push. You'll be identified as one of the people you're trying to immunize people against listening to or believing. postmodern literature, consequently, is very self-conscious and often trips over itself with self-references, a wink and a nudge to the reader not to take this all too seriously. It is double-coded like postmodern buildings with the heavy message that metanarratives are false truths (because necessarily incomplete and harmful to those forced to the periphery) and with the lighter message that this truth isn't one of those false truths (because, hey, we're not Nazis; we have a sense of humor!).

Sky High is full of these moments. My favorites are the revelation that the conflicted, liminal figure that hates Will is named Warren Peace and the appearance of Will's parents at the party being thrown in their home, unknown to them. Their arrival in full superhero regalia – tight leotards, capes, masks – and playing the scene straight as if everybody's parents dress like this (or that we see our parents this way – and aren't laughing) had me almost in tears I was laughing so hard. Any film that can poke fun at itself and my ideas of my parents this well gets a free pass to smuggle risible philosophical and political points past my faculties of discernment.

My wife Mary's favorite character was the Super Bad Girl. She had been a Sidekick at Sky High whose powers weren't appreciated, so, this being a superhero flick in need of a villainess, she vows revenge on the Heroes who treated her like dirt. Her plan is to turn them all into babies and then reeducate them so they learn to appreciate her genius and powers. For four-fifths of the movie she plays the vamp with Will to get access to the Bat Cave...

Mary thinks (and would I be sharing her thought if I thought it was wrong?) that the *Sky High* writers were contrasting their subtle, fun way of indoctrinating a generation in postmodernist dogma ("All dogma is false!") with the Dr. Frankenstein methods of the superfeminists. The sexual manipulators' "reeducation" scheme by "baby-ification" and violence does seem like a subtle hint that this is not the way for the oppressed to throw off their chains.

8.   *Nothing is what you think it is, no one is who you think they are, on the surface*

One tenet and foundation of postmodernism is the assertion that sense experience, the empirical perception of reality, while perhaps a more direct experience of what is real, is still mediated by sign, language, and representation. We do not see or sense anything as it is except through a filter or layers of mental-construction filters. "Knowing," consequently, isn't about knowing objects but examining the way we think and how we understand the things we perceive. The norms by which we know things – say, "truth, beauty, goodness" – are also historical constructions produced by or immanent within the material and social conditions they are supposed to be the objective standards for judging. "Truth" is absolutely relative, "direct perception" is delusion, "knowledge" is never certain or more than fragmented ideas shaped by our conceptions. "Truth is made, not found" (Rorty).

In story, our inability to know is best presented by the surprise ending, in which turnaround we are confronted by our misperceptions and misunderstanding of the people and problems presented in the play. The postmodern drama is either a disorienting and disconcerting flood of contradictory images and plot directions or a conventional story, maybe even a mystery, at the end of which you discover you have been totally suckered. You thought the butler did it? Ho! The narrator did it – can you believe it?

Everything you think you know from direct perception is wrong. Every one you want to believe you understand is not who you think they are. And every day you should expect to have your world and concepts and ideas of truth, beauty, and goodness turned on their heads. As Rorty said, "keeping faith with Darwin" means understanding that all our beliefs and convictions "are as much acts of chance as are tectonic plates and mutated viruses" (Pearcey, *Total Truth*, pp. 242-243).

What a happy ending! Only Disney could wrap Rorty's description of our delusion so we feel like we've just spent ninety minutes with Christopher Robin and Pooh.

9. *Unity as Ignorance, Pluralism as Deliverance*

The first point I tried to make about postmodernism is its assertion that the controlling metanarrative is the big, bad guy. The cultural myth that divides the powerful and the oppressed into a false hierarchy is the primary agency of injustice in the world. Now that we know, too, that one view or perspective is necessarily faulty and deceptive (as well as marginalizing and punishing those not sorted into the powerful group), we can understand the depth of the dangers represented by dogma, ideology, unexamined beliefs, and our individual and shared prejudices. The faux unified perspective keeps us from pursuing either the unifying view of everyone's opinion or the transcending, harmonizing way of revealing the false division of the unified view. Grand narrative = bad, even "evil." Revealing and refuting the divisive myth = good, even "heroic."

Postmodern stories have to have a division in them between the "favored" class and the "looked-down-upon" bunch. The aim of these stories is show us what a deliverer from this division would look like, a messiah, if you will, from the delusions of our prevailing myths. *Sky High*, like *Toy Story*, like *Antz*, like *Little Giants*, yes, like *Harry Potter* (we'll get back to him in a moment, trust me) and every movie and kids book I can think of that's come out in the last five years, comes through in spades.

Will Stronghold starts out as the archetype of all losers: two superhero parents and not one superpower himself. Total Sidekick and low man on the Hero Support totem pole. Then he "gets" his power and is moved to the "fast track" for Heroes. But though he has crossed the artificial line separating these polar ends of social life at Sky High School, he remains good friends with the Sidekick friends of old and eventually becomes the means by which the losers can demonstrate they are true heroes. Either by having two natures simultaneously or by showing there is only nature and the Hero/Sidekick dichotomy is a false one. Hey, the guy is Hermaphroditic – "core group" and "other" at the same time.

And pluralism being kin to godliness? The Sidekicks don't defeat the horrible villainess as individuals. Their powers aren't up to that. But working together, every one of their goofy powers proves essential to overthrow the Super Baddies plans to baby-ify every superhero and raise them up in her image. The Rainbow Coalition is invincible! Especially when led by "Hero/Side-Kick Man," the Category and Ideology Buster!

10· *The Contradictions and Ironies of Postmodernism*

Critics of postmodernism – and they are legion – find them to be easy pickings. By asserting an "absolute relativism" and a vacuum of truth, they are obliged to contradict themselves. If no knowledge is sure, then is the idea that there is no sure knowledge also necessarily false or a limited truth to which there must be exceptions? If truth is a dogma and all dogma is false, are we to neglect that "All Dogma is False" is a dogmatic position? This is shooting fish in a barrel.

Postmodernism, however, isn't dismissed so easily. First of all, it is the spirit of our times. Ironically, this self-contradicting ideology solvent has, with naturalism, become the state religion and predominant ideology of church, government, and academy in Western Europe and the United States. Laugh at it all you want for its violation of the Law of Contradiction. Your neighbor is a believer (and we are, too, more than we want to be or are able to think, alas). It's in the air we breathe.

More important, the PoMo theorists aren't stupid. In driving ratiocination and reductionism to their logical ends, they know what they are saying is contradictory. In pointing out the limits of rationalism, the better ones are aware there are no alternatives to "logocentrism" and "discursive argument." They consciously contradict themselves, nonetheless, offering paradox and contradiction as part and parcel of their absolute relativism package. "Even these ideas may be hogwash," they admit with a shrug. Hence the self-mockery mentioned above.

These contradictions and ironies, as you'd expect, are just beneath the surface of the postmodernist mythology. In *Sky High*, for example, we're being shown just how bad it is for the Sidekicks in a world made for Heroes with real superpowers. The losers in Hero Support are used and abused by the sadist "Heroes."

The funny thing is, on the way to dispelling the metanarrative that teaches us that the "powerful" are deserving and righteous, the writers of *Sky High* are obliged to create a counterparadigm that is just as prejudicial and distorted. There aren't any Hero-track students in this movie that aren't borderline psychotic. Not one. In order to get us to identify with the "losers," they are obliged to demonize the "winners." And wasn't this just the sort of polarization and "marginalizing the other" that we were being taught was evil and that we should look out for and condemn?

Maybe one good Hero and one jerk Sidekick would have made the propaganda piece this movie for the downtrodden, and for postmodernism in general, less obvious and painful a mixed message. As it is, even an antipropaganda propaganda cartoon is a little much for my entertainment.

Two quick points to wrap up this introduction to postmodern story telling using *Sky High*:

Key Four, Part One: Disney Does Derrida

1.   I know I'm going to get a bunch of email from readers saying essentially, "C'mon, John! Loosen up! It's just a kid's movie for crying-out-loud." Okay. I'll grant that revealing the stuffing of the Teddy Bear is hard for some film goers – especially those who are thoroughly postmodern and who watched this film without a second thought. It would be pretty weird, wouldn't it, if this film's message struck postmodern audiences as strange?

My point for those of you who think I'm working too hard for my film critic merit badge is only that *Sky High* would have been just bizarre and *avante garde* if not impenetrable to audiences of only 50 years ago. After the civil rights, feminist, sexual, and coming-out-party revolutions of the past four decades, though, *Sky High* is now kiddy fare, a booster shot for a country thoroughly immunized against the possibility of taking ideas seriously, especially dogmatic ideas (at least those ideas not dogmatically denouncing dogma). Movies like *Sky High* are no different, really, than other generations' propaganda films, say, Griffith's **Birth of a Nation** or Leni Riefenstahl's **Olympia**, except for their CGI and production values.

Propaganda and brainwashing, be it for racism, fascism, or for postmodernism, is still an invitation to think with the herd. The fun part is that in the case of our times and postmodern books and movies, the herd is a nonconformist herd of individualists all thinking outside the box, all attacking the box, and all neglecting the possibility that box-hatred has become the box.

2.   Again, although I have used this one fun movie to introduce ten points about postmodernism and postmodern literature, I could have used any of the last ten "current releases" my family has seen. *The Fantastic Four, Antz, Memoirs of a Geisha, Little Giants, Happy Feet*, even the *Narnia* movie, believe it or not. Read any of the interviews with the *Lion, Witch, and the Wardrobe* producer or with the actress who played the White Witch. The stories about how the director, Adam Adamson, fought with Lewis' Stepson to "empower" the girl characters and not succumb to the sexism of the story is a real hoot.

If you think what I've said about *Sky High* is an isolated instance (and more the product of my frenetic speculation than reality – the postmodernist's point?), take *Sky High* back to the video store and rent *Antz*, the movie. It's almost the exact *Sky High* story situated in an ant colony with soldier and worker ants subbing for heroes and sidekicks and Woody Allen as the Will Stronghold transcendent messiah that "thinks outside the box" and saves the colony. A propaganda piece for individualism and nonconformity – set in an ant colony! This one ends with Allen's character summarizing the action: "Y'know, boy meets girl, boy gets girl, together they reorganize the accepted social order." If only we could stop thinking in such artificial and divisive categories as "Worker" and "Soldier" ants...

This myth-busting formula, ironically, is the foot-shooting, ironic metanarrative of our age, and all of our popular movies and stories reflect it. Especially those meant for children. To include *Harry Potter*.

Postmodernism = Post + Modernism

Before we dive into the postmodernity of Joanne Rowling's books, here's the Post-It note round-up version of what postmodernism is about. It's all in the word "postmodern," as you might expect in a movement built largely on the deconstruction of language and meaning.

On the one hand, postmodernism represents a radical departure from, even a war on the imposed, rationalist order or ideologies of modernity. Think postmodern with a big emphasis on the "post" or "after." postmodernism is about exposing and eradicating all the positivism and surety of the modern period and the oppressive and crushing hegemony of the fascist, imperialist, capitalist, communist, sexist, racist, and homophobic regimes of this period. Personal conscience and self-actualizing choice are king; non-conformity, however risible as a group project or community vision, is the rule. Everyone must wear his baseball caps' bills backwards or askew to be different just like everyone else.

On the other hand, postmodernism is the radical continuation, conclusion, and exaggeration of modernity and its attendant myths. Emphasize, for this sense, the second part of postmodernity. For starters, for a movement about the eradication of dogma, it's a pretty unforgiving and discriminatory dogma. "All dogma is false and must be resisted (except this dogma, which must be taken on faith)." It is also rationalism, naturalism, and atheism on steroids and lithium. Like the moderns, the chief enemies of the postmodern are the God believers and their monolithic, hierarchical "Organized Religion." The modern writer lionizes the scientist and the soldier; the postmodern worships the university professor of linguistics and anthropology. Both shoot priests on sight – if the postmodern might forgive the pedophile predator.

In one graphic image, postmoderns are patricides, the superrational sons and daughters who use the materialist and pragmatic tools they have from daddy to murder their father in his sleep. The fact that their father himself had killed his own father and usurped the noetic throne centuries before, somehow makes this seem reasonable, even inevitable (see Martin Lings, 'Intellect and Reason,' *Ancient Beliefs and Modern Superstitions*, Quinta Essentia, 1991, pp. 58-59).

Rowling as Postmodern

Is Ms. Rowling a postmodern writer? Does that preclude her being a Christian writer, or at least her being a throwback to the Inklings? And what about her stories? Is Harry another Will Stronghold sidekick-becoming-a hero? Will all the marginalized characters (Luna, Neville, Hagrid, et alii) have to be world saviors at story's end?

At last, *Harry Potter* as postmodern myth and epic!

Read on to find out how *Harry Potter* is and is not postmodern.

Chapter 4, Key 4, Part 2
Postmodern Harry:
Joanne Rowling as a Writer of Our Times

> Majeed from Bristol Grammar School – Bristol: To what
> extent did you conceive *Harry Potter* as a moral tale?
>
> JK Rowling replies – I did not conceive it as a moral tale,
> the morality sprang naturally out of the story, a subtle but
> important difference. I think any book that sets out to teach
> or preach is likely to be hard going at times (though I can
> think of a couple of exceptions). http://www.accio-quote.org/
> articles/2004/0304-wbd.htm

I confess to loathing biographies of writers that assume because
Writer X had a crazy mom or a great relationship with dad or a history
teacher that ran away with a student that every character in any book
Writer X wrote that can be connected to their biography must be tied
to antecedent as cause and effect. Much preferable, I think, are literary
biographies that detail what Writer X was reading and thinking just
before or while writing any book.

Having said that, Ms. Rowling does seem have the attributes for
poster child of the postmodern movement. The exaggerated and always
repeated Cinderella story of her circumstances while writing the first
Harry Potter book is, after all, meaningful. She was a single mother,
freshly divorced, out of work, with dependent infant, few friends, and
nothing but a story she had been working on for some time. Worse, she
was living in a country enduring or celebrating the "Get Tough" years
of Margaret Thatcher and her successor John Major.

It wasn't the best time to be a welfare mum, living off the dole and
"the sweat of hard workers' brow." Rowling's feelings for the marginalized
and oppressed, already sharp as we know from her working on staff at
Amnesty International, only became more profound from her time
as a person treated like dirt by the powerful and predominant Grand
Narrative. That Mrs. Thatcher will live forever as Harry's pompous and
self-inflated Aunt Marge is a reflection of Ms. Rowling's memories of her

life on the periphery of the public square. She remembers vividly being on the wrong side of the arbitrary "hard-working tax-payer" – "welfare mom and cheat" divide.

[Here's a head-scratching side-note: Rowling finishing the story, a story she began while on the dole, as one of the richest people alive, of course, the first "billion dollar author," is just another of the several ironies of postmodernism. How curious is it that this woman from the far periphery of the Public Square, powerless and essentially disenfranchised, by writing a story about the evil nature of the defining metanarrative has moved from edge to center, depths to height? Only in a PoMo world where the periphery defines the center...]

Not as well known as the rags-to-riches tale are Ms. Rowling's childhood experiences as her mother died of degenerative illness. Her friends largely avoided her during this long trial and she has said the strong presence of death in these books reflects her preoccupation with these thoughts while beginning the books; at the moment of her mother's death, she explained recently, she knows she was at home writing about Harry. Ms. Rowling's enthusiastic and generous contributions to charities supporting single mothers and searching for cures for illnesses like MS and AIDS as well as her kindnesses to families with dying children point to the lasting mark the isolation and trauma of her mother's illness and death had on her. Not to neglect her efforts to free the Romanian "cage children" and help the helpless through Children's High Level Group.

And even more neglected is her major in French at university. postmodernism is born in the Algerian War with France, in large part, and its most profound voices spring from this conflict and the existentialist revolution in French culture of this period. There is simply no way that Ms. Rowling graduated with a major in French without reading heavily in the original language the writings of Derrida, Foucault, Lyotard, Sartre, and Irigaray. Alma mater, the Latin words for "nurturing mother," are used to describe our schools because they shape our beliefs and thinking as much if not more than our birth parents. Ms. Rowling's closeted mama is a postmodern, French-speaking Algerian lady with an attitude.

Anyway, on to an exploration of what this French major with scars from her life on the periphery has written about life out there... My tack here will be, again, first to write out one aspect of the postmodern view or a quality of postmodern literature and then to offer evidence that Ms. Rowling's books conform to it. Here are the ten aspects we learned about in the previous chapter for us to match up with Harry's themes, symbols, and meaning:

- Constitutive "Otherness"
- Linguistic Support
- Self-Actualizing
- Political Subtext
- Deconstruction
- Genre Blending
- Self-Mocking
- Nothing is What you think it Is
- Unity is Ignorance, Pluralism is Deliverance
- Contradictions and Ironies

- **Prejudice: Evidence of a Divisive "Grand Myth"**

The heart of postmodernism's break with the modern world view is in its belief that metanarratives describing reality or "foundational narratives" are by necessity incomplete. These myths are created within prevailing social structures to explain why the powerful have the power (because they are better than those people who are not on the higher rungs of the hierarchy). The stories shaping beliefs require both a "core group" and an "other" or "nigger" class. The cultural beliefs consequent to learning and embracing these stories in turn create an oppressed, marginalized group in the present. Prejudice, be it institutional or individual, active or passive, is the most evident marker of this destructive cultural myth. Academics call this "Constitutive 'Otherness'" and look to language for its reflection and support of this confining, divisive myth.

The postmodern writer's enemy is always the pervasive cultural belief in the Foundation story, the metanarrative, that defines and divides the world into good people and marginal "others." postmoderns are defined by their "incredulity towards metanarrative" and what "incredulity" means is that, to a postmodern person, most of the world's problems are caused by people believing in big foundation stories like "original sin" and "invisible hand capitalism" or Marxist theories of economic determination. Each of these "Founders Stories" ossifies into an ideology that is inherently and inescapably totalitarian and exclusive, dividing the world into a good core of people and a "necessary other," who, by not being part of the core group, are "bad," even "evil."

Remember when the President made his speech about the "Axis of Evil" in the world, namely, Iraq, North Korea, and Iran? The press and academics, the people who are most stridently postmodern in belief in the public square, all laughed or rolled their eyes. The more ardent wrote articles and long research papers to demonstrate that the Republican fascist and capitalist ideologue was creating this "Axis of Evil" by declaring it as such. This same group finds the current state of affairs overseas, in which these three countries are indeed lining up as our crisis foes, as confirmation of the consequences of the President's ideology, which requires an "other" enemy to rally his core electoral constituency. It can be argued, of course, that Bush was just sharing the facts as he knew them.

No matter, the key point is our shared skepticism about surety, our common belief that if you're certain about the world and what human beings are about or how we should behave, you're (a) stupid and (b) almost certainly dangerous, because your metanarrative is going to pigeonhole someone (and probably a lot of people as a group) as "evil" – and then you will go after them "just like Hitler."

Imperialism, racism, chauvinism, unrestricted capitalism, homophobia, and ardent religious belief not tempered by individualism and a touch of hedonism are the sworn enemies of the postmoderns – and you'd be silly to think the world has not become a better place in important ways because of this shared "incredulity towards metanarratives." People don't picnic at lynchings anymore.

Ms. Rowling, as a woman of her times writing PoMo myth in large part (as does almost every film director making movies today), is obliged to give us a Founders' Myth that is the cause of every problem at Hogwarts and the Wizarding World. The Myth is the story of the Four Founders and the breakup of the once dear friends, Salazar Slytherin and Godric Gryffindor.

This is the fictional metanarrative Ms. Rowling asks us to see which poisons the minds and hearts of all witches and wizards. This Grand Narrative causes not only the Gryffindor-Slytherin battle that is the good/evil axis of the storyline, but also turns each magical person into a partisan defending their quarter rather than celebrating the whole. Gryffindor is core, Slytherin is "other" from the Gryffindor side; Pure bloods are core, all other beings are "other" and "lesser" to the Slytherins. The Death Eaters are Slytherin ideology run amuck and truly evil, but Gryffindor pride and machismo are equally divisive. All of them, as partisans, share dismissive attitudes about the "Magical Brethren."

The Sorting Hat, in brief, as the vehicle of the Wizarding World's metanarrative, is the villain of the piece and says as much about itself in *Phoenix*.

> Listen closely to my song:
> Though condemned I am to split you
> Still I worry that it's wrong,
> Though I must fulfill my duty
> And must quarter every year
> Still I wonder whether sorting
> May not bring the end I fear.
> (*Phoenix*, Chapter 11, p. 206)

This division-in-keeping-with-legend colors and clouds everyone's thinking or ability to see things as they are (Dumbledore aside). It is the root of Slytherin "Wizarding pride" and Muggle-baiting and the inability of the other Hogwarts Houses and the Magical Brethren to unite. The Wizarding World's Foundation myth is divisive and oppressive to the "other." This is the core teaching of the postmodern metanarrative we live with today, as expressed in the *Harry Potter* stories.

The Sorting Hat is the real bad guy; Voldemort and the Death Eaters are just understandable consequences of the divisive myth we confirm at the annual sorting. We need a new metanarrative.

- **Consequent Wizarding World Prejudices**

The *Harry Potter* stories are largely about the many prejudices gripping the magical world of Hogwarts and beyond consequent to the

Four Founders Myth (I detail this theme in Chapter Six of *Looking for God in Harry Potter*). Three of the larger prejudices are those against (1) magical people (and creatures) of mixed blood or blood that is otherwise tainted, (2) against the poor, and (3) against those Magical Brethren who are not witches or wizards.

Hogwarts' blood problems like the others can be traced back to the "origin myth" of the Four Founders. One of these four, Salazar Slytherin, wanted only pure blood wizards in his school House, and, though Slytherin left the school after a disagreement with Gryffindor, his House remains the bastion of wizard prejudice against those Witches and wizards of mixed ancestry or those who are Muggle-born. We learned in *Order of the Phoenix* at the House of Black that this prejudice is not limited to Hogwarts but pervades the Wizarding World.

The "N" word among the Magical folk is "Mudblood," and Draco Malfoy, the Slytherin boy we love to hate, uses this word to describe Hermione Granger (as Severus Snape did as a student to describe Lily Evans). Other linguistic reflections and supports to this division based on birth and blood are "Pure-blood," "Half-blood," "Half-breed," and "Muggle-born."

Draco Malfoy doesn't restrict his prejudices to bloodlines, however, in keeping the traditions of his house and beliefs of his family. He is as disdainful, too, of those individuals and families who don't have a lot of money or the ability to have many things or live in a big house. Ron Weasley is the usual target of this prejudice against the poor – and every one of his barbs hits home, it seems, in Ron's heart. Ron, much more than his several siblings and parents, takes his lack of spending money and his hand-me-down wardrobe as if it were a great personal failing to be hidden and overcome.

As nasty as these Slytherin prejudices are (and as poisonous as they are both to the holder of the prejudice and the individuals slighted), they are held by a relatively narrow slice of the population pie. The prejudices identify the evil characters of the book as surely as the Dark Mark tattoo, but they aren't the Grand Narrative problem that threatens to bring down the Wizarding World.

That constitutive otherness is the prejudice of good and bad wizards and witches with respect to three-fourths of the world's Magical Brethren, that is, the Centaurs, the Goblins, and the House Elves. The myth was depicted in the Ministry of Magic as a statue and fount called "The Fountain of Magical Brethren."

> Halfway down the hall was a fountain. A group of golden statues, larger than life-size, stood in the middle of a circular pool. Tallest of them all was a noble-looking wizard with his wand pointing straight up in the air. Grouped around him were a beautiful witch, a centaur, a goblin, and a house-elf. The last three were all looking adoringly up at the witch and wizard. Glittering jets of water were flying from the ends of the two wands, the point of the centaur's arrow, the tip of the goblin's hat, and each of the house-elf's ears, so that the tinkling hiss of the falling water was added to the pops and cracks of Apparators and the clatter of footsteps as hundreds of witches and wizards, most of whom were wearing glum, early-morning looks, strode toward a set of golden gates at the far end of the hall (*Phoenix*, Chapter 7, p. 127).

This is the overarching belief of witches and wizards about their fellow magical beings or creatures. First, of course, is the fealty of the "adoring" centaur, goblin, and house-elf for the "noble" wizard and "beautiful" witch. As central as this joyful subservience is to the myth, those who are not depicted as "Brethren" is as telling about wizard beliefs and exclusion. There is no giant in the fountain nor is there a dementor. The non-human "brethren" in the fountain have it bad, certainly, but the real "others" or "niggers" in this representation of the magical world are those not even pictured.

After Harry's hearing, he takes a closer look at the statues:

> He looked up into the handsome wizard's face, but up close, Harry thought he looked rather weak and foolish. The witch was wearing a vapid smile like a beauty contestant, and from what Harry knew of goblins and centaurs, they were most unlikely to be caught staring this soppily at humans of any description. Only the house-elf's attitude of creeping servility looked convincing. With a grin at the thought of what Hermione would say if she could see the statue of the elf, Harry turned his money bag upside down… (Phoenix, Chapter 9, p. 156)

Key Four, Part Two: Postmodern Harry

Ms. Rowling offers us this statue as something that none of the passers-by even look up at because it is the unquestioned and unconscious belief on which the magical world and government rest, however prejudicial and nonsensical. Don't look for representatives of even the centaurs, goblins, and house-elves in the Ministry of Magic. There may be a Committee for the Disposal of Dangerous Magical Creatures at the Ministry but the prejudice against non-wizards is universal enough that there are no Magical Brethren in the Ministry or liaisons to these groups.

This blindspot in the consciousness of wizards, their exclusive hold of power and misuse of those they think of as "brethren" as well as their totally marginalized others, is the agony of the Wizarding World and the cause of the Voldemort crisis. Lord Voldemort, the Nazi and totalitarian madman of these books, is anything but an incomprehensible and aberrational evil without beginning or cause. He is only the logical extension and symptom of the prejudice against all non-wizards held by all witches and wizards with few exceptions.

That the statue is destroyed by the mano a mano combat between Dumbledore and Voldemort at the end of *Phoenix* is telling. Dumbledore explains to Harry that this myth is a lie – and that the much uglier truth it fails to represent will have horrible consequences.

> "Sirius did not hate Kreachur [his family's house-elf]," said Dumbledore. "He regarded him as a servant unworthy of much interest or notice. Indifference and neglect often do much more damage than outright dislike….The fountain we destroyed tonight told a lie. We wizards have mistreated and abused our fellows for too long, and we are now reaping our reward" (*Phoenix*, Chapter 37, pp. 833-834).

Marietta College Prof. Kathryn McDaniel's paper, "The Elfin Mystique: Fantasy and Feminism in J. K. Rowling's *Harry Potter* Series," reveals that Ms. Rowling's depiction of the house-elves is not an abstract "other" standing in for any marginalized group like the Sidekicks in Sky High. Prof. McDaniel's thesis is that the house-elves are Ms. Rowling's snapshot of modern women in the throes of digesting the victories of the second and third generation of feminists. The house-elves are, in brief, allegorical story stand-ins for housewives, the status of most

169

American and European women, however liberated in appearance.

As McDaniel's paper details, Ms. Rowling's presentation is nuanced rather than just slapstick caricature. It has to be to include a Winky (dependent but forcefully liberated against her will), a Dobby (gladly liberated but isolated and confused in his role without conventions or peer support), a Hermione (the liberate-at-all-costs firebrand feminist), a Kreacher (evidence of what life as a house-elf/-wife can do to an elf/woman – and to their masters), as well as the horde of kitchen-elves and their responses both to Hermione, the Queen of SPEW, and to the liberated house-elves, Dobby and Winky. Quite the comprehensive picture of the troubled landscape of feminism entering the 21st century. As we'll see in Chapter 6, the liberation of the house-elves may be the deliverance of the world from Voldemort.

The centaurs, following Prof. McDaniel's lead, then can be understood as those marginalized and brilliant people that live outside of the "real world" – who seem to be as caught up in the counter-mythology of racial superiority over their oppressors. The goblins work with wizards; in fact, they control the economy and the money of the world. But, historically, we know they are a group ever ready to revolt against their magical "betters."

The giants may be Ms. Rowling's caricature of traditional people who are hounded onto reservations and into ghettos, becoming only a monstrous shadow of their former greatness. The dementors, too, are an excellent depiction of what a nightmare a magical creature can become when confined to the narrow existence of its worst traits by government policy – and the repercussions on society when released from its confinement by a greater evil.

I'll leave it to you to put the names of real world minorities to each of these groups if you think this a parallel akin to "house-elves = housewives." My point is only that Ms. Rowling certainly passes the first and most important litmus strip test for postmodern literature. The fictional world she has created is a troubled place whose Grand Narrative excludes groups from power in its mythology and imposed rational order, the hierarchy of blood, wealth, and race.

The postmodern hero is the character who crosses or transcends the artificial divisions of the narrative. Bridging the conceptual divisions of other characters, this hero liberates the oppressed minority from their chains and the power holders from their delusions. Harry Potter, the hero of Ms. Rowling's books, is such a figure. He is the Chosen One, the Hogwarts Hermaphrodite described in Chapter 2, but to consciously transcend the core-other division of the Founders' metanarrative he must "embrace the Slytherin" within. Leaping this flaw of prejudice that he must overcome himself, he will be free to act as Quintessence to the polarized Four Houses and four Magical Brethren.

Harry will forgive Severus Snape and embrace the Slytherin aspect of Hogwarts to transcend his Gryffindor prejudices, either during the story in order to become the Androgyn Vanquisher or after the story to vanquish forever the partisan metanarrative that we readers have adopted along with wizard kind. How this might happen and how the Magical Brethren might really become brethren is one subject of the next chapters. Check off "constitutive other" and "language support" from our postmodern Harry checklist.

• *Choice: the Means to Self-Actualization*

The hero or heroine of any postmodern drama, as we just saw, is the woman or man who exposes the Grand Myth as a lie and who either acts as a means for a community polarized into haves and have-nots to create an inclusive culture or just transcends this polarity themselves. They take their ideas of themselves from individual conscience rather than external standards and other peoples' opinion. The key to their freedom and power is this self-actualizing internal victory.

This is, again, the *Harry Potter* story. As Dumbledore says at the end of Harry's second year, "It is our choices, Harry, that show what we truly are, far more than our abilities" (Chamber, Chapter 18, p. 333). It is not the position or wealth we enjoy because of our birth and it isn't the high opinion of others or things we can and cannot do that communicate who we are and what we're about. It is the choices we make consequent to our understanding of ourselves "that show what we truly are." (See Chapter 8 of *Looking for God in Harry Potter* for a full treatment of "choice" in these books.)

Rowling develops this postmodern, self-actualizing theme on several levels. Most obviously, there is Harry's almost never being able to do anything without creating a firestorm of controversy at Hogwarts and often in *The Daily Prophet*. The least that happens is that Ron and/or Hermione are all over him, pressing him to go left, right, up, or down away from his chosen direction, and usually we can count on the distracting and disturbing crowd approval or disapproval from his fellows in Gryffindor House. Slytherin House members and Rita Skeeter are constants of harassment, public misrepresentation, even physical assault and bullying.

The *Harry Potter* books are largely, as Ms. Rowling has said, about moral courage (CBBC Newsround, 7/18/2005, p. 8), the courage to stand by your choices for the right thing against your enemies and sometimes against your friends. Harry's victories over the adolescent desire to be liked by everyone were largely won in his agonizing fifth year when he was stripped of every positive, external token he had from school, friends, and magical community (not to mention being tortured, literally, by the school's acting Headmistress).

It was at the end of this fifth year that Harry learned he was seemingly the subject of a Prophecy in the Department of Mysteries and that his opposition to Voldemort may have been foretold. Harry's understanding of his prophesied Destiny as "Voldemort Vanquisher" is mechanical and superstitious, however, until his discussions with the Headmaster in *Half-Blood Prince* (cf., *Prince*, Chapter 23, pp. 509-512). As Ms. Rowling explained in July, 2005:

> I think there's a line there between the moment in *Chamber of Secrets* when Dumbledore says so famously, "It's our choices that define us, not our abilities," straight through to Dumbledore sitting in his office, saying to Harry, "the prophecy is significant only because you and Voldemort choose to make it so." If you both chose to walk away, you could both live! That's the bottom line. If both of them decided, "We're not playing," and walked away… but it's not going to happen, because as far as Voldemort's concerned, Harry's a threat. They must meet each other….
>
> It's the MacBeth idea. I absolutely adore MacBeth. It is possibly my favorite Shakespeare play. And that's the question, isn't it? If MacBeth hadn't met the witches, would he have killed Duncan? Would any of it have happened? Is it fated or did he make it happen? I believe he made it happen. (Mugglenet interview, 7/16/2005, pp. 5-6)

Key Four, Part Two: Postmodern Harry

Believe it or not, I don't think Shakespeare wrote MacBeth as the postmodern answer to the fate and freewill question. Ms. Rowling's interpretation, though, is the self-actualizing understanding of choice within a destiny that we would expect from a postmodern reader. And her having Dumbledore come down as hard as he does for choice over destiny or providence marks him as a postmodern guru.

Why?

Again, the critical metanarrative in any culture is the "origin myth." Like Hogwarts' Four Founders and the schism between Gryffindor and Slytherin that has echoed through generations and centuries, the origin story explains a community's understanding of why the powerful are better and more deserving than the displaced folks not in the original order. The origin metanarrative also spells out the destination or teleological point of the community which also is divisive and exclusive by necessity a la constitutive otherness.

A destiny, then, prophesied or imagined, as a postmodern person sees it, is just a mind-jam that paralyzes our ability to make self-actualizing, liberating choices. Harry is not "The Chosen One" except as much as he chooses to be; Dumbledore has liberated Harry from the metanarrative of the prophecy and popular understanding of his situation. That he chooses to do what he was prophesied to do may seem to make this a matter of splitting hairs, but, as Harry thinks in his moment of revelation:

> It was, he thought, the difference between being dragged into the arena to face a battle to the death and walking into the arena with your head held high. Some people perhaps would say that there was little to choose between the two ways, but Dumbledore knew – and so do I, thought Harry, with a rush of fierce pride, and so did my parents – that there was all the difference in the world (*Half-Blood Prince*, Chapter 23, p. 512).

Free choice tells all and means everything. Check off "Self-Actualizing" from our postmodern check list.

- *The Political Subtext: Satire of Ruling Institutions and Disdain for Authority & Rules*

The historically "modern" idea that postmoderns are most obviously "post" is that institutions and authority are, as vehicles of rational order, "good" by definition, however flawed the people running the show or in positions of authority. To a postmodern, public organizations, government or business or religious, are the vessels and hammers through which the prevailing metanarrative's nonsense is delivered, enforced, and policed every day. Institutions and authority are "bad" by definition, even evil.

No trouble here seeing where Ms. Rowling checks in. I can honestly say that I receive more mail from Christians disturbed by the rule-breaking at Hogwarts than I do about the magic controversy (and I get a lot of email about the latter as Ms. Rowling's Christian apologist, believe me). My response has been simply that any author writing satire in the tradition of Swift's *Gulliver's Travels* and schoolboy fiction in the tradition of *Tom Brown's School Days,* as Rowling hs done, is pretty much required to write about misbehaving boys and to have institutional and individual authority figures be the subject of ridicule (see "Genre Rowling" below). That's half of the answer, I think.

The other half is postmodernism, which is also known as poststructuralism. "Poststructuralism" points to the tendency of the spirit of our times to not only hold in disdain and at a skeptical distance but to pursue with some vigor the undermining and assault on "structures" that advance a totalitarian and oppressive cultural message. This is celebrated in the collapse of apartheid and the Soviet empire, noted in riots at WTO meetings, and the subject of alarm to many and cause for resistance when the Constitution, family, heterosexual marriage, and Christian participation in the public square are mocked or presented as outdated and dangerous. All these structures, as vehicles of prejudicial and confining metanarrative, are the authorities that the spirit of our times tell us to resist or just tear down.

Ms. Rowling's books and the characters in them certainly have a healthy disdain for authorities and rules, as those who write me point out. The "societal vehicles or metanarrative agencies of oppression and marginalization" take a real beating in these stories – and, frankly, I doubt it has ever been done, at least not since Swift, with such a comic touch, so deftly, or as effectively as Ms. Rowling has done it. Her attacks on Schools, Government, the Courts, and Media are merciless, uniformly scalding, and drop-dead hilarious.

She is so good at what she does that her targets applaud her, which I confess never ceases to amaze me. Teachers and librarians as a rule love these books, and most I have spoken with think Ms. Rowling is attacking the details of their work that they don't like (standardized tests, punishment of students, etc.) rather than mocking them. What a hoot! Most teachers at Hogwarts, other than Hagrid, are self-important, pompous boobs (if not also sadists, boors, or incompetent fakes) and an obstacle to students learning anything important.

And the teachers get off easy! Government officials at their best are officious idiots writing cauldron reports and investigating exploding toilets. More often, they are evil cohorts and collaborators with the pure bloods and their drive to make wizarding pride the subject of legislative action. Remember where the dangerous and ludicrous "Fount of Magical Brethren" is located. Cornelius Fudge and Rufus Scrimgeour are ridiculous at one level but always borderline wicked in their incompetence, self-inflation, and inability to do the right thing. Yet Tony Blair, who like Margaret Thatcher may only be remembered by history as the PM mocked by Rowling (Thatcher as Aunt Marge, Blair/Major in the opening chapter of *Prince*), professes a love for the books and jokes about looking for the painting on Downing Street by which the Prime Minister communicates with the Minister of Magic.

I'll discuss the media response to *Harry Potter* in Chapter 5 but I should mention here the depiction of courts and prisons. It is a sign of our times and of the condition of our legal institutions and jails, that no one is shocked or willing to defend them against their depiction in Ms. Rowling's books. The Wizengamut as we have seen it in Dumbledore's Pensieve and in Harry's hearing in *Order of the Phoenix* is a celebrity sham (Ludo Bagman standing in for OJ), a Stalinist show trial with only the pretense of fairness, or an outright assault on the innocent to advance a government position, as we saw in Harry's "hearing" in Phoenix.

And where are the guilty sent? To what are essentially torture chambers. Azkaban and the dementors are the principal nightmare of the Wizarding World and their shadow hangs over everything. Hagrid even hesitates about doing the right thing (freeing Buckbeak in

Prisoner of Azkaban) because of his fears about being sent back to the dementors and their island prison. Dumbledore is always concerned about the role the dementors have been given in wizard justice and we see in *Half-Blood Prince* that his worries about their "natural affinity" with Voldemort were spot on. No one who survives incarceration there is the better for it.

No one defends the courts or prisons against their satirical depiction in these books, though, as broad-stroked and Cruikshankian as they are. I bring this up because it explains, I think, why the students have the healthy disdain they do for rules for the sake of rules (curfews, etc.) and for their incompetent or sadistic teachers, government officials, and the powerful in general. They are intelligent postmodern human beings, in a nutshell, who see through the pretense of these "structures" and the assault on goodness, truth, and beauty each carries.

More mysterious to me is why Christian readers – and my mail almost without exception comes from thoughtful Evangelicals, Catholics, and Orthodox Christians, not from crank Fundamentalists the media present as the horde of Harry Haters – find this disturbing. Disdain for worldly authority is a PoMo virtue, but it is also, by and large, a Christian one. St. Paul is usually quoted here to the contrary because he did not believe that individual or collective slave revolts or rebellions within marriage ever led to spiritual perfection, but the thrust of the Gospels is about the world being the playground of and a planet being held captive by the Evil One.

Christ's assault on the lawyers and Pharisees as the vipers and parasites of his age, his insistence that we render to Caesar only what is Caesar's (and nothing of immaterial substance), and the doctrine that we be "no respecters of persons," of position, and the "workers of iniquity" are not a textbook for obeisance to worldly authority. I worry that Christians combating PoMo relativism and who extend this concern to their reading of Harry's breaking of rules and his friends' contempt for authority are breaking with Truth Himself to fight secular excesses of our times. I wonder if the conservative reaction to postmodern liberalism and godlessness has not erred in embracing modern, "structuralist," authoritarian thinking about church and state that are ideologies alien to radical faith in Christ.

Just a sidenote, forgive me. Check off "political subtext" and "anti-authority" from our literary postmodern checklist. Rowling gets a high pass in these PoMo subjects.

- ### *Deconstruction of Taboos, Ancient and Modern: The Meaning of Her Magic*

Having just said that Christians upset about the rule-breaking at Hogwarts are straining at a righteous gnat and swallowing a secular camel, let me reverse field and say there is something of truth in Christian concerns about the magic in *Harry Potter*. I have no doubt what I say here will be misrepresented by the crazies I usually get to debate on radio talk shows, but I don't think there is any sense in denying that the magic in *Harry Potter* undermines reader's belief in levitical proscriptions against sorcery and invocational magic. (See Chapter 1 of *Looking for God in Harry Potter* for a full discussion of 'Magic, Fantasy, and the Christian Worldview.")

This is a case book example of "deconstruction," a hallmark of literary postmodernism. Deconstruction, you'll recall, is showing an attractive alternative in story form to undermine (and passively attack) the predominant, repressive metanarrative. The whore with a heart of gold and female professional super-person, the Christ-like homosexual lovers (and rodeo cowboys?), the avenging angel black man – we recognize these cinematic and story clichés as attacks on sexist categories, homophobia, and racist denials of minority strength and virtue. It is a very unusual movie or novel in our times that does not have a hero or heroine, at least a principal side-kick, fulfilling the deconstructive role and advancing the poststructuralist argument.

Harry Potter certainly is no exception. His best friends are a "Mudblood" and the only "economically challenged" character in the series. His preferred travel companions and colleagues in battle are Neville Longbottom and Luna Lovegood, a Herbology wallflower and headcase, respectively. He is adopted by a house-elf, Dobby, that even house-elves feel is deep out in left field. These are the peripheral, slighted characters of wizardry that will be the true bane of Voldemort in the series' finale, I'm sure.

The greater deconstruction aim of the books, however, is in the magic – and it has an ironic twist. I doubt very much that Rowling was aiming to undermine biblical teaching on magic and sorcery. Her targets for "myths to dissemble in story," I'm almost certain, are not levitical law but the modern myths of material progress, materialism in general, and the idolatry of technology in particular. Magic does this deconstructive labor in a way that "instructs while delighting."

There is no wiggle room in Rowling's books for us to identify with Muggles and be anything but fascinated with magical folk, even the real jerks in that crowd. The only Muggles we meet are the Dursleys, Dudley's friends, Frank Bryce, a ticket taker at the grounds for the Quidditch World Cup, and the nameless Prime Minister. Outside Bryce and the campground keeper, both included only because we need someone for the Death Eaters and Voldemort to kill and torture, we're simply not allowed to like the Muggles, especially the Dursleys. We identify with Harry, the persecuted magical minority, in the Dursley home.

This is important because the Dursleys are the crassest materialists and status seeking conformists in recent literature. Dudley gets everything he demands and his desire-driven *Weltanschauung* is celebrated by his parents even during his tantrums and fits of disappointment and present counting. "'Little tyke wants his money's worth, just like his father. 'Atta boy, Dudley!' He ruffled Dudley's hair" (**Stone**, Chapter 2, p. 22). His room is a graveyard for computer games, racing bikes, and televisions he had to have and broke or forgot in his hurry to get the next thing.

In contrast, anyone in the Magical world interested in Muggle technology and goodies is considered something of a loon, even if it is only a hobby (e.g., Arthur Weasley and his electrical outlet collection and his childish wonder before the "fellytone"). Muggle preoccupation with things and gadgets is seen as something cute and primitive by witches and wizards. The Magical world is startlingly free of computers, iPods, even scuba gear. Their preoccupation is with magical ability and choices, both of which are internal achievements (and, as we'll see in a moment, the magic is more a measure of character than brains).

Materialism is the de facto and de jure State religion of our historical period. The methodological naturalism of physical science has morphed in the popular mind to the secular creed that things are made of measurable matter and energy – or they don't really exist. Anything immaterial or immeasurable is either delusion or not-yet-fully-understood brain chemistry. Mankind is supposed to be on a never ending escalator of material and technological progress that separates us from our primitive forebears and brings us ever closer to a worldly paradise.

The magic in *Harry Potter* deconstructs these myths just by taking place in a world where just the opposite world view pervades. Material things that can be measured are playthings for the magical person and of no consequence to the person of character. Mankind isn't evolving ever upward but devolving in descent or repeating the historical patterns of mythical founders. The integrity of one's soul is the measure of an individual's power and worth – and splitting or shattering the soul by injecting it onto or into material things as idolatry is a monstrous, self-destructive path of faux immortality.

Harry Potter, though, while effectively deconstructing the naturalist myth that matter/energy is the only reality, the myth that has become the Established Religion of American Government, also inadvertently undermines biblical teaching on witchcraft. Just as the Harry Haters love to shout from the housetops, it really is "only logical" that sympathetic treatments of witchcraft in stories and movies make the occult seem less dangerous than in fact it really is. The Christian objection to the excesses of postmodernity, that it undermines biblical and church authority, orthodox doctrine, world view, and values, has a foothold of truth, no doubt.

A better and more pressing question than "Is *Harry Potter* the gateway to Satanism and the Occult?" however, is "Who is the greater enemy of Christian faith – is it materialism or twisted occult 'spirituality' condemned by scripture?" I find this at best a rhetorical question. The materialist creed of our times has not only murdered many millions of Jewish, Buddhist, and Christian believers, especially the Orthodox Christians caught in the Soviet nightmare, but it has reduced faith to the category of subjective, individual opinion in countries where religious persecution doesn't extend to the gas chamber or gulag. It is an odd Christian believer in America who does not have more faith in General Electric and Bell labs than the teachings of their churches. Even the Fundamentalists seem to have more faith in religion per se than in God.

By retreating to Pharisaical legalism and attacking the wizardry of the *Harry Potter* novels, Harry Hating preachers and internet mavens are attacking a safe, identifiable target and creating a mechanical touchstone for believers caught up in the so-called culture war. In so doing, of course, they are both bearing false witness against a neighbor and neglecting their charge to "pick up the cross" and turn from the world.

It is, I think, one of the greater ironies of times that are almost beyond satire that Ms. Rowling's deconstructive attack on the greatest enemy to the faith, atheistic materialism, has caused her to be branded as a PoMo heretic if not the Anti-Christ by many Christian believers. Would that they were engaging with the real enemy and danger to our souls as creatively and effectively as is this thoughtful, postmodern, and, yes, Christian artist.

- *Literary Syncretism and Innovation: Genre "Rowling"*

I mentioned back in our look at **Sky High** that it was a blending of three film formulas as well as a mix of high and low art that is characteristic of postmodern story-telling a la architectural "double coding." By blurring our understanding of what it is exactly that we're viewing – superhero movie? Coming-of-age drama? B-movie camp? – the writers of that film created sufficient confusion about and fascination with the type of story we were watching that the meaning of the story was smuggled in without alarming the culture warriors.

This borrowing from seemingly unrelated categories to create a singular category or unique item outside any one category is called a syncretic approach. Syncretism and genre-jumping are means to paradigm and "mental formula" crashing. Like literary moderns, innovation is a hallmark of postmodern writing. Ms. Rowling conforms splendidly with this creed of nonconformity.

I told you that I frequently answer questions from readers about misbehavior at Hogwarts and the kids' disdain for authority figures and institutions by making reference to Ms. Rowling's writing within the genres of satire and schoolboy fiction. These two categories, though, are not half of the Rowling collection. These two are not even a fifth. Really, the *Harry Potter* stories are a seamless "rowling" together of twelve different literary genres. Rowling is the queen of the genre busters.

Key Four, Part Two: Postmodern Harry

I'm writing a book called *Harry Meets Hamlet and Scrooge: Reading The English Greats with Harry Potter* that reveals the literary antecedents and formulas Ms. Rowling includes in her marvelous brew. The twelve genres, if you want a preview, are, in no particular order (and with representative author):

- Alchemical Drama (Shakespeare)
- Detective Mystery (Sayers)
- Schoolboy Fiction (Hughes)
- Satire (Swift)
- Adventure Thriller (Orczy)
- Fantasy Fiction (Lewis, Tolkien)
- Children's Literature (Googe, Lewis)
- Manner-and-Morals story (Austen)
- Gothic Romance (Brontë, Stoker)
- Political Broadside (Shelley)
- Arthurian Legend (Mallory, Pyle)
- Hero Journey Epic (Homer, Ariosto)

I'm writing this book for two reasons besides making money (see Samuel Johnson for a sage reflection on the man who writes for any reason other than to be paid: "No man but a blockhead ever wrote, except for money"). A book revealing the debts Rowling owes to the English literary tradition simultaneously throws a bucket of ice water on the Harry Hater's mantra that the books are a "gateway to the occult" while bringing to light a whole new level of appreciation of Rowling's artistry and genius. The English tradition being almost exclusively a Christian tradition (e.g., all the authors listed with the genres above who are English, with the exception of Shelley, were committed Christians), the idea that Rowling is writing books inimical to faith but in conformity to tradition in all other respects is shown for the silliness that it is.

Rowling is quite open about her not being a boundary respecter at least with regard to literary genres She said in December of 2005 that:

> JKR: I've taken horrible liberties with folklore and mythology, but I'm quite unashamed about that, because British folklore

and British mythology is a totally bastard mythology. You know, we've been invaded by people, we've appropriated their gods, we've taken their mythical creatures, and we've soldered them all together to make, what I would say, is one of the richest folklores in the world, because it's so varied. So I feel no compunction about borrowing from that freely, but adding a few things of my own. http://www.accio-quote. org/articles/2005/1205-bbc-fry.html

In her interview with Mugglenet "reporters" in July, 2005, too, she twice made references to "the genre" in which she was writing, once with respect to hero journeys (in which she conformed to the formula of the hero finishing his struggle alone, sans mentor) and in another place in which she talks about detective fiction and breaking its rules:

JKR: There's a theory – this applies to detective novels, and then Harry, which is not really a detective novel, but it feels like one sometimes – that you should not have romantic intrigue in a detective book. Dorothy Sayers, who is the queen of the genre, said – and then broke her own rule, but said – that there is no place for romance in a detective story except that it can be used to camouflage other people's motives. That's true; it's a very useful trick. I've used that on Percy and I've used that to a degree on Tonks in this book, as a red herring. But having said that, I disagree inasmuch as mine are very character-driven books, and it's so important, therefore, that we see these characters fall in love, which is a necessary part of life. (Mugglenet.com interview, Part 2, p. 13)

In both her discussion of mythology and detective fiction, Rowling makes two direct points and a third indirectly. She says in both that she knows that static categories of writing with rules exist and that she does not think keeping these rules is important. In fact, she says, mythology has always been syncretic (therefore she is acting traditionally by mixing items and adding her own) and the "queen of the detective story genre" also broke her own rules about romance. Her third point is one she makes by talking about several types of books, tricks, and drives; she is consciously mixing and matching literary tools and categories for a melange that works.

For anyone that still thinks she is pulling this off unconsciously or "just got lucky," it is time to wakeup. When she realized she was writing fantasy fiction in addition to other categories, she decided to do fantasy differently. As she told Lev Grossman in her *Time Magazine* interview in July, 2005:

> "I was trying to subvert the genre," Rowling explains bluntly. "Harry goes off into this magical world, and is it any better than the world he's left? Only because he meets nicer people. Magic does not make his world better significantly. The relationships make his world better. Magic in many ways complicates his life." "J.K. Rowling, Hogwarts and All," *Time Magazine*, Lev Grossman, 17 July 2005

Another aspect of literary postmodernism is high-and-low art "double coding." Rowling is all aces here, too. With the alchemical formula out of Elizabethan drama alongside Nancy Drew and the Hardy Boys, in this double-coding alone we have a remarkable combination. Add in the semi-schlocky Gothic romance setting at Hogwarts Castle from old Dracula sets with a sophisticated coming-of-age orphan story a la David Copperfield and a doppelganger conflict straight out of Jekyll and Hyde and you have a book that simply couldn't have been conceived, much less written, one hundred years ago.

Check "genre blurring" and "double coding" off the postmodern checklist – and make a mental note (or twelve) that the *Harry Potter* books are a masterful introduction to English literature and a lifetime of edifying reading.

• *"No Teaching Here": The Postmodern Distance from Preaching*

The poststructuralist message is that messages are by nature exclusive, totalitarian, and oppressive to the group of people necessarily marginalized by the Grand Narrative. Literary postmodernism, consequently, self-consciously laughs at itself, turning things on their heads, to insure readers understand that there is no sermon being smuggled in here (other than that readers should be wary of people bearing sermons). Rowling shows this in her books and shares it in her interviews.

> Reporter: Your books have a theme of racism with the wizards oppressing other races and half-bloods. Do you think this has changed how people think when they read them?
>
> JKR: Do not think I am pessimistic but I think I am realistic about how much you can change deeply entrenched prejudice. So my feeling would be that if someone were a committed racist, possibly *Harry Potter* is not going to have effect.
>
> I would hope that it would make people think. I mean, I do not write the books thinking what is my message for today, what is my moral, that is not how I set out to write a book at all. I am not trying to criticise or make speeches to you in any way, but at the same time, it would be great if the people thought about bullying behavior or racism.
>
> The house-elves is really about slavery, isn't it? The house-elves are slaves, so that is an issue that I think we probably all feel strongly about enough in this room already. http://news.bbc.co.uk/cbbcnews/hi/newsid_4690800/4690885.stm

Rowling says here that, yes, she is writing about racism, bullying, and slavery, but, no, she isn't trying to win anybody over to her side about these things, because, hey, we all agree, don't we, that these things are bad? So that doesn't count as criticizing or making speeches, right?

She shows the postmodern conflict of bearing serious messages about the evil of serious message-bearers in her interview with Grossman, a certified C. S. Lewis despiser:

> And unlike Lewis, whose books are drenched in theology, Rowling refuses to view herself as a moral educator to the millions of children who read her books. "I don't think that it's at all healthy for the work for me to think in those terms. So I don't," she says. "I never think in terms of 'What am I going to teach them?' or, 'What would it be good for them to find out here?'"
>
> "Although," she adds, "undeniably, morals are drawn."

Key Four, Part Two: Postmodern Harry

The Latin motto of Hogwarts translates to "Never Tickle a Sleeping Dragon." I think this is Ms. Rowling's policy as a postmodern writer, too. C. S. Lewis wrote that he tried to "steal past the watchful dragons" in his readers' hearts, dragons of skepticism about anything suggestive of stained glass and Sunday school. Ms. Rowling's dragons are the same as Lewis', only the times have changed and with them the dragons' attentiveness. Rowling's messages are relatively nuanced and buried in comedy and narrative misdirection compared to Lewis'. Her readers will not tolerate sermons and she is not an apologist for any "doctrine" save nonconformity.

What is amusing is that the books are "drenched," as Lev Grossman might put it, in traditional Christian imagery, themes, and symbolism, "morals are drawn" undeniably and heavily, and the books are didactic, however subtle they may be compared with the Inklings or Victorian moralists. But Rowling, the supreme planner, as a postmodern writer will not allow that this is intentional.

Check off "self-mocking" and "internal contradictions" from the literary postmodernism checklist.

- *Nothing Is What It Seems – the Need for an Ever Larger View*

The single most important insight of the postmodernists is that a Unified View or Grand Myth is by definition not a full view. At best, this cultural metanarrative about beginnings and ends is just exclusive and incomplete; more often, they say, it is dogmatic, totalitarian, and oppressive to those not considered power-worthy within the myth. All other poststructuralist elements flow from this "skepticism about metanarrative."

Literary postmodernism expresses this core teaching, the contradictory Grand Myth of our times, by means of changes in the narrative voice or person a la Faulkner or in confusion or misdirection consequent to a restricted narratological perspective. In film and on television, a similar effect on the viewer is made by rapidly changing camera angles, time perspectives, and the confusion of the protagonist about what is really happening to him or her. Think MTV, 24, any snapshot sequence television commercial, and *The Matrix*.

185

Ms. Rowling's principal trick (and she has a full bag) as a writer, as we have seen in Chapter 1, is narrative misdirection. The *Harry Potter* stories are told from what is called the 3rd Person limited omniscient view, a mix of first and third person narratological voice. Harry's stories aren't told by Harry nor are they told by an all-seeing God-like narrator (3rd person omniscient). The stories seem to be told by Harry because we readers see everything Harry sees and are told what he is thinking and feeling.

These insights give us the mistaken impression that we know what's really going on, much like our perceptions and being aware of our own thoughts and feelings leads us to the mistaken belief that what we're seeing is the full truth. Every *Harry Potter* novel, except for *Half-Blood Prince*, ends with the revelation of just how mistaken we have been – and, in this, ends by fostering the idea central to postmodernism: "Don't believe everything you think."

Think of Moody's Disillusionment Charm in *Phoenix* (Chapter 3, p. 54). It makes Harry invisible or, at least, transparent. Ms. Rowling calls it a "disillusionment" charm because what you see of a person is not what they really are but an illusion. Seeing through people, grasping their front and back simultaneously and their environment that creates their reality, is seeing folks as they are, sans delusion.

Readers can take this charm as a challenge to read with more "penetration" and to avoid being duped again by the misdirection. I suspect Ms. Rowling's point may be to encourage precisely this intellectual virtue in us. Then again, it just might be that she intends to demonstrate what is axiomatic among poststructuralists, namely, that the structures of our thinking mean we will never transcend our limited perspectives and come to knowledge of anything real sans mental filters. Her track record so far is very good.

I wrote in Chapter 1 that Ms. Rowling learned this trick from her very close reading of Jane Austen and her understanding of how the narratological voice in Emma gave us "the biggest twist in English Literature." You'd be right to wonder how can this Edwardian spinster have been pioneering postmodern literary effects and tricks. The answer is fascinating.

Austen, as Rodney Delasanta has shown, was, if not a postmodern chronologically, was certainly an antimodern or postempiricist. Her books are story form responses and arguments with the sense-based empiricism and implicit materialism of David Hume. Before the full nightmare of modern myths and metanarrative were revealed in the 20th century, Jane Austen saw the dark shadows and gave us a picture of how our limited views based on sense perception (and no little self importance) blind us to our ignorance of what is really happening around us.

The recent popularity of Austen, with several television and movie productions of every one of her novels being written in her voice and the voice of other characters than the protagonist of her novels (latter day fan fiction), would be astonishing except for one thing. This manners-and-morals author of romantic fiction about English minor gentry is a woman, if not of our times (she certainly isn't), and is certainly an "early postmodern." By attacking and undermining the radical empiricism of David Hume, modernist, she anticipates the paradigm of our time by more than a century.

Does Harry have any hope of getting a larger perspective on things? Yes, he does. When Harry has a challenge, be it on the Quidditch pitch, or running the Philosopher's Stone gauntlet, or as Tri-Wizard Tournament champion, he only survives and prevails because of his team and support crew.

In *Stone*, it was Ron and Hermione that got him to the Mirror amphitheatre; in *Chamber*, it was Fawkes saving his bacon; in *Prisoner*, the terrible trio triumph again; in *Goblet*, Harry has major help with every one of the three tasks and even wins the Tournament jointly; in *Phoenix*, he takes Dumbledore's Army to the Ministry and it is the Headmaster and the Order who save his butt there; and in *Prince*, Harry is led by Dumbledore's withered hand from the Dursleys all the way to the Astronomy Tower.

Harry doesn't seem to understand how little he does without a host of help, but Ron and Hermione get it. As soon as they understand Harry is off to the wars at the end of *Prince*, they immediately enlist for the duration. They know the narrow-minded looney doesn't stand a chance without the broader perspective of a team and a variety of views.

Check off "nothing is what you think it is" and "solitude is ignorance, pluralism is deliverance." And we have a perfect record. Rowling passes every one of our tests for literary postmodernism.

Amazing! Every item on our literary postmodernism checklist checks out. I feel a little bit like the researcher with government grant money who investigates whether breast feeding is better than formula for mother and baby. How startled should I be that Ms. Rowling's books reflect the spirit and thinking of our age in some detail? Could books that denied the *Zeitgeist* be as popular as her books are? And what sort of freak of nature would she be if she weren't in many ways the product of her experience, her education, and her reading, what she calls her "creative composting"?

A Few Words About Dumbledore:

"Postmodern!" "Archetype!" "Thank you!"

The celebration of the periphery and the displaced is characteristic of literary postmodernism, whose principal lesson, in the language of Sky High, seems to be that the so-called Heroes are jerks and the real Heroes are the Sidekicks, that is, the 'Other-than-Heroes,' and the Heroes who identify with and protect them. Ms. Rowling's champions are certainly all from this upside-down school of "Misfit-as-Hero."

Run down the list of "Good Guys" in Harry Potter. Find me the character that isn't an outsider or freak from the periphery. Harry is the Muggle-raised 'Boy Who Lived' who grew up under the stairs and as a de facto orphan. Hermione is a Muggle-Born (Mudblood) brainiac in a house of jocks and fraternity boys. Ron comes from the wrong side of the tracks and is scarred by insecurities about being the youngest boy in a family of overachievers and no money. Luna Lovegood is from outer space, with a father who publishes an alternative tabloid and a dead mother. Neville Longbottom is another de facto orphan and outsider within any group to which he is attached.

And the adult "white hats"? Hagrid is a half-breed giant/wizard unable to fit in even with respect to appearance; he's too big to fit in anywhere normal. Ms. Rowling has described Sirius Black as a "case of arrested development" who looks to his friends for the family he threw off because of their darkness (Mugglenet interview, July 2005, part 1). Remus Lupin? Werewolf. Alaistair Moody? Obsessive, ever-vigilant compulsive. Nymphadora Tonks? Another freak among wizards, a Metamorphmagus and blood traitor.

Even the magical creatures and ghosts we know and like are bizarroes. Dobby is an independent house-elf, Firenze a co-operative and congenial centaur, and Moaning Myrtle and Nearly Headless Nick are ghosts whose deaths separate them not only from the living but from the company and easy fellowship of other ghosts.

All the Good Guys, in brief, are eccentric characters, well removed from the center of wizarding power by their inborn condition and conscience, who champion the helpless against the powerful because they understand being helpless. All of the Good Guys, that is, except one. . . . Albus Dumbledore.

Albus Dumbledore.

Ms. Rowling said in her July 2005 interviews that Dumbledore's intelligence is so great that he has no equal, which results in his being "isolated" and relatively "detached" (Op. cit., part 1). Dumbledore's oddity, however, magical power great enough to impress an O.W.L.S examiner even as a young student so much that decades later she recalls he "did things with a wand I'd never seen before" (Phoenix, Chapter 31, p. 711), doesn't make him less attractive to his wizarding peers. He is offered the position of Minister of Magic on several occasions, he has received every significant wizard honor, and he sits on all the right committees and panels, usually as chairman.

Nonetheless, Dumbledore is the postmodern champion par excellence. Like Will Stronghold in Sky High, he does not have to be a Sidekick, he chooses to identify with the outcasts and periphery magical folk that Draco calls riff-raff. He is the very model of a postmodern English gentleman.

Maybe you don't see right off the connections between the Hogwarts' Headmaster and an archetype of postmodernism. Here's a quick review of ten correspondences between Dumbledore and a heroic linguistics professor:

- **Academic**;

Dumbledore is a teacher and school administrator by choice. As he tells the young Lord Voldemort at his job interview, Dumbledore thinks the life of the mind more important than public service, at least than a position at the Ministry.

- **Penetrating Intelligence**;

Dumbledore is able to see past popular prejudices and beneath the surface of individuals. He has gathered around him a group of freaks with hearts of gold whose inner worth he alone among wizards was able to recognize and foster (contrast this with Horace Slughorn's "Slug Club"). Again, remember his preference in candies. When we first meet him, Dumbledore is eating a Muggle treat called lemon sorbets, the

UK equivalent of the American "zots," a sweet sucker with baking soda at its center that fizzes and delights the sucker with a surprise inside. The Headmaster likes his candy and his friends to have extraordinary, invisible, neglected qualities.

- **Discerns signs of times;**

The greatest wizard of his time is able to see the blind-spots, prejudice, and mistaken, oppressive beliefs that marginalize "others" and which characterize the predominant metanarrative. Be it discrimination against Half-giants or Voldemort's inability to understand the power of love, Dumbledore always has his finger on the piece of the truth that a person's beliefs about "What Truth Is" obscures.

- **Attacks core problems;**

The Ministry of Magic is a group of self-important bunglers that focus their efforts on bread-and-circus events like the Quidditch World Cup, risible bureaucratic paper shuffling like Cauldron Bottom Reports, or, less humorously, enforcing the imposed order of the Grand Myths and punishing the helpless and innocent (Hagrid, Sirius, Harry, "others"). Dumbledore, in strong contrast, acts independently of the herd of public opinion and the tide of prevalent beliefs to help the helpless, is an "equal opportunity employer," and is constantly on the lookout for information about the core evil of the moment (in this series, about Lord Voldemort).

- **Signifiers meaningless, humorless, interchangeable;**

And he is a linguistics man, no doubt. Recall his speech at the banquet following the sorting of Harry's class, in which he said, "Welcome to a new year at Hogwarts! Before we begin our banquet, I would like to say a few words. And here they are: Nitwit! Blubber! Oddment! Tweak!" "Thank you!" (Stone, Chapter 7, p. 123). Harry remembers this talk years later at Dumbledore's funeral.

> A little tufty-haired man in plain black robes had got to his feet and stood now in front of Dumbledore's body. Harry could not hear what he was saying. Odd words floated back to them over the hundreds of heads. "Nobility of spirit". . . "intellectual contribution". . . "greatness of heart". . . It did not mean very much. It had little to do with Dumbledore

as Harry had known him. He suddenly remembered Dumbledore's idea of a few words, "nitwit," "oddment," "blubber," and "tweak" and again had to suppress a grin. . . What was the matter with him? (*Prince,* Chapter 30, pp. 643-644; thanks to Odd Sverre Hove for this reference)

Harry then recalls Dumbledore's facility in Mermish. Dumbledore alone among wizards made the effort to lean the languages of other magical creatures.

Dumbledore is a good postmodern linguistics man because he suggests openly that words are not reality or signifiers of real things but humorous toys that do little more than reflect the mental filters of the speaker. These toys, however, are at the heart of things because only through them can we see what is real, namely, these filters.

His seemingly nonsense collection of words, for instance, reveals his focus and concern with the disenfranchised and the prevailing beliefs that ostracize or over-correct them: "nitwit" is a word of derision for someone seen as less capable than others, "oddment" is a word for something extraneous or left over, "blubber" is a word for whale fat used to describe obese people, and "tweak" is the act of adjusting by little bits what seems out of order back into alignment.

The "tufty-haired" eulogist at the funeral tries in vain to capture in platitudes the reality or essence of Dumbledore. Harry remembers the first words he heard Dumbledore say – a man fluent in many languages and who understood language itself – and has before him the man whose life was about protecting the "oddments" derided by others with unkind names about their way of thinking or physical persons and who are endlessly "tweaked" into conformity to the prevalent Grand Myths. Dumbledore's four words are a veiled rebuke and a warning of the dangers in the Sorting Ceremony that has just taken place. Each word is one that a newly sorted First Year would use to define him or herself in contrast with the "other" houses (e.g., new Ravenclaws see themselves as brilliant and call others, "nitwits").

- **Deconstruction of Prophecy Text;**

For an academic, Dumbledore doesn't do a lot of conventional teaching. We know that he was a Transfiguration professor but only see him practice the craft outside of a classroom. The sole text we see him discuss – a transfiguring discussion it turns out – has to do with the prophecy that seems to link Harry to Voldemort as his vanquisher.

We shouldn't be surprised by now to see him deconstruct this text and reduce its meaning to Harry's understanding of its meaning. The prophecy, he insists, is meaningless except for the meaning Voldemort and Harry have given it. Harry is transformed from something of a fatalist who is prisoner or subject to a fate and reality outside his free will to a self-actualizing hero able to confront the Dark Lord because of his choice to confront him. Dumbledore, the words man, reveals for Harry that texts are meaningless and deceptive; the reader and his understanding are the meaning and the reality of the text.

- **Music lover;**

After the *Harry Potter* series is completed you may expect an avalanche of books and dissertation theses on such topics as "Music in J. K. Rowling's Hogwarts Saga," and (ahem) "postmodernism and Alchemy in *Harry Potter*: the Frenetic Interpretations of Fandom" will quickly follow. About the music, just two quick "notes" (sorry).

First, the only song sung at Hogwarts is the school song, which everyone "bellows" at the end of the Sorting Banquet. Dumbledore acts as conductor, instructing everyone to "pick their favorite tune," and

> Everybody finished the song at different times. At last, only the Weasley twins were left singing along to a very slow funeral march. Dumbledore conducted their last few lines with his wand when they had finished, he was one of those who clapped loudest.
>
> "Ah, music," he said, wiping his eyes. "A magic beyond all we do here!" (*Stone*, Chapter 7, p. 128)

Dumbledore is alone among the adults, it seems, to have this appreciation of music. Ms. Rowling tells us that when Dumbledore announces it is time for the school song, "Harry noticed that the other teachers' smiles had become rather fixed" (op. cit., p. 127). Besides foreshadowing the heroic death of the Weasley twins in the last book, this passage is exceptional in Dumbledore's urging everyone to sing their favorite tune and his saying music is the more powerful magic when compared to Hogwarts wand-work.

The invitation to listen to your own drummer and sing your own song is the mantra of our individualist and nonconformist age. The teachers grimace because the "singing" must be cacophonous and singularly unpleasant. To Dumbledore, however, this "singing together separately" is something like the "Aims of Education" and moves him to tears.

The only other songs we hear in the books, leaving out the Weird Sisters dance band in *Goblet* and Molly Weasley's favorite tunes at her Christmas party, are Quidditch chants, Mermish puzzle ditties, Snape's life-saving incantation over Malfoy "that sounded almost like song" (*Prince*, Chapter 24, p. 523), and Fawkes' song in the *Chamber of Secrets* and after the Astronomy Tower debacle. Dumbledore's beliefs about music and his relationship with Fawkes mean we'll have to come back to this point in a later chapter.

- **Indifference to teacher's didactic abilities and students' conformity to standards;**

Professional educators as a rule are the most officious group of rule-keepers and enforcers on the planet. Their job is largely about creating law-abiding citizens, and school is mostly about training the innocent to conform to arbitrary and meaningless standards (time schedules for classes, recess, and eating, test scores and grades for sorting into hierarchy according to one characteristic, etc., ad nauseam, ad infinitum). We see a lot of this at Hogwarts, especially in the year-long reign of Dolores Umbridge, super-professional educator. How teachers read the *Harry Potter* adventures and don't understand themselves and their institution as being skewered mercilessly in them is something that completely escapes me. Rowling presents teachers and school as simultaneously hilarious and tragic, even evil.

Dumbledore, however, is something like what an existentialist would be if Headmaster. He does not overthrow all the demeaning conventions of the institution (can you say N.E.W.T.S. and O.W.L.S.?), nor does he hold exacting standards for teachers, all of whom are borderline incompetent, overly serious and self-impressed, or sadistic. His only standard seems to be that they not be Lord Voldemort.

He fails, too, to treat "smart" students differently or better than "dumb" ones. He is most concerned, it seems, with manners and the details of respect ("Professor Snape, Harry") everyone is due, from Professor Trelawney and Hagrid, even to his evident enemies like Dolores Umbridge and the Minister of Magic. Dumbledore, unlike his fellow faculty members seems ever onguard against letting his perception be clouded by labels, prejudicial stigmas, and pigeon holes. Which, again, is the defining characteristic of a postmodern intellectual.

It is no accident that, as David Colbert and Travis Prinzi have pointed out, many of the members of the Order of the Phoenix have names similar to the more famous members of the so-called Fabian Socialists of the early 20th Century. These intellectuals, including a few of Ms. Rowling's favorite writers, were socialists wanting reform without the coerciveness and unpleasantry of Marxist revolution. As Prinzi explains:

> Simply put, the Fabian Society believe[d] in slow, eventual change, not revolution. This was one of their early defining characteristics, in fact. They are a socialist society, but different from Marx in his belief that equity would come about by a lower-class revolution. Rather, they believed in gradual change over time. In fact, a parody of their philosophy goes something like this: "What do we want?" "Gradual change!" "When do we want it?" "In due course!"
> http://swordofgryffindor.com/2006/06/08/fabian-society-post/

Dumbledore doesn't want to remake the world; he just wants a safe place in which people can grow up over time and come to their senses.

• **Student of his own thoughts;**

We are not surprised, consequently, that it seems Dumbledore is the only witch or wizard to own a Pensieve and spend time examining his own thoughts. Professor Snape borrows the Pensieve, but only, it seems to "protect" his thoughts from Harry during Occulmency lessons (just as likely he left them out for Harry to see), not as a tool for self-reflection and understanding. This is Dumbledore's domain.

• **Careful of his influence over others.**

As "how we think" equates with "reality" to the postmodern, the greatest crime is the act of undue influence, indoctrination, or of "brain washing." The greatest injury possible to a human being – which injury is the aim of government, media, and educational institutions by and large – is to shape or twist a person's thinking into cement channels like Swiss rivers so it has little to nothing of the freedom or direction it had at birth. If the principal virtues of postmodernism are "tolerating all but the intolerant" and "respect," the greatest vices are disrespect and patronizing others like colonial masters on a plantation.

Dumbledore exemplifies these virtues and deplores these vices. He disappears, in fact, from the stage in *Order of the Phoenix* because he fears his very presence is causing an unfortunate response in Harry, something like misplaced transference. He is loath to have this effect on anyone, even if it is something he is not doing but which is coming from within Harry, and respects Harry enough to let him fight this internal battle alone.

Ms. Rowling has said about Dumbledore and Hagrid that the Headmaster will help the Gamekeeper out of his psychological ruts – but only after he "stewed a bit."

> My sister said to me in a moment of frustration, it was when Hagrid was shut up in his house after Rita Skeeter had published that he was a half-breed, and my sister said to me, "Why didn't Dumbledore go down earlier, why didn't Dumbledore go down earlier?" I said he really had to let Hagrid stew for a while and see if he was going to come out of this on his own because if he had come out of it on his own he really would have been better. "Well he's too detached, he's too cold, it's like you," she said! [Laughter] By which she meant that where she would immediately rush in and I would maybe stand back a bit and say, "Let's wait and see if he can work this out." (Mugglenet interview, 16 July 2005, part 1)

Dumbledore is no man's nursemaid or "facilitator."

The only student with comparable penetration if much less respectful is Hermione Granger. The object of the wizarding equivalent of racist remarks because of her Muggle parents, she champions the oppressed if seemingly happy house-elves. Hermione alone among the students seems to get the Sorting Hat's call for Inter-House Unity. She shows that she understood as early as *Goblet* that the Gryffindor/Slytherin divide must be crossed because she goes to the ball with Viktor Krum, the water-quality (aka Slytherin) champion in the Tri-Wizard Tournament, despite her Gryffindor loyalties.

Black Hats: Ms. Rowling's Archetypal Postmodern Villains

The *Harry Potter* Good Guys, then, like those in every postmodern novel, are both the freaks that have been made freaks by the myths shaping our thinking and the brilliant people whose understanding and virtues penetrate and transcend these myths. The Bad Guys are postmodern Bad Guys, too, which is to say, they are "modern" and champions of the repressive regimes of the power holders and the attendant myths.

I give you Lord Voldemort, his Death Eaters, and, for the most part, Slytherin House. Tom Riddle, Jr., is a power obsessed modern, a Nazi wizard who becomes increasingly monstrous as he continues to embody his Muggle-hating, weakness-despising ideology. The Dark Lord and his followers are caricatures of fascist personalities whose almost total lack of self-awareness and of love are their very real weaknesses.

And love here is not just a Hallmark card sentiment. It is the power by which Harry will be able to defeat Voldemort, Dumbledore says repeatedly. Behind a door in the Department of Mysteries, a door that cannot be opened by conventional magic, is power that is simultaneously unknowable, unquantifiable, and capable of transcending death. As the Headmaster explains to Harry:

> "There is a room in the Department of Mysteries," interrupted Dumbledore, "that is kept locked at all times. It contains a force that is at once more wonderful and more terrible than death, than human intelligence, than the forces of nature. It is also, perhaps, the most mysterious of the many subjects for study that reside there. It is the power held within that room that you possess in such quantities and which Voldemort has not at all. That power took you to save Sirius tonight. That power also saved you from possession by Voldemort, because he could not bear to reside in a body so full of the force he detests. In the end, it mattered not that you could not close your mind. It was your heart that saved you" (*Order*, Chapter 37, pp. 343-344).

Dumbledore repeatedly tells us that Lord Voldemort does not understand the power of love. In one visit he and Harry take into the Pensieve, we see Dumbledore confront the Dark Lord with this failing to his increasingly anguine face:

> "Certainly," said Voldemort, and his eyes seemed to burn red. "I have experimented; I have pushed the boundaries of magic further, perhaps than they have ever been pushed –"
>
> "Of some kinds of magic," Dumbledore corrected him quietly. "Of some. Of others, you remain . . . forgive me . . . woefully ignorant."
>
> For the first time, Voldemort smiled. It was a taut leer, an evil thing, more threatening than a look of rage.
>
> "The old argument," he said softly. "But nothing I have seen in the world has supported your famous pronouncement that love is more powerful than my kind of magic, Dumbledore."
>
> "Perhaps you have been looking in the wrong places," suggested Dumbledore. (*Prince*, Chapter 20, pp. 443-444)

Dumbledore seems to believe that Voldemort is not only ignorant of love's power, but that he is incapable of understanding it. As he said to the 11 year old Harry after his first encounter with the Dark Lord:

> "Your mother died to save you. If there is one thing Voldemort cannot understand, it is love. He didn't realize that love as powerful as your mother's for you leaves its own mark. Not a scar, no visible sign . . . to have been loved so deeply, even though the person who loved us is gone, will give us some protection for ever. It is in your very skin" (*Stone*, Chapter 17, p. 299).

Remember, Dumbledore believes that love is a mystery and a magic that "is at once more wonderful and more terrible than death, than human intelligence, than the forces of nature." He suggests even that it is the power, too, that allows us to transcend and win some victory over our human mortality. As he said to Harry in the denouement to *Prisoner*:

> "You think the dead we loved ever truly leave us? You think we don't recall them more clearly than ever in times of great trouble? Your father is alive in you, Harry, and shows himself most plainly when you have need of him" (*Prisoner*, Chapter 22, pp. 427-428).

I discuss the theme of "Love over Death" in the tenth chapter of *Looking for God in Harry Potter*. I bring it up here to close my discussion of the many ways Ms. Rowling is best understood as a postmodern writer. It is a fitting ending because "love" is the antithesis of a "Grand Narrative," overarching ideology, or founding myth. Love only works "locally," that is, between individuals or in community. Love, as fluid and untenable as it may seem, even ooey-gooey as Valentine candy, is a reality that transcends time, space, and even boundaries like death.

Quirrelldemort preaches to Harry in front of the Mirror of Erised a modern, nihilistic catechism. "There is no good and evil, there is only power, and those too weak to seek it...." (*Stone*, Chapter 17, p. 291). Ms. Rowling offers the relatively elastic and individual postmodern solution to this Nietzschean *Übermensch* monologue via her story of an orphan boy and his friends from the Island of Misfit Toys who defeat the Power seekers and their will to power with love.

Conclusion

I've got good news and bad news.

First, the good news.

You now have a grasp of what postmodernism is and the several important ways Ms. Rowling is a writer of her times writing for a postmodern audience of readers. The *Harry Potter* books reveal her disregard for conventional and historical genre lines and taboos, her "incredulity toward metanarrative," that is, a loathing of dogma and ideology in an almost dogmatic fashion in choice of themes, narratological perspective, and story line, and her profound suspicion of and skepticism about the motives of institutional carriers of these metanarratives (school, home, government, media, everyone it seems but "organized religion").

Even one or two generations ago, these books would have seemed recklessly avant-garde and radical for "kid-lit." Now the pluralistic themes are the "common sense" of our age. Understanding postmodern literature and *Harry Potter* as a postmodern period piece gives you a remarkable heads-up in grasping why these books are as popular as they are. They jibe with how we see the world nowadays.

The bad news?

You've only got half the story.

Great writers and great books are simultaneously of their historical time periods and somewhat timeless, with story, symbols, and themes that touch on not only what makes us what we are as products of our age but what makes us human, regardless of our fashionable beliefs. And the greatest writers, the Shakespeares, the Austens, the Dostoevskys (would that there were bunches of them!), do something more. While representing and embodying their historical periods, by transcending their age, they also critique it and hold it up against a standard of truth, beauty, and goodness.

Ms. Rowling is, on one level, your "typical postmodern writer," cranking out politically correct stories about the big, bad founding myth and the heroic struggle of those marginalized by it. As we'll see in the next chapter, she is one of the harshest critics of our times and of many of the tenets of postmodernism. Hidden in this criticism is probably the clearest evidence that she is "a postmodern's postmodern."

Read on to find out how Ms. Rowling is and is not like the Inkling writers with whom she is often compared (and how her recent comments about C. S. Lewis reflect her poor understanding of his work), not to mention explorations of why the postmodern critics despise her work alongside Christian Harry Haters and why the Harry Haters really hate the magic and the rule-breaking at Hogwarts. You're right if you guess it doesn't have much to do with the Bible.

Chapter Five   Key 5

Traditional Symbolism OR
Postmodernism on its Head

Our first clue that Joanne Rowling is not your died-in-the-wool, card-carrying poststructuralist writer is the reception she has received by those saluting the PoMo banners and manning the barricades of relativism. Her reception by Ivory Tower academics and the doyens of Culture (capital "C") has been anything but pretty.

Ms. Rowling is a media darling, and, frankly, this is bizarre, if it is true that, as a postmodern, you'd expect them to have a lot in common. Reporters, as a rule to which there are few exceptions, are graduates of the "better schools" and, as such, they are almost always true believers in the Gospel of Lyotard, Derrida, and Foucault. What is weird about their adoration and ardent defense of Ms. Rowling is that it happens despite her doing everything possible to show her disregard for news people and journalists.

Every media character in her books is a boob or a villain. Her caricature of Fleet Street in the Daily Prophet is anything but subtle or flattering.

> "So the *Daily Prophet* exists to tell people what they want to hear, does it?" said Hermione scathingly.
>
> Rita sat up again, her eyebrows raised, and drained her glass of firewhisky.
>
> "*The Prophet* exists to sell itself, you silly girl," she said coldly. (***Phoenix***, Chapter 25, p. 567)

Rita Skeeter and the profit-focused *Prophet* aside, Rowling herself is indifferent, even hostile to publicity. She only does interviews at the release of books and movies, I assume because of contract obligations with her publishers and Warner Brothers, or in association with her remarkable charity work. Her wonderful website, www.jkrowling.com, is her direct link to her fans, with whom she communicates regularly and without the media intermediaries that would necessarily spin her story in unflattering or unnecessary ways.

So why the love affair of the news media for this woman that is so queerly one-sided?

My best guess is that it is a function of the old adage, "the enemy of my enemy is my friend." There are only two stories or "sure things" that have to be included in every story about *Harry Potter* and Joanne Rowling: her rags-to-riches Cinderella story of rising from the dole as welfare-mum to being "richer than the queen" and that "Christians burn her books." The only religious group American reporters love to bash or at least make look ridiculous is not the Islam of Muslim terrorists ("a peace-loving religion") but Christianity of any flavor, especially the sort of folks that can be called "Fundamentalists" or "conservative members of the Religious Right."

Harry Potter, in academic language, is an excellent vehicle with which to bash the "Christian superstition metanarrative." The Press loves to find token Christian Harry Haters at every *Harry Potter* film or book release to show just how stupid and out-of-step the Bible Belters really are. No matter how badly Ms. Rowling treats journalists in person or in her stories, I have to doubt the Press will stop celebrating her "genius" as long as points can be made against Christian faith. Which is to say, "until she publishes her first non-Harry story."

Strange as the media's embrace of Ms. Rowling has been, the response of academics and culture mavens is just as peculiar, if almost exactly opposite.

Academy Indifference and Hostility

I have just argued that Joanne Rowling is the poster child postmodern author and the perfect model of a poststructuralist "gentleperson." A good clue that we're missing something by saying this is the meanness of commentary and the barrenness of criticism coming from the universities and the book review journals of the literati. If Ms. Rowling's books were as postmodern as I've been arguing, certainly the postmodern establishment and taste-makers would have embraced her with open arms.

Hasn't happened.

If you take *The New York Times* as the mouthpiece of those-in-the-know, that is, "All the News That's Spun for the Real Thinking People Everywhere," their treatment of Ms. Rowling and her books reflects the arms-length posture of the culture mavens with respect to *Harry Potter. NYT* Columnist William Safire noted famously that the books are "not worthy of serious adult attention." A novelist beloved by literary critics but unknown to most *Harry* readers, A. S. Byatt, wrote a scathing critique of the *Potter* books and their audience, "*Harry Potter* and the Childish Adult," that *The Times* ran as a featured column about "Ms Rowling's secondary world, made up of intelligently patchworked derivative motifs." Worse,

> Ms Rowling's magic world has no place for the numinous. It is written for people whose imaginative lives are confined to TV cartoons, and the exaggerated (more exciting, not threatening) mirror-worlds of soaps, reality TV and celebrity gossip. Its values, and everything in it, are, as Gatsby said of his own world when the light had gone out of his dream, "only personal". Nobody is trying to save or destroy anything beyond *Harry Potter* and his friends and family....
>
> It is the substitution of celebrity for heroism that has fed this phenomenon. And it is the levelling effect of cultural studies, which are as interested in hype and popularity as they are in literary merit, which they don't really believe exists. It's fine to compare the Brontes with bodice-rippers. It's become respectable to read and discuss what Roland Barthes called "consumable" books.
>
> There is nothing wrong with this, but it has little to do with the shiver of awe we feel looking through Keats's "magic casements, opening on the foam/Of perilous seas, in faery lands forlorn". http://www.telegraph.co.uk/news/main.jhtml?xml=/news/2003/07/10/npott110.xml (A.S. Byatt, "*Harry Potter* and the Childish Adult," NYT, 7/7/05)

Charles Taylor at *Salon* wrote a wonderful response to this patronizing, self-important criticism by an envious author ("A.S. Byatt and the Goblet of Bile") in which he revealed that Ms. Byatt has a penchant for dismissing publicly those whose books sell much better than her "numinous" masterpieces. The point is that *The Times* thought this condescending and dismissive calumny worthy of its pulpit and faithful congregation of know-betters.

The *Times* doesn't restrict its disdain for the *Potter* books to its editorial pages and literary reviews, however. In the summer of 2001, *The Times* made the first changes to its popular "Best Seller List" features in more than a decade by creating a separate "Children's Book" list that would be below the Fiction/Non-fiction and Paperback sales listings. Why?

Well, because Ms. Rowling's books, which Harold Bloom at Yale had dismissed as "mush," had dominated the Fiction Best Seller top three spots for more than eighteen months, and *Goblet of Fire*, the fourth book in the series, was about to be published, no doubt taking still another place. Enough is enough, decided the *Times*, and Ms. Rowling was cast from the heights of *The Times'* lists to the juvenile department in the subbasement of the listings page.

> "It was startling to me that they would choose the moment when the fourth *Harry Potter* would be hitting No. 1 on the adult list," says Barbara Marcus, president of the Scholastic Children's Book Group, J.K. Rowling's American publisher. "The *Times* became a spoiler of it all. I always believed that best-seller lists are just that, and they should be recording and reporting the bestselling books in the country." http://archive. salon.com/mwt/feature/2000/08/16/bestseller/index.html

How wonderfully naïve. What makes this move especially comic is that booksellers have noted that more than 50 percent of the *Harry Potter* books they sell are to adults who are not buying them for children. The *Times'* decision to track and list them as Children's books, regardless, reflects their agreement with Ms. Byatt about the poor taste and limited intelligence of Harry's reading audience. These are books for children and "childish adults."

And if the doyens of literary accomplishment at the *Times* have been bad, the Ivory Tower folk may have been worse. Harold Bloom says he read the first *Potter* novel and then wrote an article he titled, "Can 35 Million Book Buyers Be Wrong? Yes." He concludes his dismissal of the series as being unworthy of comparison with *The Wind in the Willows* and the *Alice* books of Lewis Carroll by writing:

Key Five: Postmodernism on its Head

How to read *"Harry Potter and the Sorcerer's Stone"*? Why, very quickly, to begin with, perhaps also to make an end. Why read it? Presumably, if you cannot be persuaded to read anything better, Rowling will have to do. Is there any redeeming education use to Rowling? Is there any to Stephen King? Why read, if what you read will not enrich mind or spirit or personality? For all I know, the actual wizards and witches of Britain, or America, may provide an alternative culture for more people than is commonly realized.

Perhaps Rowling appeals to millions of reader non-readers because they sense her wistful sincerity, and want to join her world, imaginary or not. She feeds a vast hunger for unreality; can that be bad? At least her fans are momentarily emancipated from their screens, and so may not forget wholly the sensation of turning the pages of a book, any book.

And yet I feel a discomfort with the *Harry Potter* mania, and I hope that my discontent is not merely a highbrow snobbery, or a nostalgia for a more literate fantasy to beguile (shall we say) intelligent children of all ages. Can more than 35 million book buyers, and their offspring, be wrong? Yes, they have been, and will continue to be for as long as they persevere with *Potter.* http://wrt-brooke.syr.edu/courses/205.03/bloom.html (WSJ, 7/11/2000)

Would that Bloom were alone in his willing blindness to the complexity and depth of these supposedly witless, illiterate fantasies. In 1999 the judges of the Whitbread Prizes (now the Costa Book Awards) passed over *Prisoner of Azkaban* by one vote and gave Ms. Rowling the consolation prize of a special "Children's Book Award." We'll come back to the Whitbread Prize in a second; more important is what critical attention the *Potter* books have received from academics to this point.

There are more than fifty guides to *Harry Potter* in print today but only six that have been generated by literature and other professors at American and UK universities. If you have a minute, go to Amazon.com and look them up:

Reading Harry Potter : Critical Essays (Contributions to the Study of Popular Culture) by Giselle Liza Anatol (Hardcover - May 30, 2003)

The Ivory Tower and Harry Potter: Perspectives on a Literary Phenomenon by Lana A. Whited (Hardcover - Dec. 2002)

Harry Potter's World: Multidisciplinary Critical Perspectives (Pedagogy and Popular Culture) by Elizabeth E. Heilman (Paperback - Jan. 2003)

J.K. Rowling's Harry Potter Novels: A Reader's Guide (Continuum Contemporaries) - Unauthorized by Philip Nel (Paperback - Oct. 2001)

Irresistible Rise of Harry Potter by Andrew Blake (Hardcover - Dec. 12, 2002)

Scholarly Studies in Harry Potter: Applying Academic Methods to a Popular Text (Studies in British Literature) by Cynthia Whitney Hallett (Hardcover - Dec. 5, 2005)

Of these books, only Andrew Blake's is overtly hostile. Blake, the Head of Cultural Studies at King Alfred's College and author of **Salman Rushdie: A Beginner's Guide**, is symptomatic of the approach of many if not most of the academic treatments in the other collections. He sees the books as the "literary equivalent of French Fries" and examines them as a cultural artifact with his Marxist literary criticism tools. They are popular, in brief, because they are products cleverly packaged for consumption with minimal difficulty and for marketing to the broadest possible audience.

Blake, again, is the exception in his enmity for the books, but his posture relative to the book is typical of academic treatments thus far. He is shocked and disappointed that we are celebrating the English public boarding school and its privileges in children's literature of the 21st century. Similar politically correct arguments based on cultural categories outside the artistry of literature are made in articles in the first three collections (listed above) on "Gender Identity and Issues," "Cultural Hegemony," and "Interpretative and Sociological Perspectives."

While more sympathetic than Blake to Rowling's achievement, there is an unfortunate failing in these collections of academic articles to explain the books' literary merits or the reason for their unprecedented popularity in ways that distinguish them from Blake's position. Despite some excellent individual pieces that more than justify their purchase at even twice the price, these books left me disappointed.

I don't want to explore the various ways of reading *Harry Potter* as a text on race and social class or to read about the various ways Hermione's subservience to the boys reinforces negative gender stereotypes. I expect the Academy to tell me why the books are so popular through an exegesis of their meaning and the author's artistry, not walk me through a primer in cultural studies that leads me nowhere.

(An aside: Philip Nel's brief book, that is now outdated and has always been the smallest of the introductions to Harry and Potter-mania, remains the best academic guide produced by a university professor that I have seen for its consistent sobriety and insight about the series.)

In all fairness, the reason academic criticism is so thin and unsatisfying now is because the folks on tenure tracks or with full professorships aren't going to comment publicly and in depth until the seventh and concluding novel in the series is published. This is simple prudence and I'm not blaming anyone for not risking their reputations on *Harry Potter* before they've read the whole thing. I am looking forward to the avalanche of University Press books that will be printed, I'm sure, within a year of *Deathly Hallows'* publication.

Having said that, the treatment of *Harry Potter* by those academics who have dared the waters this early as something of a "cultural artifact" to dissect in a sociology lab and as a "vehicle of the oppressive metanarrative" supporting gender, race, class, and sexual orientation bias and oppression is bizarre. They seem to be saying without hesitation that Ms. Rowling, postmodernity's champion and feature attraction, is not quite postmodern enough.

Consider the children's book author, Phillip Pullman, who has won the real Whitbread Prize, the biggest prize for books in the UK, in 2001 for his *The Amber Spyglass*. Pullman, referred to at a *Harry Potter* conference as "the gold standard" in children's literature by a respected professor in that field, is a public and zealous atheist, who attacks the Christian Church in his books explicitly as the agents of oppression, more to be feared and decried than the schools, the media, or the government. Issues of sex, race, and political correctness are his measures of value.

For example, Pullman, who is called "the UnLewis" by British critics because of his hateful comments about C. S. Lewis and especially Lewis' books for children, once told an audience of children at a book fair that, "I realised that what he was up to was propaganda in the cause of the religion he believed in. [*Narnia*] is monumentally disparaging of girls and women. It is blatantly racist. One girl was sent to hell because she was getting interested in clothes and boys." http://books. guardian.co.uk/guardianhayfestival2002/story/0,11873,726818,00. html.) About himself, he is equally frank: 'Blake once wrote of Milton that he was a "true poet, and of the Devil's party, without knowing it". I am of the Devil's party, and I know it.' http://observer.guardian. co.uk/international/story/0,6903,542616,00.html

Pullman is the champion celebrated by academics and Prize committees, although Rowling has, of course, won her share of prizes and honorary degrees. What is lacking in her postmodern resume? Or is she justifiably considered a second-class writer when compared with Pullman? What departures and "compromising failings" did we miss in the last chapter's review of *Harry Potter*'s postmodern qualities?

If we take a second look at the series, what we will find is that, in addition to being in so many ways a child of our age, Joanne Rowling is also a conscious critic of the excesses and failings of our time. She is, probably, an uncomfortable subject for academics because she often seems to be pointing to the failings of poststructuralism and the unexamined preconceptions of the postmodern university.

Let's take a look back.

Voldemort and Dumbledore

We ended our discussion of Rowling's postmodernity with reviews of her villainous and heroic mages, Tom Riddle, Jr., a.k.a., Lord Voldemort, and Albus Dumbledore. Voldemort seemed an archetypal modern baddie, just the sort of power-focused crazie bent on destroying the weak and marginalized that all readers, but especially postmodern ones, love to hate. But Voldemort can also be understood, especially after the revelations of *Half-Blood Prince*, as a picture of postmodern man and a vignette-critique of the excesses of our time.

He is, post-Horcruxes, simply a shattered person, whose soul and humanity have been deposited in physical objects as a means to a mechanical, murderous immortality. He is himself a "deconstructed text," that no longer has an independent existence or value. Even though we learn about his painful childhood in an orphanage and about his mother's trials, Ms. Rowling never suggests there is something understandable or pitiable in the evil person Tom Riddle chooses to become in his pursuit of power.

He is also not a conceptual evil that can be parsed, broken down, and made relative, "the product of external forces outside his control." Rowling presents her prime villains and his henchmen as a very real wickedness, the product of human error and choice, that must be resisted at all costs, even death. Voldemort may be a doppelganger, or Harry's shadow figure, but even as an internal struggle writ large as external drama, the nature of fantasy fiction, Rowling never soft-pedals the reality of Riddle's wickedness, his culpability for his condition, or the necessity of resisting this evil courageously and sacrificially.

This shows her departure from postmodern relativism and conceptuality. At the same time it proves Ms. Rowling's quintessentially postmodern attack on the hyperbole and silliness of the postmodern metanarrative.

Odd Sverre Hove, a friend and editor in Denmark, shared with me some notes from a lecture he attended by Dr. Anssi Simojoki and thoughts of his own about Rowling's departure from "orthodox postmodernism:"

> In Europe deconstructionism and Jacques Derrida's linguistic philosophy (or "structuralist semiotics") seem to have a strong influence. Greek semeíon means "sign," and "semiotics" is "sign theory." Deconstructionists demand the deconstruction of any message, since they are by nature totalitarian and repressive, and in reality the result of endless plays of language. By consequence all interpretation of texts and signs are equal, and there is no such thing as a "correct interpretation." Consequently there are loads of narratives, but no truths.
>
> Against structuralist semiotics, author and philosopher Umberto Eco in his philosophical writings has advocated a strong criticism: Derrida semiotics cannot function outside the philosophic chambers. A pilot running an airplane is using semiotics when he interprets the signs of his instrument panel, basically in the same way as a Bible scholar interpreting the Hebrew or Greek

Bible. If the pilot started interpreting his instruments according to Derrida, he would soon crash his plane. Umberto Eco's (and Charles S. Pierce's) alternative semiotics is called "pragmatic semiotics."

According to Eco there is no way of verifying interpretations in Derridean semiotics. Interpretation is a two-way-process between text and interpreter; nobody can tell whether an interpretation is false or true. Opposing this, Eco defends a three-way-relationship between text, its object, and its interpreter. In a three-way relationship, verification is often possible. A text about sparrows may be polysemic, meaning that several interpretations are possible. But interpreting it as being about soap instead of about sparrows is a verifiably false interpretation.

Traditionally the process of searching for truth is described as similar to following a river in the desert after rain. The river gradually narrows and finally disappears in the sands, and finding the truth is accordingly impossible.

But according to Umberto Eco the real situation is totally different. To be human is to be all the time totally surrounded by the truth, it is to live in a lasting bombardment of signs in an incredible variety of rich meaning. Truth is an enormous giant, bombarding us with signs. If we learn to interpret them correctly, these signs may open the doors and allow us to recognize Truth.

The next question is whether this is relevant in understanding how JKR relates to deconstructionism.

In *Stone*, chapter 7, Prof. Dumbledore gives a short welcome speech just after the Sorting Hat had placed Harry in Gryffindor:

> "Welcome!" he said. Welcome to a new year at Hogwarts! Before we begin our banquet, I would like to say a few words. And here they are: "Nitwit! Blubber! Oddment! Tweak!" .... "Is he a bit mad?" Harry asked Percy uncertainly. "Mad?" said Percy airily. "He is a genius! Best wizard in the world! But he is a bit mad, yes. Potatoes, Harry?"

It seems this is a set-up to be followed up by the pay-off in *Prince*,

Key Five: Postmodernism on its Head

chapter 30, in the middle of Prof. Dumbledore's funeral:

> A little tufty-haired man in plain black robes had got to his
> feet and stood now in front of Dumbledore's body. Harry could
> not hear what he was saying. Odd words floated back to them
> over the hundreds of heads. "Nobility of spirit" ... "intellectual
> contribution" ... "greatness of heart" ... it did not mean very much.
> It had little to do with Dumbledore as Harry had known him. He
> suddenly remembered Dumbledore's idea of a few words: "nitwit,"
> "oddment," "blubber," and "tweak", and again had to suppress a
> grin ... what was the matter with him?

My guess, then, is that JKR here gives a limited "yes" to
postmodernist deconstructionism. There is a meaninglessness
in much use of language which is laughable and alienating,
laughable even in a funeral.

But on the other hand, the total concept of the six books
is a rejection of Derrida semiotics, because the books are so
overloaded with signs claiming to carry very clear meaning.
postmodernism is here fighting postmodernism.

Look how Harry is verifying the ability of carrying meaning
even in the eulogy phrases. This is a three-way-semiotics. Harry
knows it when words about Dumbledore carry no meaning.

Ms. Rowling seems to be more in line with Umberto Eco's
semiotics, doesn't she? (HogwartsProfessor.com forums,
discussion of postmodernism, 1/8/2006)

Indeed, she does, Odd. The postmodern correction of postmodern
excesses made by Eco, Pierce, and others allows for a greater reality
or truth than the filters through which we sense reality. Rowling's
use of traditional symbols as vehicles of meaning reveals her not
only as a proponent of Eco's pragmatic semiotics but as a "giant's
helper," bombarding us with signs from Truth for our edification and
enlightenment.

She is not a postmodern and a relativist for whom "evil" is only
a reflection of one's being in bondage to a Grand narrative (with a
peripheral 'other' that is by definition "evil"). Ms. Rowling, while
attacking exclusive conceptions that oppress innocents because of
accidents of birth and circumstance, simultaneously affirms the reality

of evil and the necessity of fighting it tooth and nail.

Her "perfect man," Albus Dumbledore, seems superficially to be the postmodern superman, a linguistics professor who jumps into a phone booth and returns as the greatest wizard of his age. In his tutoring of Harry on choice and prophecy in *Half-Blood Prince*, he preaches the deconstructionist party line ("the Prophecy itself is meaningless; it's what you think about it and choose to do that makes it real"). He is also no stickler for rules, arbitrary categories, or especially worried about other people's thinking, no doubt because he understands them as relatively value-barren signs. Dumbledore is our heroic "Academic without blindspots," but complete with sense of humor and a delight in adventure.

But Dumbledore isn't a cartoon superhero version of Derrida.

For one thing, he's anything but a relativist. Dumbledore spends no little time trying to teach his former students in the Ministry that Voldemort is really back. There is a genuine good and evil, true and false, and the Headmaster is our heroic example of a man resisting error and evil with his life and his love to the very end (or at least to the beginning of the end in *Half-Blood Prince*).

Albus is also not an egalitarian. He despises those who put on airs, of course, especially the wicked and self-important, but he accepts that he is not "just another wizard." Dumbledore's several comments about his own cleverness, followed by his reassuring "if I say so myself," reminds us he is not Uriah Heep or burdened with a false sense of modesty.

More to the point, Dumbledore is sacrificial in his love for others. Qua postmodern and professor of linguistics, loving sacrifice of self would be contradictory behavior, if not deicide; this wizard is not the paradigmatic individualist who maintains that "the signified becomes real in the signifier's mind" (i.e., that the *cogito* translates as "*deus factus sum*," that the thinker is God, creating reality in thought). Love, and sacrificial love especially, is greater, more real, than thought and self, even more real than life and death. In this and many other ways, Dumbledore is perhaps the key Christ figure, especially in *Prince*'s Stygian Cave and on the Astronomy Tower (see "But Obviously Dumbledore is not Jesus" at http://hogwartsprofessor.com/?p=22).

Rowling the Feminist

It is hard to overestimate the influence of J. K. Rowling's favorite author, Jane Austen. Beyond the voice she uses to tell her stories and the consequent narrative misdirection that give each novel its "big twist" ending, Ms. Rowling follows her beloved Georgian mentor's lead philosophically and morally.

Philosophically, Rowling consciously or unconsciously takes Austen's position contra David Hume and empiricist thought (again, please read Rodney Delasanta's *First Things* article, 'Hume, Austen and First Impressions,' June/July, 2003). Austen attacks the "knowledge is only had through sense impressions" as a premodern and Rowling follows her lead as a postmodern. The surprise ending always reminds us how what we thought was true because of what we thought we saw is hopelessly colored by our prejudices and preconceptions.

So far, so good, in so far as Rowling is speaking the deconstructionist party line here. Rowling goes further, however, in emulating Jane Austen in what at least one reviewer has called her "manners-and-morals fiction" (Joan Acocella, "Under the Spell," *The New Yorker*, 31 July 2000). You don't have to think that *Harry Potter* is "just about 'shipping'" to see that much of the book is keyed to relationships and right behavior.

Ms. Rowling's books are not the drawing room dramas of low gentry society in the early 19th century, of course. There is, on the other hand, plenty of metanarrative about what constitutes virtue and vice in both Austen and her apt pupil. Ms. Rowling is politically correct enough to liberate her characters and allow them to grow and change and even act in boorish fashion.

Scenes that are meant to be risqué, fortunately or unfortunately, especially the snogging scenes with Ron wrestling publicly and amorously with his girlfriend, come off as somewhat prudish; no adolescent reading these chapters thinks it is a must for them to emulate. Rowling, like Austen, is heartily moral, in addition to being realistic and up-to-date, without ever seeming to be "moralizing." Call it post-postmodernism.

While an A. S. Byatt might find this less than numinous and drivel fit for those only able to enjoy "family romance," it represents a subtle shift away from relativism that few notice. I suspect, that one of the spurs that keep academics and culture mavens from embracing Rowling is her nuanced critique of housewives specifically and feminism in general via her depiction of house-elves and Hermione.

If you accept, as I do, Kathryn MacDaniel's thesis that the house-elves in *Harry Potter* represent the spectrum of postmodern women's situation in the world today (see previous chapter), we're left with a peculiar departure from postmodern dogma. Hermione, the feminist liberator of housewives, I mean "house-elves," is an insightful, postmodern crusader who is unaware of her excesses and self-importance.

Isn't there something ironic and just plain mean or patronizing in wanting to liberate the house-elves against their will? Weirder still, hasn't Hermione lost her bearings in *Half-Blood Prince* when she hexes people she doesn't like just for the advantage of her friends? A little Slytherinesque, no?

Remember that feminism per se is postmodernism's central victory in the public square and especially in literary criticism and linguistics. The popularity and noncontroversial place of so-called "Slash" fan fiction in fandom, in which writers, mostly women, create homosexual novellas and novels to empower themselves by recasting characters' sexual orientations, is a measure of the degree to which feminism rules the roost in book circles. Remember Pullman's first and most damning critique of Lewis' *Narnia*? "It is monumentally disparaging of girls and women.... One girl was sent to hell because she was getting interested in clothes and boys." Heaven, forbid. Off with his head!

Ms. Rowling, in her detailed portrayal of different types of house-elves and of their crusading liberator presents some aspects of feminism as problematic, even as a Grand Narrative needing deconstruction before good people are treated as things by an exclusive and oppressive ideology. Again, this is not conventional but a dynamic poststructuralist fiction that isn't afraid to cast down its own idols (even if it means being snubbed by the ideologues in the literature departments).

Existential epistemology: Character counts

If postmodernism has a signature science, it is linguistics. Written and spoken language is the primary vehicle of metanarratives, and the attack on these oppressive myths has largely been won by revealing the sexist/racist/imperialist, etc., language of texts and popular idiom. It has been the deconstruction of language that has given scientific standing to the postmodern mission and that has fostered social policy to create equal rights, multiculturalism, and a culture of aggressive tolerance (in which only the intolerant cannot be tolerated). Tom Wolfe is said to have commented that, according to postmodernism, "language is merely one beast using words as tools to get power over another beast" (quoted in Pearcey, *Total Truth*, p. 243).

In Hogwarts, language is especially powerful because magic is a function of spoken spells for all witches and wizards except those skilled in nonverbal spells. Ms. Rowling, however, seems to be turning the semiotic message of Lyotard and the gang on its head. The spells don't have their power because of the unexamined messages they carry from cultural narratives. Quite the contrary, the language of wizards is not value-laden because of the meaning of the words (which, it seems, no wizard understands; Latin is not a subject at Hogwarts). Spellwork has its power from the harmony of the wizard with the Logos or Creative language of God.

No doubt that seems a real reach to you, but in magic you really only have two options, incantational magic and invocational (explained in chapter one of *Looking for God in Harry Potter*). Either you call down spirits and demons to do your will, that is, invocational sorcery, or you use words that somehow harmonize with the mesh and music of creation with spellwork. Incantation is just the fancy word for "to sing along with, to harmonize." Hence, Snape's "muttering an incantation that sounded almost like song" over Malfoy in *Prince* (Chapter 24, p. 523).

There is no sorcery or calling on demons in the *Harry Potter* stories. None. At. All. What's curious here is that bad people can be wizards and witches according to this scheme of things and the specific limits Rowling puts on her magic; as the creator of her subcreation, she sets all the magical parameters (no raising a corpse from the dead back to real life with wand work, etc.).

It strikes many people as odd when I explain this traditional distinction, that bad wizards and witches can perform magic. If it involves harmonizing with the divine speech underlying the created world, shouldn't magic be something only for the saintly? Well, yes, and that is why in the real world good and bad magic is neatly divided between holy persons who act in communion with God's will and sick-oes that think they can safely make deals with or subdue demons to

215

do their will.

In fiction, though, especially in Ms. Rowling's Wizarding World, everyone can perform incantational magic, regardless of their virtue or lack of same (and often times, it seems, the virtuous are less accomplished than the wicked). You go to school, you practice, you learn the spells and the wand-work.

In this Wizarding World, there are limits, however, to what learning can do for you. The wisest wizard in the *Harry Potter* stories intentionally restricts his knowledge by not studying the Dark Arts or, at least, by not using them. Prof. McGonagall says as much to Dumbledore on Privet Drive in the first chapter of the first book. It's not until *Half-Blood Prince* that we learn why, beyond a prudish nobility, a wizard would restrict his knowledge or skills in this way.

During the only conversation the Headmaster tells Harry it is "essential" he understand, Dumbledore explains to the boy wonder why Harry has never been tempted to practice dark magic or follow Lord Voldemort:

> "You are protected, in short, by your ability to love!" said Dumbledore loudly. The only protection that can possibly work against the lure of power like Voldemort's! In spite of all the temptation you have endured, all the suffering, you remain pure of heart, just as pure as you were at the age of eleven..."

He then tells Harry why the Dark Lord cannot see what a dangerous enemy he has created in Harry Potter:

> "I do not think he understands why, Harry, but then, he was in such a hurry to mutilate his own soul, he never paused to understand the incomparable power of a soul that is untarnished and whole." (*Prince*, Chapter 23, p. 511)

Purity and integrity of soul, when filled with love, are unstoppable, transcendent powers that a mutilated, soiled spirit cannot comprehend or equal.

This is not generic postmodernism but a postmodernist critique of postmodern excesses resulting in something more like premodernism. Call it "traditionalism," or, better, "philosophical realism." It's a big step away from "there is no good or evil" semiotics.

Postmodernism tells us that metanarrative evil or a value-neutral good is conveyed by speech, even that these evils or goods have no existence independent of speech and our ability to perceive them. Speech creates "truth" and what little reality there is in words.

The most important type of speech in the Wizarding World, namely, spellwork, isn't folks using words that reflect nothing more real than their understanding of what the word's mean (philosophical nominalism). The power of your speech and spellwork is your relation with what is real. A witch or wizard can know all sorts of magic; their power consequent to this knowledge, however, as Dumbledore explains it to Harry in *Half-Blood Prince,* is restricted by the quality of their being rather than by the quantity of information, wicked or benign, they have learned.

Patristic scholars call this existential epistemology and it is a hallmark of traditional thinking, the distinction between "scientia" or "episteme" (knowledge) and "sophia" (wisdom). The more virtuous you are and the greater purity and integrity you have retained equates to how much more powerful and wise you can become because you will have access to the very fabric of creation and to the Creative Energies of God. Knowing a lot does not give you this kind of power. Far from it. In a way, seeking knowledge and power just to have them is to guarantee your fall.

The Thomistic formula for this is "concupiscence darkens the intellect." The bumper sticker version is "sin makes you stupid." Lord Voldemort's fate is largely predicted in the Gospel passage about the poor (in spirit) losing even what they have and the rich getting even more than they have now. This is why Luna and Harry can see the Thestrals; their experience of death has expanded their ability to perceive things. Character counts even with respect to what and how much we can know.

Wait a minute. I see a bunch of you whispering in the back saying, "This guy is NUTS." I can understand that you might think I'm crazy for thinking these books are largely about what words mean and what people think words mean. But let's look at one of the first scenes in *Philosopher's Stone.* Mr. Dursley sees a cat reading a map, remember?

It was on the corner of the street that he noticed the first sign of something peculiar – a cat reading a map. For a second, Mr. Dursley didn't realize what he had seen – then he jerked his head around to look again. There was a tabby cat standing on the corner of Privet Drive, but there wasn't a map in sight. What could he have been thinking of? It must have been a trick of the light. Mr. Dursley blinked and stared at the cat. It stared back. As Mr. Dursley drove around the corner and up the road, he watched the cat in his mirror. It was now reading the sign that said Privet Drive – no, looking at the sign; cats couldn't read maps or signs. Mr. Dursley gave himself a little shake and put the cat out of his mind. As he drove toward town he thought of nothing except a large order of drills he was hoping to get that day. (**Stone**, Chapter 1, pp. 2-3)

So what? Well, Ms. Rowling is asking us to look at Vernon Dursley and to draw some conclusions from his behavior. He sees a cat looking at a map and reading a street sign. This sign or event that he has witnessed does not jibe with his understanding or concepts of what is and isn't possible and he therefore fails to see the reality of what he saw.

Mr. Dursley is looking at the sign, "a cat reading," but he "cannot read the sign" or understand the event because postmodern human beings (fat cats?) per se cannot read reality except in so much as the filter of their metanarratives or world-view allow them to see it. Much of the rest of this opening chapter is the war within Vernon Dursley as the magic of the world at the far periphery of his vision continues to distract him and he struggles to explain away what he is looking at (but not reading) with his prejudices and misconceptions (and, truth be told, his fears).

We don't like Mr. Dursley. He's a nasty, mean-spirited, self-important buffoon. I think we don't like him, too, because he is rather like us, sad to say.

Contrast this with the ending of that book, where Harry stands before the Mirror of Erised and sees the Philosopher's Stone, it becomes real, and drops into his pocket. Dumbledore describes this accomplishment as something nigh on superhuman in **Half-Blood Prince**:

> In spite of all the temptation you have endured, all the suffering, you remain pure of heart, just as pure as you were at the age of eleven, when you stared into a mirror that reflected your heart's desire, and it showed you only the way

to thwart Lord Voldemort, and not immortality or riches. Harry, have you any idea how few wizards could have seen what you saw in that mirror? Voldemort should have known then what he was dealing with, but he did not! (*Half-Blood Prince*, Chapter 23, p. 511)

Mr. Dursley looked at a cat on the street and saw himself. He supposed the cat was just an animal without rational powers and certainly not with magical abilities. He saw in this ironic vignette what postmodern theorists see when they look at human beings.

Harry looking into the Mirror of Erised, on the other hand, is supposed to see a reflection of his mental categories, i.e., those things that will be most to his advantage (wealth and immortality, essentially, freedom from want and death). Everyone sees this because this is all we are able to see as animals whose view of things is constricted to our individual conceptions and desires.

Harry's desire, Dumbledore explains, was to get the Stone, not for his advantage but because he had to resist Voldemort. Why did an eleven-year-old want to do this, at the risk of his life? Because he loved his "mum and dad." Love allows Harry to transcend his ego-self, the Stone he sees in the Mirror is real, and becomes his. Love allowed him to see the reality Quirrelldemort could not, and, as remarkable, to own what is most real, the means to immortality and spiritual riches.

You guys in the back are telling me these books aren't a primer in semiotics? Maybe you're nuts. Or maybe you're just Mr. Dursley looking at a cat reading the signs; you're not only going to deny what you're seeing, you want to tell me the signs don't exist. Maybe.

Back to Ms. Rowling and what her stories seem to be telling us about signs and what they mean, if anything, beyond our conceptions. Believe it or not, getting this will help you figure out how the books may end.

Dumbledore's description of Harry's great power, his capacity for love, if we assume that Harry is a real human being (at least as compared with Mr. Dursley, who seems a shadow of a human being), tells us that Ms. Rowling is a postmodern realist. Let me unwrap that label.

Philosophically or logically speaking, a realist isn't just the pessimist's name for himself or someone who denies the existence of anything not quantifiable matter and energy. Just the opposite, really. A philosophical realist is the opposite of a nominalist. What realists and nominalists disagree about, in plain speech, is whether words and ideas reflect real things or just conceptions. The nominalists won the day centuries ago, like it or not, and things have been on a downhill slide ever since (see Whithall Perry, *The Widening Breach*, Quinta Essentia, 1995, for more on this watershed event in western intellectual history).

When I say that Rowling is a postmodern realist I'm almost saying she is a "square circle." Hold on for a minute and I'll do my best to talk myself out of this seeming contradiction.

A postmodern writer as a rule is a nominalist who believes that signs or words as vehicles of our mental conceptions are everything, quite literally. Worse, as much as these conceptions of ours are trapped in oppressive Grand Narratives, everyone except the linguists revealing these logocentric traps we're in are up the creek without a paddle to experience anything greater than their confining ideas. Our only way to freedom is by self-actualization consequent to our resistance to the metanarratives reflected in our speech and thinking and recreating ourselves. Good luck in that.

A philosophical or logical realist, on the other hand, posits that signs have real referents that are both conceptual and actual because they exist in Universals. Realists use the word [realism] to mean that all seeming reality in our world is entirely infused by the sole ultimate Realty of the Universal or Ideas propounded by Plato. These are the Informing Essences, Archetypes, Exemplars, and Qualities.... The Scholastics taught that the Universals are *ante res* [before the specific things], *in rebus* [in things], and *post res* [after things], reasoning that their existence is prior to, within, and subsequent to outward things....

Realism in later times has come to signify the notion that matter and sense objects have a concrete reality in their own 'right', they being considered to embody a true existence independently of Ideas....

Nominalism is the term that describes the view taken by the opponents of Scholastic Realism, namely, those who say in substance that there are no universal essences, a stand which comes down to the realism of our day [called epistemological or natural realism]. (*Widening Breach*, Chapter 4 'Realism to Nominalism: The Watershed,' p. 59)

Love is the most important reason why the *Harry Potter* books have to have been written by a realist rather than a nominalist. Love is the power "at once more powerful and more terrible than death, than human intelligence, than forces of nature" (*Phoenix*, Chapter 37, p. 843). Love is what Harry must embody to defeat Voldemort, simple as that.

Love is greater "than human intelligence" means that it is beyond conception, universal, and what is most real. St. John the Theologian sums up traditional belief on this by saying succinctly that "God is love." And vice-versa. This is a position a nominalist or an orthodox poststructuralist cannot hold. The most real thing informing all things of the sense or mental conception is a Universal. Things don't have reality independent of this power.

So what does being a postmodern realist mean?

It means, if you are a PoMo Realist, that you agree with almost of all the conclusions about the confining metanarrative on men like Mr. Dursley that are held by the postmoderns and you bewail the oppression of those excluded by these filters that block out the real. But, and this is all the difference, while you understand this is the condition of almost every human being, you cannot hold this is the limit of human understanding or believe that because most people cannot transcend metannarative that there is no reality greater than this.

Human beings are obviously designed to love and to receive love. Love is an undeniable power and reality outside of conception; it is universal to humanity, if, sadly, subject to human perversion, hatred, and partisanship.

Here's a quick look at the several reasons besides the centrality of love for the position that Rowling is a realist rather than a nominalist, however important it is to understand her postmodern beliefs.

Sparing Church

Every age has its "nigger." The whipping boy of modernism, the child of the Enlightenment, logical positivism, and the materialist Reign of Quantity, was "organized religion." Traditional or "blind" faith was represented as the enemy of progress and reason by Communist ideologues and hagiographers of the "advance of science" alike. In fact, if there is a metanarrative of the modern period, a myth that defines that age, it might be that "science and reason are winning the war with superstition, unexamined myths, and the opiate of religion." It was not a heroic time for Churchmen except in terms of producing martyrs of the faith in numbers greater than any previous period.

Postmodernism, as I've said, is largely modernism on steroids. Chesterton is supposed to have said that if you take away a man's gods, he will not believe in nothing; he will believe in anything. When God "died" in the modern period, his declared death created the vacuum of belief of our age, in which everyone is "spiritual" (not wanting to admit to being a crass materialist) and few are "religious."

In postmodern literature, though, we see the vestiges or the final step of modernism. Poetry, drama, and novels in several ways served as the last bastion of criticism of science, commerce, and the myth of progress through the modern period which explains the number of clergy, the sons and daughters of clergymen, and devout Christians in the 19th and 20th centuries (Gerard Manley Hopkins, George MacDonald, Jane Austen, T. S. Eliot, Lewis, Tolkien, Williams, Sayers, Goudge, etc.). In the postmodern period, however, we have serious writers attacking organized religion to free the oppressed.

Given Eliade's thesis that popular entertainments serve a religious function in a profane culture, this taking of the last sanctuary of faith perhaps was inevitable as modernism comes to a close. Novelists who attack the faith of millions like Rushdie are lionized for their heroism when it gets the response they might have expected if religion is indeed the dangerous boogey they are exposing (as the world saw in the reaction of Muslims to *Satanic Verses*). They are lionized by press and academics, too, even when they assault the church which doesn't issue fatwahs.

As evidence, read *The New York Times* piece on Philip Pullman, "The Man Who Dared Make Religion the Villain" (6 November 2000, B1). How daring, really, does one have to be to make Christians the badguys and the "Institutional Church," the Mordor habitation of plotting clergymen, as Pullman does in the *His Dark Materials* trilogy? No more daring than the author of the Christian-mocking and church-bashing *Da Vinci Code*.

So what? Ms. Rowling, in her *Harry Potter* novels, attacks every organization that is the vehicle of the oppressive metanarrative that excludes and demeans those not celebrated as "central" in the Grand Myth. She guts the media, satirizes government folly, self-importance, and ineptitude savagely, and portrays the justice system and prisons as arbitrary systems of organized injustice and torture. Schools? They get a comic beating perhaps more serious than her other targets. I am always startled, as I've said, to see teachers and librarians say how much they love these books. Ms. Rowling, unless I am much mistaken, thinks schools are a tragicomedy of the first order.

But she spares the church.

There is no mention of church, clergy, or religious faith of any kind in the books, that is, outside the few holidays in the books (which have no sense of "holy days" about them) and the several times Harry prays to the unknown god for things to happen (e.g., "Accio Firebolt!" he shouted. Harry waited, every fiber of him hoping, praying…,"*Goblet*, Chapter 20, p. 353). Ms. Rowling's decision not to attack the professionally religious in her books can be explained in several ways.

Most obviously, her story does not involve the church as it does school, media, government, and courtrooms with their gulag just off-stage. Ms. Rowling is a satirist of the Swiftian breed and a caricaturist a la George Cruikshank (to whom she tips a hat in the name of Hermione's cat). She is not primarily a satirist, however, but an incidental one.

She creates mocking, borderline vicious portraits of Margaret Thatcher (Aunt Marge), Tony Blair (the Prime Minister), newspaper reporters, lifeless teachers (Professor Binns), and torture chambers that are supposed to be just places of incarceration. Ms. Rowling is not going out of her way to attack these individuals and institutions (Aunt Marge being an exception…), though, the way that Swift creates magical countries for Gulliver to visit as vehicles for his acid narrative. Rowling mocks the people and institutions that get in the way of her story.

Ms. Rowling, in sparing the church, is firmly in the English fantasy tradition, too. Lewis famously said he was trying in his stories to "smuggle the Gospel" past the "watchful dragons" in his readers' hearts, dragons ever mindful of any religious message or stained glass imagery. Tolkien, Goudge, and MacDonald likewise all refrain from churchy scenes in their mythic stories, books that are relatively transparent vehicles of religious content.

But, it must be noted, these writers were putting pen to page when the resistance to the excesses of modernism was largely literary. In the postmodern period, the doyens of the academy and the world of letters have jumped ship and started to attack "organized religion" after the fashion of the Spartacus Youth League. Ms. Rowling, in being in step with tradition, is very much a non-comformist with postmodern conventions.

As a self-proclaimed iconoclast and genre-convention buster, this exception to her postmodern qualifications is noteworthy. It even qualifies as a postmodern critique of postmodernism. The orthodox postmodern position, she seems to be saying, has a remarkable blindspot. Its prejudice and hatred of orthodox spiritual traditions, inherited from the modern celebrators of material progress and science at war with superstition and ignorance, has become its own oppressive metanarrative.

This may be hard for American readers to grasp because we are inundated with media scare-messages about the culture war and the designs of the "Religious Right" on individual liberties and the like. Rowling seems to understand, however ignorant her Christian critics may be, that the martyrs of the Grand Narrative of modernity were the Jews to National Socialism (6 million), the Tibetan Buddhists to the Chinese Communists (1.2 million), and the Russian Orthodox Christians to the Soviet Communists (as many as 40 million died from gunshot, gulag, or created famines between 1918 and 1988).

These incomprehensible numbers of martyrs to the Grand Myth of modernism certainly dwarf the supposed victims of our age's myths and metanarratives, namely, more than western women, American blacks, or homosexuals everywhere. Ms. Rowling, as a professed Christian, has chosen not to kick this slaughtered horse or pretend it is the vehicle of oppression that Pullman and others would have their readers believe.

Transcendent Postmodern

Sparing the church from caricature and satire is not the only or even the most important departure Ms. Rowling makes from orthodox, which is to say "nihilist," postmodernism. The morality of her stories, their transcendent symbolism, and the alchemical meaning and structures of her books are evidence of her being a postmodern realist rather than just another nominalist writing fantasy.

In her interview with *Time* magazine's Lev Grossman, Ms. Rowling took real pains to distance herself from the moralist or evangelist some writers (to include this one) have said she is:

> And unlike Lewis, whose books are drenched in theology, Rowling refuses to view herself as a moral educator to the millions of children who read her books. "I don't think that it's at all healthy for the work for me to think in those terms. So I don't, she says. "I never think in terms of What am I going to teach them? Or, What would it be good for them to find out here?"
> "Although," she adds, "undeniably, morals are drawn."
> (Grossman, J.K. Rowling Hogwarts and All, *Time*, 17 July 2005)

We'll return at the end of this chapter to J. K. Rowling and C. S. Lewis, but this quote should be taken as is. Ms. Rowling insists as a postmodern that she is no moralizer, telling folks in her stories, subtly or not so subtly, what she thinks they should do or not do. As she said in her CBBC Newsround Q&A session with children reporters:

> I would [hope] that [*Harry Potter*] has made people think, I mean I do not write the books thinking what is my message for today, what is my moral, that is not how I set out to write a book at all. I am not trying to criticize or make speeches to you in any way, but, at the same time, it would be great if the people thought about bullying behavior or racism.

Nonetheless, as she says, "undeniably, morals are drawn." In her answer to a question about which Hogwarts she would be in if she were a witch being sorted, she reveals how much she values moral courage and how she "wrote it into" her story.

> Well, I would want to be in Gryffindor and the reason I would want to be in Gryffindor is because I do prize courage in all its various ramifications. I value it more highly than any other virtue and by that I mean not just physical courage and flashy courage, but moral courage.
> And I wanted to make that point in [the] very first book with Neville, because Neville doesn't have that showy macho type of courage that Harry shows playing Quidditch. But, at

the end, what Neville does at the end of *Philosopher's Stone*
to stand up to his friends and risk their dislike and approval
is hugely courageous so I would want to be in Gryffindor.
(CBBC Newsround, Edinburgh, ITV, 16 July 2005)

Beyond the contradiction here with her assertion that she doesn't
write messages into her stories deliberately, we have the obvious point
that having the courage to do the right thing is important, even the
most valuable virtue, to Ms. Rowling. She obviously isn't a nihilist; nor
is she a relativist in her postmodernism.

There's some reason to think she leans toward the multicultural
agenda of our times and the ignoring of differences in the name of blind
tolerance. Take for example her thoughts on whether the "Bad Guys"
at Hogwarts are really bad:

> But they're not all bad. They literally are not all bad.
> [Pause.] Well, the deeper answer, the non-flippant answer,
> would be that you have to embrace all of a person, you
> have to take them with their flaws, and everyone's got
> them. It's the same way with the student body. If only they
> could achieve perfect unity, you would have an absolute
> unstoppable force, and I suppose that craving for unity
> and wholeness that means that they keep the quarter of
> the school that maybe does not encapsulate the most
> generous and noble qualities, in the hope, in the very
> Dumbledore-esque hope that they will achieve union,
> and they will achieve harmony. Harmony is the word.
> (Mugglenet interview, Part 3, 16 July 2005)

We'll return again to Ms. Rowling's idea of "harmony" momentarily,
but it would be easy to make too much of her not wanting to say "all
the Slytherin students are evil." How can the writer of books about the
importance of moral courage, i.e., the ability to discern the difference
between right and wrong coupled with the resolve to champion the
right whatever the consequences, be called a relativist or nihilist? Ms.
Rowling departs from the value-denying trend of our times in writing
value and virtue laden stories. Even if written in largely postmodern
language, these books are not nihilist or relativist messages.

Key Five: Postmodernism on its Head

The symbolism she uses, too, is a departure from postmodern understanding and practice. In using traditional symbols from English literature, she implies a very different understanding of the world than postmodern writers like Pullman and Brown in addition to elements of a specific faith. The traditional symbols that pervade *Harry Potter* are the fifth and last key the serious reader needs to unlock the books and understand Potter-mania.

I wrote about the traditional symbolism at work in *Harry Potter* in Chapter 9 of *Looking for God in Harry Potter* (Tyndale, 2004, pp. 83-100). I won't repeat what I wrote there except to make two points; (1) the symbols in the books are almost exclusively Christian, and (2) they work as well as they do because of the iconographic power of literary symbols.

About the symbols being predominantly Christian, this is understandable, even to be expected. Ms. Rowling professes a Christian faith personally. The English literary tradition, too, is Christian in form and substance until well into the 20th century in the same way Tibetan culture is Buddhist. The writers, their characters, and the audience of readers were almost without exception Christians reading as Christian believers.

What is unusual is the number of symbols she uses from this tradition, their frequent appearances in the story, and their importance in understanding the meaning and power of the books. These aren't glosses on the page but the meat of the story. The wicked Basilisk and Nagini straight from the Garden in Genesis and the Christ-representing Phoenix, Unicorn, Hippogriff, and "Golden Griffin" (Griffin d'or) among others are central to the narrative line.

They have their power because they are not allegorical stick figures ("Mr. Worldly Wise Man is Bunyan's portrait of neighborhood know-it-alls and television news commentators") but symbols doing what symbols do. Allegory and signs are just transparencies for worldly realities you are supposed to switch out. If you read Tolkien's *The Lord of the Rings* as an allegory of WWII (and I urge you not to), your task as reader is to translate all the characters and places into historical players and countries in that conflict. Sauron is Hitler, the Shire is England, et cetera, ad nauseam.

Symbols in contrast represent other-worldly realities that have more reality, more being than anything of this world. Because of correspondent qualities between the symbol of the figure and this supernatural reality, the symbol acts as a conduit of being into the receptive reader as an icon or sacrament is a conduit of grace to a believer.

The heavy use of symbols, consequently, in an author's work, especially when they are not just decorative (or cut-and-pasted in to mix genres as a postmodern architect might to double-code), points to a belief in the implicit reality and priority of supernatural worlds. Even in a postmodern text or a book with many postmodern qualities, the worldview of symbolism is that of philosophical realism rather than nominalism – and a signature deviance from the atheism and this-world-liness of poststructuralism per se.

Alchemy as Antidote to Postmodernism

Some of the more thoughtful critics of the books, especially those who compare Ms. Rowling and the Inkling writers (meaning almost always Lewis and Tolkien), complain that the Wizarding World of Ms. Rowling's books are mundane and modern despite their magic and symbolism. These critics inevitably tell us the *Harry Potter* novels have no "Emperor-beyond-the-Sea" standing in for God the Father in Narnia and no *Silmarillion* cosmological myth to let us know the good wizards are really angels of God.

As we noted above, Ms. Rowling has gone to some lengths in recent interviews to make clear to her defenders and detractors that she is not writing cardboard evangelical pieces and she does not think of herself as a moralizer in any way (however moral her stories may be). What is funny to me is that the scaffolding on which the stories are built is alchemical, and, like it or not, this is at least as strong a pointer to Christian cosmology as Lewis' Emperor or Tolkien's *Silmarillion*.

The alchemical backdrop and scaffolding in *Harry Potter* is not meaningless stage setting. It is, more likely than not, the key (yes, a hidden key) to understanding Ms. Rowling as postmodern realist and the reason these books are as popular as they are.

Alchemy is a surgeon's or engineer's course in Four Element physics. The engineer in our profane world takes the finding of theoretical sciences and lab determinations of stress limits for materials and the tensile strength of wire to build bridges and towers that are anything but conceptual. A surgeon takes the findings of biological research and anatomists to figure out how to open a body, remove or replace body parts and disease, and to close the body again.

The alchemist takes Four Element understanding of the natural world to accelerate the natural processes of sanctification and communion towards the human supernatural end. He thinks this is possible because Four Element physics or natural sciences are not restricted to understandings of matter and energy but predicate the existence of natural phenomena on supernatural and contranatural levels of existence.

In brief, the complementary and contrary qualities of traditional physics (fire and water, earth and air; hot and cold, moist and dry) like the more obvious complementary contraries of the natural world (night and day, summer and winter, male and female, etc.) are symbols and reflections of the Creative Principle "through whom all things were made." The Word/Logos or Tao is the resolution of contraries, hence its being known as "love" and "peace" among other things, but its creative work is distinguished by contraries which point to their opposite and to their resolution and origin.

The alchemist works with the contraries of metallurgical purification and transformation to participate symbolically and personally in the process himself. The "alchemical work" is less about creating a philosopher's stone to change lead into gold than a means by which the alchemist sympathetically purifies and transforms his soul. [Again, those readers interested in the history or meaning of alchemy should read either Titus Burckhardt's *Alchemy* or his *Mirror of the Intellect*, both of which Ms. Rowling seems to have studied.]

I hear someone saying "What?!" and someone else muttering, "So what?" Fair questions.

The criticism of Rowling's books made by Christians comparing her to Lewis and Tolkien, beyond the magic controversy, is that Hogwarts and the Wizarding World in general, however "magical," has a profane or flat worldview without any edifying suggestions or evidence of the supernatural. This is silly on the face of it given the depth and uniformity of Ms. Rowling's use of traditional Christian symbols, but the alchemy is perhaps a more compelling rejoinder.

The alchemical scaffolding of the stories is based on traditional Four

Element physics, the core reality of which is a Word/Logos metaphysics. The Word/Logos as Creative Principle, of course, is the heart of Christianity. The historical Incarnation of the Logos, after all, is the beginning or arche of Christian faith. The magical world of Hogwarts, consumed as it is with the power of the pure soul, the unification of the Four Houses and four Magical Brethren, is at least as Trinitarian in cosmology as anything Lewis or Tolkien wrote.

Why? A Trinitarian cosmology has to have three parts, usually divided into natural, supernatural, and contranatural. The contranatural is the most real realm and most unlike the world of time and space which it creates and suffuses. The natural world has contact with the contranatural world through symbols and sacraments that act as windows and conduits between worlds and which act as supernatural means between the two. These realms are not distinct or separate "places" or "locales" like a three-storied building but three dimensions existing simultaneously in every place and moment.

Ms. Rowling's subcreation is dynamically Trinitarian in just this way. There is the mundane natural world of the Muggles. The magic of the Wizarding World as incantational magic points to the existence of a supernatural realm through which humans act as an Image of and commune with the God Who creates by His Word/Logos. The discussion of souls that is the necessary backdrop to the Horcrux subplot and Harry's ability to defeat Lord Voldemort as Quintessence or Love or androgynic resolution of contraries, also assumes a supernatural realm.

This Love, the power that Dumbledore describes as "more wonderful and terrible than death, than human intelligence, than forces of nature" (**Phoenix**, Chapter 37, p. 843) in being greater than nature transcends and informs nature and the supernatural. Love, the force to defeat Voldemort and which overcomes death, in its being "the origin and resolution of contraries" is the contranatural realm and the end (telos) of alchemy.

This explains the power, meaning, and popularity of Ms. Rowling's books, as well as her seeming fence-sitting as a "postmodern realist." There isn't chaos or nihilism at the cosmological roots of Hogwarts but "harmony" and the means to transcend the natural world. As Dumbledore says at the Welcoming Feast in **Stone**, the magic of music is "beyond all we do here!" (*Stone*, Chapter 7, p. 128). Ms. Rowling goes further in her comments about harmony.

> If only they could achieve perfect unity [at Hogwarts], you would have an absolutely unstoppable force, and I suppose it's that craving for unity and wholeness that means that they keep the quarter of the school that maybe does not encapsulate the most generous and noble qualities, in the hope in the very Dumbledore-esque hope that they will achieve union, and they will achieve harmony. Harmony is the word.....
>
> It is the tradition to have four houses, but, in this case, I wanted them to correspond roughly to the four elements. So Gryffindor is fire, Ravenclaw is air, Hufflepuff is earth, and Slytherin is water, hence the fact that their common room is under the lake. So, again, it was this idea of harmony and balance, that you had four necessary components and by integrating them you would make a very strong place. But they remain fragmented, as we know.
>
> (Mugglenet interview, 16 July 2005, part 3)

The alchemical idea of "harmony and balance" (balance being another word for resolution) that is both the underlying cosmology of this subcreation and a large part of the story's ending (see next chapter) is the "structure" Ms. Rowling offers as her poststructuralism. Instead of conventional structures that are necessarily exclusive and oppressive qua metanarratives or Grand Myth, Ms. Rowling gives us love, harmony, and balance as transcendent principles that inform profane reality and the successful pursuit of which are the answer to all natural strife.

This postmodern realism, then, is anything but wishy-washy. The *Harry Potter* books are not straddling postmodern nihilism and conventional Christianity. Ms. Rowling, as a postmodern, writes contra racism and bullying behavior and against all the vehicles of the oppressive, exclusive metanarrative. *Harry Potter* in this regard is not much different than *Sky High* or every other PoMo movie script and children's story celebrating minority rights and preaching heroic tolerance.

Ms. Rowling, though, as a postmodern critic of poststructuralism, points to transcendent reality, the principles undergirding natural reality, as structures that are not static or exclusive. Love, harmony, and balance, which Principles it is the work of seven-staged alchemy to achieve or incarnate, are the answer both to the trap of founding myths every culture must have and the nihilism and relativism consequent to the postmodern mission to deny and attack all founding myths.

Ms. Rowling's solution in story form to the dilemma of postmodern times, what I'm calling postmodern realism, is also an explanation for the overwhelming popularity of these books around the world as well as the disdain and disgust she inspires in certain quarters. Let's look first at the Harry Haters.

The religious ("fundamentalist") Harry Haters do so because she is so very much a postmodern poster-child attacking biblical proscriptions on magic with her deconstruction of the archetypal "bad wizard." The Ivory Tower and culture mavens looking down their nose at Harry are put off because Ms. Rowling is insufficiently postmodern. Her morality and celebration of courage, as well as her beliefs in greater realities than matter and energy evident in her use of traditional symbols and existential epistemology (not to mention souls that live after death!), are disqualifiers for a postmodern's blessing. If only she had included a Slytherin clergyman rather than the affable Hufflepuff friar....

I don't think it is an accident that Christians whose soteriology and theology is mechanical ("systematic") and based on the authority of human understanding, i.e., a Pharisaical or legalistic approach to grace and the encounter or communion of the human person and God, find Rowling repulsive and dangerous. The response of the "true believing" Harry Hater has at least as much to do, beneath the surface objections to the supposed occult elements of her story, with her embodying and championing the anti-fundamentalist, anti-metanarrative, unloving position so cogently.

The controversy and condemnation Ms. Rowling's books have caused in the seemingly antipodal but similarly conservative or self-preservation minded communities of the Ivory Tower and Bible belt (if each feigns a flexible, liberal front) are reactions to their intuitive perception of her postmodern realism. The Christians with a Pharasaical mindset don't care for the postmodernism undermining their exclusive claims to a mechanical salvation – and the traditional realism based on a Word/

Logos metaphysics in her books is incomprehensible. Pharisaical and metanarrative surety, like sin, makes you stupid.

If you understand the world-wide return to religious fundamentalism (and away from Orthodoxy) as search for pre-postmodern certainty in "order" and "wicked other," aversion to *Harry Potter* makes a lot more sense. Most Harry Haters I have met are sincere and well-intentioned believers. I worry, though, that their concerns about these stories spring from the reaction, contra-postmodernism, against a world suddenly devoid of meaning. This trend has had the ironic effect of turning radical faith in Christ oftentimes into a modern ideology and legalism, a mechanical faith which I think is obvious in the false witness against a neighbor (Ms. Rowling is, after all, a professing Christian), Pharisee-isms, and faith litmus-strip work of Harry Hating culture warriors.

The "intellectual" or academic side of the Harry Hating camp, which of course has nothing but disdain for their Christian doppelgangers, see that Rowling is insufficiently modern (no church bashing) and postmodern ("good vs. evil? How 19th century!"). The philosophical realism of her work we see in its literary alchemy, which, though taken directly from an important stream in English literature, is invisible to most. A. S. Byatt, Harold Bloom, and most every literature professor I have spoken with (with the exception of those who are Medieval and Renaissance wonks) miss this entirely. Bloom is perhaps the greatest living authority on Shakespeare and certainly he could lecture ad lib on the alchemical and four element images in *Taming of the Shrew* for hours in some detail. When he reads *Harry Potter*, though, the books are "clichéd" and "slop" and not equal to Great Books of the Western Canon like *The Wind in the Willows*.

Some have said this critical blindness is bitter jealously (again, see Charles Taylor's *A. S. Byatt and the Goblet of Bile* in Salon). A more charitable and challenging explanation is that we cannot see what we cannot understand, a restriction not from inborn inability but an acquired inability to see reality as it is because our beliefs have restricted our soul's ability to perceive reality's multivalence and several dimensions. Again, see St. Matthew 25:29 and Martin Ling's exposition of same in *The Eleventh Hour* (Quinta Essentia, Chapter 3, "And from him that hath not...," pp. 15-44).

To postmodern ideologues, a postmodern critique of the unexamined metanarratives, excesses, and blindspots of poststructuralism itself is necessarily wrong-headed. An implicity premodern assault on the prejudices and myths of modernity, too, is simply incomprehensible. I'll leave it to you to explore and unwrap the ironies of the postmodern Grand Inquisitors being blind to how their several preconceptions have restricted their view into categories of "good" and "wicked other."

Why We Love Harry

Having tried to explain how Rowling's postmodern realism has put off her critics in some churches and most universities, I should say the obvious, namely, why this view and the engaging stories that have grown out of it have so captured the world's imagination.

In English Literature 101 or the common-sense equivalent, we know that to understand an author we should know something about the times in which an author lived if we are to understand their perspective and specific concerns fully. Unless your literature professor was a historicist or Marxist, though, you wanted to know something more. You wanted to know what about the author's work made it edifying and important for you, who, as likely as not, do not share the writer's prejudices and blindspots.

When we read books and really want to get at them, then, we're searching for the historical as well as the transcendent or timeless qualities of any book and perhaps the intersection of these qualities, if any. *Harry Potter* shouldn't be an exception to this rule, and, given the popularity of Ms. Rowling's stories, it is probably logical to assume her books sell as well as they do because of their joint timeliness and their "forever" appeal to humans regardless of their time period.

My *Looking for God in Harry Potter* (Tyndale, 2004) is a book length treatment of the timeless and transcendent qualities of the *Harry Potter* novels. I argued there that these books are as popular as they are because their symbols, themes, and meaning touch the human heart with eternal verities and realities for which contact the heart is designed and hungers, especially in a profane world. This is the traditional realism of Ms. Rowling. If I overstated her didactic or evangelical purpose in this book while trying to slay the Dragon of Christian objections to *Harry Potter*, the truth of my thesis seems to have survived this hyperbole.

Ms. Rowling's Harry is as popular as he is because in her books about this boy wizard she profoundly and simultaneously embodies and criticizes the *Zeitgeist* or spirit of our times. This last she does both unconsciously I think as a member of the subset "postmodern," by just breathing the air of the world in which we live, and deliberately as a critic and observer of the wreckage and successes consequent to the world's departures from modern and traditional moorings.

The *Harry Potter* books are as temporal and topical on one level as a newspaper, speaking to us from within our historical period's concerns and showing us the limitations and blind spots of these ideas. They are simultaneously transcendent and transforming; they speak to us about the human condition, point us to unchanging verities, and transform us alchemically by our sympathetic identification and sharing in the changes in her storys' players.

It has been said that "postmodern Literature," as such, is an impossibility. postmodernism is at base a technique for unraveling and revealing the metanarrative of texts, and as soon as anyone begins to write from within this perspective, they should be obliged to unwind its preconceptions. Not much of a narrative line there.

But there certainly is a "literature for postmodern people," a story-telling that embodies the genre-crashing and remolding of our times, the nihilism and doubt that pervades our age, not to mention our iconoclasm and skepticism about all dogma and authority. From the syncretic madness of The Matrix movies, to the pop culture celebration of diversity and choice in everything from The Berenstein Bears to Disney's Sky High, we see the postmodern spirit shaping our stories and entertainments and reinforcing our shared beliefs and concerns.

As we saw in the last chapter's review of the *Harry Potter* books against a check-list of the qualities of postmodern literature, Ms. Rowling qualifies on every count. Though we discussed the seeming "gaps" in her poststructuralist resume above, these "failings" are on a second look proof of her greater postmodernism. Ms. Rowling is perhaps nowhere more postmodern than in insisting on critiquing and exposing the painfully restrictive consequences of the metanarrative of postmodernism.

Instead of the unexamined nominalism and relativism of the postmodern period, Ms. Rowling offers us stories reflecting a poststructuralist's structure, namely the Principle of Love, Harmony, and Balance we see in her use of alchemical topoi and in her symbols and story reflecting a Trinitarian cosmology. This is not a restrictive metanarrative or the vehicle of an oppressive ideology; Love is a contranatural force permeating reality that is capable of defeating death.

Harry Potter offers us a baseline for behavior, what we can call a "morality," to counteract the excesses of our "if it feels good, do it" age. Harry's stories also come with a backdrop of eternal reality with which we can, even must have contact to be fully human. This, combined with her reflection of our age's concerns and beliefs in a great story with engaging characters, makes for one powerful tale.

Is this a formula, then, for global sales that are off the chart? Combine (1) artistry and story-telling genius, (2) an echo of eternity in traditional symbols and cosmology, and (3) an edgy relevance to our times so there is a powerful resonance with readers everywhere? I think that combination of art, symbol, and topical relevance really is the explanation of her success.

There is a magic in Ms. Rowling's postmodern realism, though, beyond these three elements. Her magic is the way her realism or traditionalism answers the question or satisfies the need we all feel for meaning that is not moralizing and for virtue that is heroic and uniting rather than divisive. The transcendent elements of her story fill the vacuum created by the radical skepticism of our time with a magic that cannot be deconstructed because it is atemporal and about love. Ms. Rowling has hit the trifecta jackpot – and we are all the richer for it.

Conclusion

I said at the beginning of chapter four that my thoughts on Ms. Rowling as poststructuralist grew out of a lecture I heard on the modernism of the Christian writers called the Inklings (Lewis, Tolkien, Chesterton and Charles Williams, most famously). I'd like to conclude with some thoughts about the differences between these Christian writers as moderns and Ms. Rowling as a postmodern realist and Christian.

Andrew Lazo at Houston Baptist University argues cogently that the Inklings are best understood first as modern writers dealing with modern themes and issues. The important difference between Lewis and Tolkien, he says, and Eliot and Pound, is only in their answer to Pound's demand that everyone writing "Innovate! Innovate! Innovate!" The Inkling response is not to deny change or the modern impulse, but to insist that writers and readers are best served by "renovation" and rehabilitation of the best forms and topoi of traditional writing.

To Lewis, this meant that writing, a la Spenser, was about "instructing while delighting" and being relatively open with his didactic and evangelical purpose. Aslan's sacrifice on the Stone Table is a powerful image but not especially subtle or sneaky (how watchful were those dragons really?). The alchemy of his *Space Trilogy* and the astrological underpinnings of *Narnia* are not in-your-face artistry but their Christian message is.

If Lewis and Tolkien are modernists writing in reaction to the same questions and issues that provoked all writers of the modern era, albeit as moderns in opposition to the unexamined convictions of modern people, I think the same might be said about Rowling as a postmodern writer. She is exploring the same problems as her contemporaries and she has the same seeming superficiality and lightness that makes her satire comic and winsome. And like the Inklings as "modern medievalists," as Lazo calls them, Rowling works as a postmodern traditionalist critiquing postmodern ennui, deconstruction, and reductionism.

Her Voldemort, for example, is the most powerful indictment of the humanity of our times I have read in any book not written by Guenon, Schuon, Lings, or Perry. Voldemort is an idolator, an egotist, fragmented, friendless, and a slave to his fears of death. He is the Twin Enigma ("Tom Riddle") or schizophrenic dualist become a man "fleeing mortality" ("Voldemort"). Because the man Cornelius Fudge calls Lord Thingy, the postmodern man, is Harry's doppelganger and the person Harry must come to terms with, I think Harry will become the signature literary figure for our historical period, as Frodo is for moderns.

Ms. Rowling's intention in writing, however, when compared to the Inklings seems more therapeutic and cathartic than didactic. She denies in all her interviews that she is trying to teach her readers anything beyond moral courage, and that she offers it only as an afterthought. Lewis' paintings in *Narnia* are meant to suck readers in and change them even against their will by the experiences they have in Aslan's world sailing with Prince Caspian in search of the lost Kings. Rowling's paintings are engaging but only open up if you know what to say to them or what point to touch on the canvas.

If we are meant to take these experiences of living paintings as metaphors for a reader's relationship with the book being read, as I think we are meant to do in both cases, Rowling clearly thinks art is powerful stuff and that it should not force its message on those not ready to penetrate beneath the surface of their own volition. I don't think Lewis or Tolkien share this sensitivity or respect for the individual – or that Rowling has the confidence and faith that the Inklings did in the message they were sharing. *Harry Potter*'s transcendent elements are all in place but you have to reach out to grasp them or they will roll off your back.

Plato wrote famously in his Seventh Epistle that he had never written a word of philosophy because anything properly the subject of contemplation could not be reduced to words and anything written could be shown by those skilled in disputation to be false (341-344). Ms. Rowling perceives the Inklings, rightly or wrongly, as primarily moral educators rather than artists – and herself as an artist with platonic reservations about the appropriateness of writing to instruct, even while delighting, a reservation in harmony with the spirit of our times and the beliefs of her audience.

On to the Finale

Which thought brings us to the end of our one-by-one discussion of the five keys the serious reader needs to unlock *Harry Potter* and force the door on *Deathly Hallows*.

It's all very well and good to understand Ms. Rowling as a postmodern realist, but does that help us figure out what happens in the last *Harry Potter* book? Yes, I think it does. And now that we've seen a lot about each key and how it works, isn't it time we see how they work together to figure out what really happened in *Half-Blood Prince* and what may happen in *Deathly Hallows* to bring the story to a proper alchemical, postmodern, and "big twist" ending?

Read on for one dilettante reader's best guesses about *Deathly Hollows*, guesses made using the five keys of this book.

Chapter 6

Deathly Hallows SWAGs
Based on the Five Keys

When I was living in Japan in the 90s, I worked with American computer and communication geeks who were certifiably brilliant. One of their favorite acronyms that they tossed about every day while trouble-shooting satellite systems connecting the Pacific Rim with Pearl Harbor was "S.W.A.G." If one tech doubted something another had said, for example, he would ask, "Is that for real or just a SWAG?" I learned that a SWAG was the opinion of an expert, his or her best guess, but not something he or she could demonstrate from the facts. SWAG stands for "Scientific Wild-Ass Guess." Better than a shot-in-the-dark, certainly, but still a guess.

Don't let anybody kid you. When talking about the finale to *Harry Potter*, the best anyone can do is throw out some SWAGs. There will be SWAGs that aren't systematic or scientific in any sense of the word that will hit bull's-eyes. And the best guesses from the smartest readers in fandom will likely be proven all wrong.

Having made that disclaimer, let's have some fun. Here are my SWAGs for your consideration, comment, and correction.

It's All About the View from the Astronomy Tower

All guesses about what will happen in the last *Harry Potter* novel turn on what you think happened on the Astronomy Tower in *Half-Blood Prince*. We have Harry's point of view and beliefs about what happened on the Tower, but we know this perspective is remarkably undependable and restricted. Harry never knows either what Voldemort is planning or what Albus Dumbledore and Severus Snape are up to.

How you choose to understand the Tower events is critical because it colors how you understand all the back story which, in turn, will determine the direction you think the finale is headed. There are three solid ways of understanding the scene on the Astronomy Tower. I will only be choosing one to explore the back story and series finale but will

239

lay out here all three options I find credible.

Ms. Rowling has clarified Dumbledore's end-of-story condition in answers to questions at a reading she gave with John Irving and Stephen King at Radio City Music Hall in New York, 2 August 2006. "Dumbledore is definitely dead," she said without winking or crossing her fingers. As "dead is dead" in these books, all three variants of what happened on the Tower differ only in when Dumbledore dies and what death means.

The question, then, is:

(1) "Does he die on the Tower?" or

(2) "Does he die both a year before the Tower and again on the Tower?" or

(3) "Does Dumbledore die before the Tower but not on the Tower at all?"

The first perspective, "Dumbledore dies on the Tower," is the narrative line. It supports our assumption that Harry's view of things is correct. Albus Dumbledore is murdered by black hat and black-hearted Snape, whose true colors (silver and green as well as blackguard black) are finally revealed. Harry's job in Book 7 is destroying Voldemort and his Horcruxes with the side mission of revenging his beloved, martyred Headmaster by killing Snape.

The second variant, "Dumbledore dies again on the Tower," is that Harry's view is substantially correct; Snape does blast Albus with a killing curse that does "kill" him. The difference here would be that Dumbledore is already dead. This scenario rests on the "Stoppered Death" theory explained in the chapter on narrative misdirection. Severus saved Dumbledore's death with the "Stoppered Death" potion when the Headmaster failed to disarm (ouch) the Ring Horcrux. The stopper on Albus' death is for an unknown period and perhaps needs "refreshing" as does Polyjuice potion. From this view, Dumbledore's argument with Snape that Hagrid overheard, if it ever happened in fact, is the Headmaster's insisting that Severus unstopper him at the fitting time to save Draco, Severus, and allow him to carry on for the Order. Severus here wears a white hat, albeit stained by a mercy-killing of sorts.

The third variant, "Dumbledore is dead – but he doesn't die or die again on the Tower," is the view first suggested by Joyce Odell, the Red Hen (see *Who Killed Albus Dumbledore?* Chapter 6, for her magisterial tour of the back story and the events on the Tower). According to this perspective, Dumbledore is not who he seems to be. There is either a Dumbledore ghost on the Tower or a Polyjuiced stand-in.

Who could be the faux Dumbey? How about the only New Guy to appear in the series whose secret we haven't learned? The Astronomy Tower Dumbledore could be played by Horace Slughorn. Sally Gallo of The Leaky Cauldron champions this view in her fascinating look at the historical stage magician Horace Goldin who is Slughorn's twin (see Ms. Gallo's essay, also in *Who Killed Albus Dumbledore?* Chapter 4). Ms. Gallo's view allows for the possibilities that the real Dumbledore is already dead (unstoppered, alas), near death off-stage, or simply invisible, "taking the safety of his students seriously" in the face of a Death Eater invasion.

An important variation on Ms. Gallo's theory posits two Polyjuiced Dumbledores in the last chapters of *Prince*: Severus playing the Headmaster in the Cave and Sluggo picking up the drama on the street in Hogsmeade. Wendy B. Harte explains the many pointers to this possibility on her Live Journal site and the one dedicated to speculation consequent to *Who Killed Albus Dumbledore?* (Zossima Press, 2006; see book for details about this online LJ).

Ms. Rowling's Radio City Music Hall answers, especially to the question poised by Salman Rushdie and son, tell us that, yes, Dumbledore is dead, and suggest simultaneously that Severus is not a bad guy. This suggestion and what we have learned using the five key patterns we have identified and explored makes the first perspective (Harry's belief) hardly credible. No narrative misdirection, no mistaken identity, no staged deaths, no New Guy secrets, and a rather flat set of circumstances for the literary alchemy and postmodern themes to play out on. No way.

Not to mention the weird plot points Dumbledore's death on the Astronomy Tower raises, as in, "Where's Fawkes?" The loyal bird makes it to the Ministry to cover Dumbledore's back in *Phoenix* but can't be bothered to be on the Tower in *Prince*? It's possible, I guess, that Fawkes was caught napping, but a real failing in the story if true.

I think we need to pull out the simplicity razor of Steve Vander Ark.

Steve, webmaster at the venerable *Harry Potter* Lexicon online, has seen more *Harry Potter* theories and speculation than any man living, though the Lexicon only posts the facts as they are presented in canon. He argues publicly and privately that the only thing history has shown to be true of speculation about where these stories are going is that this guesswork is always wrong. The most common mistake in this guesswork has been over-thinking the problem. Lexicon Steve argues cogently that the solution to the storyline will be both relatively simple and something we never would have guessed in a million years.

Steve's sobriety in this assessment and the now vivid clarity of Ms. Rowling's statements about a dead Dumbledore certainly push us heavily towards accepting either Harry's view or seeing the murder on the tower as a mercy killing, that is, if we think Severus is a good guy. The weight of all the patterns and themes, however, push us at least as hard away from the narrative line and Harry's jaundiced view. The sober money after Radio City and with respect for Lexicon Steve's insights is on Door #2, Stoppered Death Dumbledore dying twice.

But who here is sober?

Not me, certainly. Illustrating what is going on in these stories, which, after all, is my job here, is better served by mixing metaphors with clichés, hence my "climbing out on a limb." I'm going to argue from the perspective that (1) Dumbledore is either totally incapacitated in his Stoppered Death or only able to act for very short periods by the Tower melodrama at the end of *Half-Blood Prince* and, either way, (2) there is some remarkable scrambling going on to stage his death on the Astronomy Tower.

Dumbledore is dead at the end of *Half-Blood Prince* and unable to be brought back from death but his stopper may very well be intact. He won't "do a Gandalf," then, and rise as an even stronger wizard, but before he embraces his death "as the next great adventure," he will be able to sort things out with Harry, Voldemort, and Severus.

The bizarre and seemingly more unlikely story for this possibility is a lot more fun in the telling than the other ones.

My back story explanation which follows is taken almost whole cloth, however, from Ms. Odell's essay in *Who Killed Albus Dumbledore?* and her longer posted writing at www.RedHen-publications.com and from other friends I'll mention below. Ready or not, here are my SWAGs about what really happened before the Astronomy Tower, what Severus and Albus have been up to all these years, and a little about what could happen in the series conclusion. "Five Key Checklists" in hand? Let's go.

The Five Key Checklist

Quick review time. Before we jump into what might have happened and what could happen, we need to check the keys that will open this mystery in back-story and coming events.

- **Narrative Misdirection:** The big trick of the books is Ms. Rowling's suckering us, her readers, into trusting the veracity and scope of Harry's perspective. We don't have enough information or the objectivity to understand how narrow the view we're getting really is, so we buy into it. Voldemort uses the same trick on Harry with the information he shares in the Diary/Horcrux in *Chamber* and he does it again in *Phoenix* via the Hallway Vision that haunts Harry's dreams. We should be expecting a big twist surprise that shows how incredibly deceived Harry has been – and, perhaps, a narrative misdirection stunt on part of the Good Guys to fool Voldemort.

- **Alchemical crucible** – The last book promises to be the alchemical rubedo, which promises quite a few "red" deaths, the resolution of contraries, and Harry's perfection in love. We may even have an alchemical orphan to begin the Great Work again and we should expect quite a few echoes from previous books' endings, especially the first book's. Look for the heroes, Gryffindor/Slytherin Hermaphrodites all, having resolved the great division of the Wizarding World, to become agents of love. As the rubedo is the revelation of the albedo rather than new work, *Deathly Hallows* should feature the disclosure of everything that happened in *Half-Blood Prince* that we didn't see or understand for what it was.

- **Hero's journey/Repeated elements** – Despite what Harry said at the end of *Prince* about not coming back to Hogwarts for his seventh year, this is only a statement of his intentions. He'll be back and hit almost every part of her ten-step checklist, to include, I think, a Dumbledore denouement of some kind, believe it or not. In addition to this formula, *Deathly Hallows* will repeat the several story elements found in each of the first books, meaning revelation after revelation of what Harry missed in *Half-Blood Prince*, focus on his scar as the link to Voldemort, sharing at last the Grand plan of the Dark Lord in *Prince*, pull the scales from our eyes to see all the mistaken identities and one or two staged deaths, and, last but not least, tell us Professor Slughorn's secret that every New Guy has. And did I mention a Voldemort takeover of Hogwarts?

- **Postmodern Myth** – Ms. Rowling writes as a postmodern realist. As such we should expect the collapse of the core magical metanarrative that divides and diminishes the Wizarding World in the story's closing reconciliation of Gryffindor and Slytherin. Think *Romeo and Juliet*! Not until we have a resolution of the conflict by combat, however, between the Nietzschean Death Eaters that celebrate oppression and those they attempt to exclude and oppress, with a come from behind victory of the underdogs and the marginalized. And did I mention we'll have a few revelations highlighting our limited ability to understand because of the fog of our prejudices? Start thinking, "house-elves."

- **Traditional Symbolism** – Beyond the alchemical images of the wedding, the grave, and the resolution of contraries in love that *Deathly Hallows* promises, I expect the last book to highlight the Christian theme of Love/Christ's victory over death with the Christ symbols already present in the story and the storyline with the addition of dragons and a sacrificial, loving death to defeat Voldemort as an echo both of Calvary and Lily's death. It's the magic of the wand-cores that will make a difference.

All together, if the five patterns we've explored really do open their meaning, the reader putting down *Deathly Hallows* should be moved by the continued celebration in story form of Love beyond sentiment, a metaphysical physics and the human alchemy, as the true reality above partisan ideologies and Grand narratives. The reader should also be stunned by the big twist Ms. Rowling has pulled off

Now to the back story!

The Back Story

The real Story is all about Severus Snape, not Harry/Volde, and about Severus' war against the prevailing metanarrative of the Wizarding World. What is Snape's mission? (1) Destroy the Nietzschean *Übermensch* dimension of the Slytherin quarter, (2) reconcile with Gryffindor, and (3) rewrite the Grand Narrative on the basis of Love, a supernatural power that cannot become a divisive ideology. The apprentice to Dumbledore is attempting to pull off something like "nation building," what we can call "Political/cultural Alchemy and Transfiguration."

We know what Harry sees. We usually learn something about what Lord Voldemort has been doing off-stage at the end of Harry's adventure each year. What we never learn is what Severus and Albus have been doing and thinking. Using the Red Hen's speculation as my springboard, here is what they could have been doing.

Snape grows up tutored by Eileen Prince (Irma Pince = I'm a Prince?), tortured by his Muggle and vampiric father (Filch?), and is figuratively adopted by Albus Dumbledore as one of his special student projects when he arrives at Hogwarts. The Prince family crest or coat of arms is red and gold a la Gryffindor, so our Half-Blood Prince may be undercover in Slytherin from the very beginning. His brilliance as student, self-possession, and devotion to Dumbledore makes him the perfect disciple/alchemist to win the Greater War against Voldemort and the Death Eaters. Snape is a Dumbledore man, trained in Occlumency, and is planted within Voldemort's ranks from the git-go after his graduation from Hogwarts.

After Dumbledore learns the prophecy from Trelawney, he and Snape decide Severus will become a seeming double-agent to plant half the Prophecy in Voldemort's ear so he will create or at least try to create the Chosen One. Dumbledore tries to protect both the Longbottoms and Potters but Pettigrew, with a bumbling assist from Sirius, opens the Potters' backdoor to the Dark Lord. Because of the Horcrux disaster in Godric's Hollow I'll explain in a minute and perhaps a special charm or two of Lily's, Harry survives and Volde becomes VaporMort. Pettigrew hides the wand Horcrux. Harry becomes the philosophical orphan destined to be the Gryffindor/Slytherin Rebis who vanquishes Voldemort.

Heroic Snape, however, is trapped at Hogwarts because of this twist. The plan was for Voldemort to be consumed and distracted by the Prophecy. While he was hunting for the Longbottoms and the Potters without success, Dumbledore would be hunting Horcruxes. They have assumed Voldemort was creating Horcruxes from the time of Lord Voldemort's Hogwarts interview with the Headmaster. The Headmaster destroying the six Horcruxes would have enabled Severus to kill the Dark Lord from within his inner circle and capture the Death Eaters.

Sirius' blunder, however, not only blows this plan up, it condemns Snape to a life underground, literally and figuratively, until Voldemort returns. If Dumbledore reveals his heroism and Snape acts the part of goody-goody, he will be attacked by unrepentant Death Eaters. He will also have no value in the continuing effort to purify Slytherin House and its alumni/ae or in the war he and Dumbledore know is inevitable on Voldemort's return. The larger, metanarrative war, too, has not been won, so Severus continues to play the role of Slytherin/Death Eater to maintain contact with the Malfoys and other Pure blood Slytherins as Head of House. Dumbledore and Snape expect Voldemort's eventual return because of their Horcrux suspicions and plan a counterattack. As Joyce Odell points out, how many curses can there be that change a wizard's face when performing them?

Snape hates Sirius because his bumbling not only killed the Potters, it also condemned him to a life in the Slytherin dungeons waiting on a possibility, his magisterial genius concealed under a servant's basket.

Snape plays this part most carefully and sadistically with the Potter boy and his Gryffindor buddies when Harry arrives at school. Severus must never allow himself to be seen as weak or soft in the Slytherin understanding of the Wizarding World partisan differences, lest an accomplished Legilimens find the chink in his armor and expose him.

Dumbledore will cover him with the Ministry and faculty; Snape plays to the Slytherin purebloods through their children. He never shows the smallest kindness to Harry -- and Harry from the very beginning learns to play the proud Gryffindor and hero (clueless dimwit and eleven-year-old that he is). Snape's bitterness about what has amounted to his necessary confinement because of Harry's "victory" over Voldemort (and favored status with Snape's only friend) makes "playing" the sadist an easy task for the Potions Master.

One of the better lies that Severus tells Bellatrix in "Spinner's End" is that he did not pursue the Dark Lord after his seeming demise in Godric's Hollow because "I believed him finished." Bellatrix thinks she is the only true believer. Hardly. Snape didn't pursue him, but with Dumbledore, he had few doubts that Vapormort was still alive. Just the rumor of his Horcrux fascination would be sufficient for that.

From the very beginning of the series, Dumbledore and Snape know that Voldemort is back or plotting his return. Even in *Stone*, they are working to frustrate his return, but they are very much aware of his coming and what he wants, hence the efforts to protect the Stone and intimidate Quirrell (without revealing they know he is Voldemort's agent, even Quirrelldemort). In *Chamber*, they learn about the Horcrux diary that enabled a Riddle-as-memory comeback. In Prisoner, the dynamic Dumbe-duo discover what really happened at Godric's Hollow and begin their active search for Horcruxes while doing everything possible to forestall Voldemort's return.

No luck. In *Goblet*, the Dark Lord is reborn and Snape picks up where he never really left off, very grateful that Dumbledore insisted for sixteen years that he keep up the pretenses that enable him to act as savior in VoldeWar II. Even if Crouch/Moody had survived, that Death Eater wouldn't have been able to tell tales on the Potions Master. Harry hated Snape because of his almost unbridled sadism in and out of class; everyone knew that and could give vivid "for instance" stories to prove the enmity.

Dumbledore even expected a kidnapping during the school year and Harry to be used in a black resurrection ritual (Albus knows the Dark Arts, remember, he just doesn't use them). He is anticipating what Voldemort must do to return to a body with Pettigrew's help; the blood of his enemy will be on his requirement list, especially if he wants to overcome the protection Harry's mother's blood sacrifice gave him and that Aunt Petunia sealed by taking baby Harry in – the "bond of blood" magic that has protected Harry from Death Eaters for eleven years at the Dursleys and from Quirrelldemort in *Stone*.

Voldemort leapfrogs that blood barrier by using Harry's blood in his reconstitution and is able to touch him afterwards. But Dumbledore has his famous, momentary "triumphant gleam" when he learns of the fact, because now the Gryffindor and Slytherin extremes have met and been melded within Voldemort's physical person. The conductivity and complementarity of the Red & Gold, Green & Silver extremes are now embodied in the Dark Lord. Because Dumbledore knew about the Prophecy and the Priori Incantatem effect likely to take place if Harry and Voldemort ever did battle, I think it's safe to say the Headmaster felt Harry was up to this challenge – even that he let it happen.

So the Dark Lord is a Gryffindor/Slytherin androgyne post-*Goblet* just as these factions have been joined incarnate in Harry since his parents' murder and he was gifted with the Horcrux scar. It's no accident that after Voldemort is reconstituted with Harry's blood and the sacrificial love of his mother that the bond between them through the scar becomes so much stronger, as it does in *Phoenix*, and Harry starts speaking in ALL CAPS!

Rowling all but told us that nothing would be the same after *Goblet*:

Rowling said that *Goblet of Fire* is the turning point in the series, the critical book. "Book Four is the end of an era for Harry. He's been very protected until now." "Harry's horizons are literally and metaphorically widening as he grows older." She has also said that *Goblet of Fire* represents "the end of an era in the context of the whole series of books. For Harry, his innocence is gone." (Penny Linsenmeyer, *Harry Potter for Grown-ups*, http://www.hpfgu.org.uk/faq/rowling.html)

Everything changes when Voldemort gets his body back. We are on the road to the resolution of contraries and of the metanarrative's divisive work. Harry's alchemical change moves into hyperdrive, also known as the alchemical nigredo, in which the old man is "killed, putrified, and dissolved into the original substance of creation, the prima material, in order that it may be renovated and reborn in a new form" (Abraham, p. 135). This is the agony of Harry's experience in *Phoenix* as everything ego-laden about him is stripped from him except his core identity as prophesied Deliverer.

But this story is not really about Harry. He is not consciously doing the work of alchemy as an alchemist; he is the stuff of the Great Work through which the alchemist is working. Dumbledore is that Alchemist and Severus is his Master Apprentice. Snape is consciously working to transform the Slytherin component of the Four Houses in resistance to Voldemort and become the Slytherin/Gryffindor androgyne or hermaphrodite that will remake the Wizarding World metanarrative in Love. [The Hermaphrodite you recall from your AP literary alchemy class is a preferred alchemical symbol for the Philosopher's Stone or the transcendent end of Alchemy.]

Voldemort's search in Phoenix is only partially about the prophecy. His central quest has been to know for certain where Snape's true allegiance lies. The Dark Lord lives in a black-and-white world and the s/he double-agent in his inner circle is a great distraction. Voldemort needs to know the whole prophecy, word-by-word, to find out if Snape told him the truth about what Trelawney said at least as much as he wants to know the rest of her vision.

Hence, too, Harry's Occlumency lessons in **Phoenix**, disastrous as they are.

Snape/Dumbe know that Voldemort is after the prophecy and that he is in Harry's head, hence the guard duty at the Ministry and the Headmaster's distance from Harry all year. They are replaying the plan that almost worked when Harry was an infant, namely, preoccupy Voldemort with the prophecy search while gathering and destroying Horcruxes. Snape proves his allegiance to the Dark Lord by failing to teach Harry Occlumency, a sop that Dumbledore and Snape know can be staged easily enough so it seems that Snape was refusing to do what Dumbledore has ordered him to do (and Harry obliges his Twin Riddle's plans, complementary antagonist that he is, by not practicing on his own). The Pensieve was baited with Snape's worst memory to draw Harry in and give Severus the excuse he needs to break off the lessons.

Beginning with *Order of the Phoenix*, we not only see a change, then, in Harry's struggles and in Voldemort's plans. Severus and Albus are on a radically different track, too. By the time **Phoenix** begins, they know

Harry has become a transmitter of sorts, a walking minicam through which the Dark Lord can see through Harry's eyes. Harry, when he is remarkably relaxed, can look through Voldemort's eyes as well. More important, though, is the reverse action on Voldemort's end.

Because our view is restricted to Harry's experience, we don't know what Lord Thingy or what the Headmaster and his apprentice are up to. If Harry is able to see accidentally into Voldemort's world, it seems logical that the Dark Lord, an accomplished wizard to say the least, could intentionally work the Scar-O-Scope in the opposite direction. What we see in Harry's rage from beginning to end of *Phoenix*, his feeling-snakes move inside him when near Dumbledore, and his schizophrenia (the several times he feels his head splitting along his scar) are the side-effects of Lord Voldemort's learning to crawl behind Harry's eyeballs and look out.

Severus, no doubt, hears about the Dark Lord's new ability and warns the Headmaster, who elects to stay off-stage and pretend he is no special friend of Harry's. This serves, of course, to protect Harry and guard the Prophecy and Snape's secret for as long as possible. More important, it buys time for the Good Guys to be Horcrux hunting. Reread *Phoenix* from the perspective of the Order knowing that Harry is carrying the Dark Lord's camera inside his head. Everything from the Advance Guard escorting Harry to Grimmauld Place (almost certainly while the rest of the Order makes a diversionary attack on Voldemort and the Death Eaters to be sure the Dark Lord isn't "tuned in" that night) to Molly Weasley fighting with Sirius about how much Harry can be told takes on an entirely different and richer meaning. The ALL CAPS fireworks Harry puts on in the early chapters are signals that Voldemort is on the scene and, excited for some reason, not practicing his Occlumency very successfully.

Dumbledore's tactic with Harry almost works. As I said, we are back to the plan that the Order was working on before the Potters were murdered: distract and delay Voldemort from his larger ambitions with a side-show while Dumbledore seeks-and-destroys Horcruxes so that Severus can kill Voldemort and have the death be final.

Unfortunately, Sirius Black blows it again! His interference (in switching secret keepers) exposed the Potter family to Voldemort's attack on their home in Godric Hollow years ago. In *Phoenix*, his rushing contra instructions to the rescue and getting killed in the Ministry means Dumbledore has to tell Harry (and Voldemort; that's not just Harry tearing up the Headmaster's office!) almost everything he knows about the Prophecy. Again, little wonder Snape hates Sirius and there isn't a memorial service for Harry's godfather.

So the Dark Lord's bumbling Death Eaters don't get the prophecy, doggone it, and Snape's true identity and loyalties escape confirmation or denial once again, at least in the showdown at the Ministry of Magic. In Dumbledore's office, however, Voldemort does learn the details of the Prophecy – with the special spin Dumbledore gives the story with respect to who delivered the partial message to Voldemort. Professor Snape is not named; Dumbledore says only that it was an "eavesdropper" who was "detected only a short way into the prophecy and thrown from the building."

Dumbledore knows in this speech that he is performing for both Harry and Lord Voldemort, who is watching through Harry. Harry's rage leaves little doubt that he is experiencing the presence of perhaps the most evil wizard who ever lived. See how careful the Headmaster is. He has to spill a lot of information, and, no doubt, he met with Severus before going to the office to tell him what he would have to do and say.

Which brings us to the action of *Half-Blood Prince*.

Dumbledore can no longer pretend he isn't Harry's beloved guardian. That secret is history after the drama in his office at the end of *Phoenix*. The question is, "What now?" Voldemort has seen that his taking over Harry's sight causes a big change in Harry, a visible change people are bound to notice. The Dark Lord doesn't stop doing it, however; he just changes how he does it. No doubt, the Dark Lord learns he must be perfectly calm when looking through Harry into Hogwarts; after his defeat in the Ministry, his poor anger management shows in Harry's wrecking crew performance.

Severus and Albus cannot turn off the minicam or safely pretend any longer that the Headmaster isn't Harry's ally in the "beat Voldemort" game. Their only workable option is to stage every interaction they have with Harry to feed Voldemort convincing information that is bound to distract and upset the Dark Lord – and to deceive him. The action of *Half-Blood Prince* is the story of Albus Dumbledore and Severus

Snape's writing a tale of narrative misdirection to do to Voldemort what Ms. Rowling does to us.

They do this by restricting what Voldemort learns through the Scar-O-Scope to information that will lead him to draw the wrong conclusions because of his prejudices, that is, by the pull on his thinking created by what he wants to think. Voldemort thinks Dumbledore is a besotted, weak old man consumed by sentimentality and thoughts about "the power of love." The Headmaster plays the part of the "Dumbledore Voldemort Thinks He Knows" expertly in the showdown in the Headmaster's office at the end of *Phoenix*.

Since Voldemort's incarnate return in *Goblet*, Dumbledore and Snape have been waiting for the Dark Lord to give the order for Severus to kill Dumbledore in public or in such a way that there is no doubt that (a) the Headmaster is dead and (b) Severus killed him. It is inevitable because it is an all-or-nothing test that will resolve the question of Snape's loyalty without a doubt. Voldemort finally gives the order after being defeated by Dumbledore in the Ministry at the end of *Phoenix*, and the dynamic duo prepare to act out at last the plan they have made to stage this death so that Snape will seem to all present to have done the dastardly deed. Albus plans his own survival, of course.

Enter the Ring Horcrux fiasco. Or is it the Ring Horcrux stage-prop piece-of-genius?

If you hold to the second view of the Tower events, that Severus slays the Headmaster in an agreed upon mercy killing, this is where the paths separate with the third view. According to the theory behind Door #2, the ring Horcrux destruction accident is fatal but Severus "stoppers Dumbe's death." Dumbledore for the remaining part of *Prince* is the answer to Snape's question, namely, "the difference between an Inferius and a ghost." We don't know if the "stopper" in the Dumbe-death bottle is a semipermanent fix, if it has to be boosted periodically as does Polyjuice, or if it has an expiration point that cannot be pushed back, say, for just a year or part of a year. Whatever this potion's qualities, the death and stoppering aren't the tragedy it might have been because Voldemort had already told Snape to kill Albus; now they could plan on their staged death performance at year's end with Snape taking the cursed DADA position for the year remaining.

Accepting that Dumbledore does indeed blow it and dies a stoppered death by botching the Horcrux destruction or manipulation (trying to use it as a Ring-o-Scope?), this stopper potion gives Dumbledore and his allies time for Horcrux research and Chosen One Training with Harry. Albus leaves the blackened arm visible so the world will see and confirm Snape's report to Voldemort about the injury and the old man's frailty. He undertakes his research project and training in the same evening in late June by visiting the Dursleys to get Harry and by recruiting Professor Slughorn, Riddle-Horcrux memory reservoir.

Voldemort pulls a switch, though, as soon as he learns from Severus about Dumbledore's wound and fragility. He pulls the death mission from Severus and gives it to Draco. Now the Dumbey-duo's problems are compounded by the need to save the Malfoy boy and by the spies Voldemort sends into the castle.

I'll get to Voldey's spies in Hogwarts during *Half-Blood Prince* in a second. First, scroll back a bit though and reexamine one assumption; that is, that Dumbledore blew the Horcrux disarming work on the ring and was dis-armed himself, fatally.

You know, I don't buy it.

If Horcrux destruction were such a horribly complicated business, wouldn't Dumbledore have mentioned that to Harry sometime during the course of *Prince*? If the greatest wizard of the age took a hit that left his arm horribly disfigured, wouldn't that almost require a note of caution if not detailed instruction about how to handle these things, how to neutralize them without being toasted? You'd think.

There is something bizarre here, though, something that makes me think we don't know what really happened with the Ring Horcrux. I find it very unlikely that Dumbledore was gravely wounded by the attempt to destroy this Horcrux because he never attempts to explain to Harry how to do it so he isn't killed.

This makes sense if (a) the Headmaster knows Harry-as-Horcrux can destroy them without injury, (b) he has already destroyed all the Horcruxes except Harry's scar so there's no reason to worry, (c) his injury didn't come from trying to destroy the Horcrux but to use it, or (d) any combination of these possibilities. The narrative line, however, that Dumbledore, the greatest wizard of the age ™, was blasted by the Horcrux when attempting to destroy it, that Harry is going to be finding and destroying Horcruxes, and Dumbledore says not one word to him about the dangers is goofy.

If we assume, though, that Dumbledore didn't blow the ring destruction, we have to figure out why the heck he'd make such a public show of his infirmity and eventually tell Harry what happened. He does it to confirm Severus' false reports to Voldemort about the Headmaster's condition and activities – that he is Horcrux-hunting and that he is relatively weak and vulnerable to attack. Harry's minicam picks it all up and projects it on Voldemort's home theatre screen.

Which brings us back to the theory introduced in Chapter 1, of Snape and Slughorn playing Dumbledore via Polyjuice potion. One slip in front of the Scar-O-Scope and Severus' head will be blown off by Voldemort and his gang. Why not have Severus, an obviously Oscar caliber actor and Nobel Prize Potion maker, do the Dumbledore honors through Harry's sixth year? This way Snape can know exactly what the Headmaster says to Harry and to the Dark Lord so he is never caught flat-footed in discussions with Voldemort later.

Severus and Albus expand their staged death plan by necessity to include Rubeus Hagrid and Horace Slughorn. They write the script of Harry's every encounter in *Half-Blood Prince* with the Headmaster, played brilliantly by Snape, with Slughorn, and even with Hagrid. It's all about tripping up the Dark Lord.

So let's assume for a moment the Headmaster is off-stage hunting Horcruxes and that the ring Horcrux destruction story is a red herring or "distractor," if Dumbledore has in fact "died" of some cause and been stoppered. Snape is playing Dumbledore's part so he has the information he needs and can pass the information he wants to Voldemort in the quantities and in the sequence he chooses. He deliberately presents a Horcrux story through Harry in their Voldemort-Horcrux tutorials that is probably ten to twenty years out of date.

If the horribly scarred arm is a stage prop that the Potions Masters and Dumbledore hope will act both as a token of Dumbledore's identity and as a distractor, the plan is for it to divert any attention from the Dumbledore impostor's unusual behaviors. And Snape as Dumbledore is unusual, no? He baits the Muggles by barging into their home and banging drinks against their heads before beating them up verbally for being abusive parents. Not very Dumbledoresque. Then he pokes his wand hard into a piece of furniture he thinks is a wizard in disguise?

Weird.

In *Prince,* Dumbledore is clearly a different man in several ways than the Headmaster we met in the first five books. Ms. Rowling plays fair. Three times in the first five chapters she makes the point to us through Harry that we shouldn't believe that people are who they say they are (the flyer from the Ministry, Dumbledore/Snape's discussion of same with Harry, and the conversation between Arthur and Molly Weasley on his return from work). This is overdone if there isn't someone important who isn't what he or she seems to be.

Now that you have to consider it a possibility that Professor Snape is not only the most interesting character in the book but that he is also writing the story, I hope you'll think it worthwhile to go back to the end of *Phoenix* and read *Prince* as a *Harry Potter* adventure and mystery meant to ensnare and deceive Lord Voldemort. Believe me, if Dumbledore and Snape are writing *Half-Blood Prince* and Snape is starring in two lead roles, it's an entirely different book. It certainly makes narrative misdirection essential to understanding what both Ms. Rowling and her most important character are doing.

The literary alchemy key is important, too. This key tells us that the staged *Prince* story, in which what happens won't be revealed until the climax, is exactly what we should expect before *Deathly Hallows.* As crazy as the Polyjuicing Dumbledore theory may be, with the idea that Severus, Horace, and Hagrid stage a drama for Voldemort using Harry's scar Horcrux mind-connection as a minicamera, we should be looking to learn in the rubedo (*Hallows*) what already happened in the albedo (*Prince*). There should be nothing but revelations of transformations that have already taken place in previous stages.

I half expect Severus' Parthian shot as he fled the Hogwarts grounds was Snape closing the camera opening. The "white-hot, whiplike something" hit Harry "across the face," "slammed [him] backward into the ground," and knocked the wind out of him while "spots of light burst in front of his eyes" (*Prince,* Chapter 28, p. 604) This "whip-like something" destroyed the Horcrux opening on Harry's forehead so Voldemort could no longer see what Harry was doing now that Severus wasn't there to produce the play. "Show over." The literary alchemy and the narrative misdirection keys both tell us this is exactly the kind of revelation or unveiling we can expect in the rubedo.

And this play-within-a-play, narrative-misdirection-on-top-of-narrative-misdirection, is a super-duper reinforcer of Ms. Rowling's postmodern messages that (1) the prejudices consequent to beliefs in the metanarrative blind us to reality and (2) that the subjectivity of our thinking makes understanding reality impossible; at least, impossible until love becomes the filter through which everything is understood.

And we're certainly getting an overdue portion of repeated elements like how dumb Harry is, Harry's cluelessness, Lord Voldemort's plans off-stage, the importance of Harry's peculiar scar, new guy Horace having a secret, faked deaths, and mistaken identities. Dumbledore only appearing at the Sorting Feast and his funeral with two wizards playing his part the night of the Astronomy Tower tragedy in three acts certainly qualifies as "mistaken identities." Harry is so clueless as to who is who that he is reading his worst enemy's textbook all year in Potions and unknowingly acting in Snape's play.

But there are other folks who aren't who or what they seem. Could there be Death Eater spies in Hogwarts?

Pettigrew and Bellatrix Undercover

Spies?

Of course. The point isn't just to kill Dumbledore; Voldemort is struggling to determine Snape's true aspect, Gryffindor or Slytherin? He also isn't leaving this Albus assassination to a boy who has already been bitten by a werewolf and who is terrified by thoughts of his family's imminent death. He sends two of our friends from Spinner's End into Hogwarts.

First in, Peter Pettigrew. (See Swthyv's essay, Chapter 5 in *Who Killed Albus Dumbledore?* for the detailed back story to Pettigrew and his work as a Polyjuice pretender.) As a rat Animagus thoroughly familiar with the literal ins and outs of the school, he easily evades detection and sets up shop in the Room of Requirement, working on the Vanishing cabinets, brewing Polyjuice potion, and browbeating Draco. He lets Bellatrix in through the Shrieking Shack tunnel one night; she makes it to the Room of Requirement under the cover of an Invisibility Cloak.

With their cauldron of Polyjuice potion at hand, they snag both Remus Lupin as he patrols the halls on the seventh floor (if Fenrir Greyback hadn't already delivered him to Voldemort) and Sybill Trelawney when she comes to deposit her empties. Pettigrew grew up with Lupin as a fellow Marauder and can imitate him easily; Lupin's assignment of "keeping track of the werewolves" allows for him to disappear and reappear as he likes (lunar phase permitting).

Trelawney's isolation in her Tower, semi-constant drunkenness, and bizarre character make her a ready mark for impersonation as well. Polyjuiced Lupin (hereafter P!Lupin) has to break off the romance with Tonks lest she see through the change. Professor Trelawney, of course, is just plain nutters in the minds of everyone on campus so no one notices any change in her behaviors. The switcheroos give the Dark Lord the eyes and ears he wants in both Order of the Phoenix meetings and the faculty room. Snape had better not file a report at Death Eater Central that leaves out any information this year.

The reasons for believing Trelawney is actually Bellatrix for much of *Prince* or just the night of the book's climax are:

- Her dead-on accurate predictions on the night of the Astronomy Tower stage-set;

- The need for more competent help-on site than just Peter Pettigrew;

- Trelawney's telling Harry that Snape was the prophecy deliverer; and

- Her absence from the battle and faculty meetings that night.

The problem is the need for so much Polyjuice potion, which Bellatrix needs every hour while teaching and which Draco uses to disguise his student help. Draco has to spend time with the Potions Master to get his Wolfsbane potion every month (it is a bite, not a Dark Mark, that he shows Burgin on Nocturn Alley); he begins stealing the necessary ingredients for Polyjuice potion from Slughorn's stores soon after school begins.

Sluggo has a secret; the story formula nigh on requires that. The question is, is his secret that he is a Black hat or a White hat? And when does he declare for which side? I argued at some length in *Who Killed Albus Dumbledore?* that Horace is "EVIL Slughorn" and that he came to this commitment during the school year when he realized how far from Horcrux success the Good Guys were – and when he realized there were serious Bad Guys loose in the castle.

That's a possibility. I think it more likely, though, that Horace has been on the Good Guys' side for a long time. He has been a Dumbledore man ever since. In fact, he shared the full memory of his conversation with Tom Riddle, Jr., to Dumbledore years ago, probably soon after his interview with the young Voldemort. When Dumbledore-on-the-Tower talks to Draco about faking deaths and hiding people, he's talking about Sluggo and men like him who have helped the Order and are in serious danger because of it. Slughorn faking his own death before we meet him is a pointer to this possibility.

If he hasn't been in on the charade staged in front of Harry's Scar-O-Scope from the beginning of *Prince* (and I think he has), he certainly decides over the Christmas break to wear a White Hat, in fact, to wear Albus' hat ("albus" in Latin means "white"). The memory-turnover when drunk at Aragog's funeral is a staged scene to give Voldemort a false idea of where the Good Guys are in their search for Horcruxes. Horace checks with the Good Guys before going to Hagrid's hut to see if now is the time to provide Harry with the memory. I suspect Snape, with or without Dumbledore, would not have given him the high sign if they didn't already have all the Horcruxes in hand.

Y'see, Dumbledore, Snape, and, yes, Horace have figured out they have multiple guests on campus, too. The dynamic Dumbe-duo, unlike Harry and his readers, conform to MoM security measures and to much higher ID standards and have ways of confirming identities. They know what's going on in the Room of Requirement and allow it to happen.

But their time is running short. Dumbledore and Severus know that the Cabinets cannot take forever to be repaired. The Death Eater assault on the castle could come any day. How can they stage Dumbledore's death in such a way that Draco doesn't kill anyone and Severus isn't caught on the unfortunate side of an Unbreakable Vow?

Assume, for the sake of controversy and simplicity, that Hagrid's supposedly overhearing an argument between the Headmaster and Severus didn't really happen. Hagrid relays the scene to Harry in

Chapter 19 of *Prince* only to confirm through the scar-cam what Severus told Voldemort, namely, that he and Dumbledore were fighting. Severus may have had to tell the Dark Lord that Dumbledore was trying to get him to kill Voldemort, in a mirror of Voldemort's demands on Snape. Hagrid's aside to Harry has the desired effect of assuring the Heir of Slytherin that his boy refused the assignment.

There are at least two scenarios for the Tower staged murder that are credible and still big twists. The first is that Dumbledore is not present but in a condition of Stoppered Death somewhere off-stage. This requires a double Dumbledore drama and substitution that night with both Snape and Slughorn playing his part. The second possibility is that Dumbledore is on the Tower, weakened by the Horcrux ring destruction and Lake Inferi adventure or not. Let's start with the Horace-Polyjuicing-Dumbledore version.

Horace's being in on the staged death in three acts makes the whole thing possible. Horace and Snape put their potions savvy together and come up with their plan for the night the Vanishing Cabinets are repaired and the Draco trap for Dumbledore/Snape is to be sprung on the Astronomy Tower. It's the same plan, only with Horace standing in for Albus.

The Good Guys had to make sure Dumbledore in some form or another was on the Tower so Draco can be seen trying to kill him – and presumed to have died in the attempt. "They can't kill you if you're already dead." Severus and Sluggo know the Death Eater's plan for an Astronomy Tower trap either because Snape has explained the best way to "get Dumbledore" (on his way back from Hogsmeade, drawing him in with a Dark Mark) to Voldemort with the essentials necessary for Staged Death or because they have learned the details of the plan from Voldemort, his underlings, or by tapping the Room of Requirement.

The biggest problem Severus and Horace have in staging this salutary drama (for Draco, at least) is Harry Potter.

> "Enough," said Dumbledore. He said it quite calmly, and yet Harry fell silent at once; he knew that he had finally crossed some invisible line. "Do you think that I have once left the school unprotected during my absences this year? Tonight, when I leave, there will again be additional protections in

place. Please do not suggest that I do not take the safety of my students seriously, Harry." (*Prince*, Chapter 25, p. 550)

With the Death Eaters arriving and the Staged Death to perform on the Tower, the challenge is insuring the safety of Hogwarts students before and after the trial at altitude. With Severus taking Dumbledore's part as a Polyjuiced twin and removing Harry from the school grounds on the pretense of a Horcrux mission in the Cave, the primary danger to students and the staging on the Tower is removed. Harry is taken off-campus so he doesn't do his "saving-people-thing," at which, alas, as Rebis and supposed Chosen One, he is undeniably, really very good. Harry is the potential proverbial wrench in the works who, if present in the battle below the Tower, would have made the performance on the Tower probably a non-starter.

Which brings us to the night of the crisis in *Prince*.

When the alarms go off in Dumbledore's office that the repairs to the Cabinet in the Room of Requirement have been finished, Slughorn and Snape send Jimmy Peakes to Harry with a summons. Harry flies to Dumbledore's office. On the way, though, he stumbles upon Polyjuice!Trelawney (Bellatrix) who seems to have been just thrown out of the Room of Requirement. She tells him that someone is in there celebrating...

Alas, Harry doesn't make the reaction she expects. She knows he's been trying to get into the Room for months and has laid a trap for him. If he asks for her help to get into the Room of Requirement, what she plans on his asking, he can easily gain access – and will be taken away in a Vanishing Cabinet and ultimately to the Dark Lord before the fun on the Tower. But Harry, incredibly, balks at entering the Room and instead insists that P!Trelawney come with him to Dumbledore. She refuses at first but then hits upon a better course.

P!Trelawney turns the conversation in the queer direction of her first interview with Dumbledore – and reveals that Severus Snape was there when she finished making the prophecy. This contradicts Dumbledore's version of the event in which the eavesdropper "was detected only a short way into the prophecy and thrown from the building" (*Phoenix*, Chapter 37, p. 842). Who is lying?

P!Trelawney and Dumbledore are both lying. With the Red Hen, I doubt Snape was at the Hog's Head that night before, during, or after the prophecy. But Trelawney definitely knows it was Severus that delivered part of the prophecy to Voldemort – and, because of what Voldemort saw in the Headmaster's office at the end of *Phoenix*, she knows that Dumbledore kept this information from Harry.

Dumbledore lied to Harry so he would understand how Voldemort only got half the Prophecy and so that he wouldn't know Severus was the messenger. As Joyce Odell explains, the Headmaster and Snape had made a calculated release of the prophecy to draw Voldemort into the dead-end pursuit of the Potters and Longbottoms, both of whom were protected by Fidelius charms. Dumbledore's few mistakes are correspondingly big ones, remember? But how was he to know Sirius would blow the plan?

P!Trelawney lied to Harry on the way to Dumbledore's office to put him into a frenzy. No doubt she knows there is no love lost between Harry and Snape or perhaps she thinks this is an excellent test of this enmity. Harry pops positive and petulant, which serves both her purposes.

She doesn't have to see Dumbledore one-on-one because Harry goes into shock and forgets about her in his rush to confront Dumbledore with what he has learned. Which confrontation, Bellatrix realizes, will cause a riot among the Good Guys the night the Death Eaters are coming to set their Dumbledore/Snape trap. It isn't as good as capturing Harry, but it's a quality bonus for the playacting she had to do outside the Room of Requirement.

Thus P!Albus (Snape on Polyjuice) or the Severus who plays Dumbledore with a Switching spell unlike any we know, consequently, has quite the surprise! Good thing he has taken a Felix Felicis chaser with his Polyjuice potion. Severus tips his hand by sending Harry to the dormitory for his Invisibility Cloak (Dumbledore had told him to keep it on-hand at all times) but, given Harry's rage at his entrance, P!Albus is on a roll. While listening to Harry rant about how evil he is, Severus only bites at him once (the I-never-leave-the-castle-unprotected chastisement). The guy has remarkable self-control, no?

The adventure in the Cave is only a morality play staged for Voldemort's edification (see "But Obviously Dumbledore is Not Jesus" at HogwartsProfessor.com for details of the symbolic stage work at Lake Inferi) to set up the return drama on the Tower. Dumbledore or Severus had gone there long before and briefed Severus and Sluggo on his return about what the place was about. They know the Locket in the basin is a fake; in fact, Mundungus had been sent to the House of Black to pick up the real piece months ago (Harry runs into him in Hogsmeade as he delivers the Locket to Aberforth, an Order member, with a few other stray items he found here and there at 12 Grimmauld Place).

If you think it's Sluggo playing Dumby at Lake Inferi, you're in good company. Sally Gallo explains cogently the several times P!Albus or "Faux Dumby" slips into Slughorn-isms and melodrama during the cave trip in her essay featured in *Who Killed Albus Dumbledore?* (Zossima Press, 2006). Ms. Gallo has traced the Horace Slughorn character to a famous stage magician of the late 19th century named Horace Goldin, a disciple of the Great Albini and author of the stage biography, *It's Fun to be Fooled!* We'll return to Goldin to discuss his signature magic trick on the tower. I think Wendy B. Harte is right, though, in saying it is Snape in the cave.

Incidentally, nothing happens to faux-Dumbledore in the Cave at the basin. Slughorn probably has brewed the green nasty in the basin himself, perhaps from the greens and acromantula venom he collected the night of Aragog's funeral. Nasty stuff, you'd think, but whoever is playing Dumbledore is no idiot. He takes a bezoar with his twelfth drink and gives the same great "rattling gasp" that Ron gave in *Prince*, Chapter 18, when Harry forced one down his throat.

The rest is just inspired melodrama. From the finding of the chain to Charon's ferry boat ride to the battle with the Inferi, P!Albus and Felix run the table – and Harry resembles nothing more than the audience volunteer called on stage to witness up close the lady being sawn in half. My favorite touch is the "I am with you" sentiment that the seemingly broken Faux Dumby offers Harry at Chapter's end.

P!Albus/Snape isn't broken; he's prepping for the Grand Finale on the Tower. In describing this first scenario without Dumbledore, I will be combining Joyce Odell's insights from the Red Hen collection (the feature of the *Who Killed Albus Dumbledore?* essays) with Ms. Gallo's theory that it is Horace Slughorn/Goldin that falls from the Tower, not the Headmaster.

Wendy B. Harte makes the excellent point that Harry is probably hit with a Confundus charm from Snape while in Hogsmeade, hence the "for one horrible moment Harry's imagination showed him more Inferi creeping toward him around the side of shops, but he blinked and saw that nothing was stirring" (*Prince*, Chapter 27, p. 579). There is a switch in the Dumbledore players here, namely, the switch from Snape to Sluggo, as Ms. Harte suggests, or from Snape to the genuine article Dumbledore.

P!Albus (Horace) collapses in Hogsmeade "paler and damper than ever" and calls again and again for Harry to get Severus, knowing that the Dark Mark will be seen in a moment over Hogwarts and they will be flying there directly. The near-dead Headmaster is suddenly super-powered again, outracing Harry to the Tower while simultaneously disarming the complex spells preventing broom riders from flying over Hogwarts Air Space. Hmmm.

He sends the Invisible Harry to get Severus for the final act of the drama but Draco bursts onto the scene. P!Albus hits Harry with an inaudible Freezing Charm and loses his own wand when Draco blasts him with the Expelliarmus spell. Harry is locked in place so we know the live camera is in place for broadcasting to Voldemort's flat screen TV home entertainment center at the Malfoy's mansion. Let the show begin!

I confess that very few people believe that Sluggo has it in him, even on more than a teaspoonful of Felix Felicis, to play the forgiving and heroic Dumbledore that we see on the Tower with Draco and then with Greyback and the Death Eaters. I don't know why. As Ms. Odell and Ms. Gallo explain, he isn't sick or critically weakened by the Cave journey – and, if Dumbledore has been off-stage in a stoppered death state, his time, when not searching for Horcruxes, could have been spent planning how to save Draco and fake his own death. Surely Horace's script is fairly detailed.

Remember that Snape/Dumbledore twice tells Harry how "extremely able" and accomplished a wizard Slughorn is, despite his faults. This is not Professor Sprout or Gilderoy Lockhart but the Potions wizard who taught Severus Snape and Lily Evans. P!Albus is a stretch for Horace, certainly, but he is a great wizard.

Anyway, back to Horace Goldin's best trick. Ms. Gallo tells us that this stage magician's show stopper was to "catch a bullet" fired at his chest, catching it with, of all things, a wedgewood plate. He would hold out this plate with its visible wedged bullet – the slug of Slughorn? – to the audience and the verifying volunteer to inspect after miraculously surviving the near point-blank shot. Joyce Odell explains how the Dumbledore ghost or stand-in does almost the same thing on the Tower.

First, Severus aims the Avadra Kedavra death curse at P!Albus' chest where it hits him "squarely." This curse is "unblockable" in the sense of not having a countercurse or an enchantment that can be used to protect you. Physical objects, however, are excellent protection against the spell. Dumbledore uses parts of the Fountain of Magical Brethren to this effect in his battle in the Ministry with Voldemort. Goldin/Slughorn is just holding a metal plate against his chest. Forget the wedgewood!

Second, the force of the curse "blasted [Dumbledore] into the air." This is not the usual effect of this curse on a human or living target. The Riddles weren't found "blasted" in their Dining Room, the spider Crouch/Moody hit with an AK in Goblet wasn't blown across the room, and Cedric Diggory just "[fell] to the ground" beside Harry in the graveyard after being hot with the killing curse. It took Sirius an "age to fall" after being hit "squarely in the chest" with the death curse.

Faux Dumby, in effect, anticipates the force of the blast against his chest plate and jumps backwards over the wall as if he were "blasted." He stayed close to the wall all through his conversation with the young Malfoy, just in case the little monster was able to blast him without his being able to prevent it.

Third, "for a split second, he seemed to hang suspended beneath the shining skull, and then he fell slowly backwards, like a great rag doll, over the battlements and out of sight." Levicorpus spell (inaudible) from P!Albus or Severus followed by a series of Hovering Charms to slow his fall onto a bed of Cushioning Charms prepared by Hagrid, Severus, or Sluggo earlier that evening.

And, then what? Again, Ms. Odell has an explanation. P!Albus transfigures the chest plate into grass or a stone he can toss to one side; no sense sharing this plate with his anticipated audience. He opens the locket to be sure Harry finds the R.A.B. message inside it (or Hagrid if Harry does not get there first). Last but not least, he pours a little Draught of Living Death into his hand, transfigures the vial into a grasshopper, and drinks out of his palm.

Hagrid collects the body after everyone has marveled at it sufficiently and takes it to Fawkes. The phoenix rewards Dumbledore's loyal servant by weeping copiously over the fallen Sluggo, both reviving him from the Draught of Living Death and the Basin Backwash and restoring him to Horace Slughorn out of his Polyjuiced state and his death-curse, crash-landing bruises. He's a mess when he arrives at the Faculty Meeting ("[he] looked the most shaken, pale and sweating") but he's still "on message." He is shocked, simply shocked that Snape could have done this and argues for the closing of the school.

He knows the Death Eaters are still in the school, after all, and rightly worries for the safety of the students, not to mention his own security issues, now that the Dark Lord has watched Dumbledore's death and Snape the Playwright is gone from Hogwarts for good. What's to keep the Death Eaters still on deck from settling old scores?

The alternative scenario to Dumbledore off-stage in a stoppered death condition consequent to the Horcrux ring destruction while Horace Slughorn stands in for him on the Tower is simply that Dumbledore himself takes over for Snape in Hogsmeade and acts out his own death on the Tower. Here Dumbledore stays behind in the castle to protect his students while Severus takes Harry and his Dark Lord camera out to Lake Inferi so the stage can be set for the big show in their absence.

The drama plays out the same way except that the old man is not as strong as everyone on the staging crew thought. The blast in the chest and trip to the base of the Tower kills him. Sluggo stoppers Albus' death there in the way we have been describing Snape stoppering the Headmaster's death after the Ring Horcrux debacle. Fawkes' song and tears are to preserve Dumbledore in his suspended de-animation, i.e., the "dead" Dumbledore represented in his Hogwart's office portrait who is really only sleeping the sleep of those nearly departed.

I probably don't need to point out that, regardless of which scenario you prefer, Harry missed all this. Without Sally Gallo, Wendy B. Harte, and Joyce Odell's help, I never could have imagined it, married as I have been to Harry's perspective.

No surprise about Harry missing things, though! Harry believed what he saw on the Tower without question because it confirmed his metanarrative-driven beliefs that Slytherin is evil and that the Head of Slytherin House is beyond evil.

This mistaken interpretation of what he saw, which becomes common knowledge (much like Pettigrew's staged death became "common knowledge" in the Wizarding World about Sirius' guilt) is Snape's best cover. Voldemort now believes that he has conclusive proof that his double agent is a "Lord Voldemort Man" in Dumbledore's seeming execution on the Astronomy Tower. Severus will be Voldemort's best man and the Order of the Phoenix's top target. P!Lupin makes sure of that with his comments confirming Harry's myopic interpretation of events in the Infirmary over Bill Weasley's body.

Insanely complicated and impossible? Hardly. This is not the nightmare of duplicitous difficulty that it could be. Dumbledore is not an especially hands-on Headmaster. Severus only has to play the role on occasion; his most frequent conversations as Headmaster are with Harry who never checks anybody's identity and who, let's face it, is not the sharpest knife in the drawer.

Severus, after passing the Dumbledore baton to Slughorn or Dumbledore, beats it back to the castle in time to take the Polyjuice antidote and "blast" the Headmaster or his stand-in from the tower. Hagrid plays his grieving part admirably, Fawkes stays off-stage appropriately, and Severus resumes his part as a deep plant in the heart of the Death Eater inner circle. Lest Voldemort continue to use Harry to see what is going on when Severus cannot direct the events on stage, he disarms the Horcrux on Harry's forehead before Buckbeak/Witherwings tries to kill him.

So... at the end of *Half-Blood Prince*, Dumbledore is "definitely dead." (1) He could have died in the Horcrux destruction accident and had his death stoppered by Snape the summer before the school year begins as Cathy Leisner suggests. (2) He could have died on the Tower after being unstoppered in the Cave and blasted by Snape. If the narrative line is the word of truth, he died on the Tower with his boots on and there was no stoppering or Fawkes-crying-a-river to save him. Or (3) he could have died in an elaborate staging of his death for Harry's Scar-O-Scope and had this death stoppered by Horace at the base of the Tower with an assist from Fawkes.

The formulas and five keys point to Dumbledore being "only" dead in the way of Stoppered Death. Joyce Odell's back-story of Severus and Albus in cahoots from the very beginning – and what they've been doing all these years – along with Sally Gallo's explanation from stage magic history and W. B. Harte's thoughts on Severus as P!Dumbledore, are very compelling. I urge you to pick up a copy of *Who Killed Albus Dumbledore?* (Zossima Press, 2006) today to read their stuff.

Horcruxes, Harry, and Hermaphrodites: The Grand Finale

All we're left with after the invisible back-story is what happens in the last book.

I have no idea of how it will turn out, other than the assumption that Voldemort will not survive the tale's end. Steve Vander Ark of the *Harry Potter* Lexicon is probably spot on in his predictions that the ending will be both simpler than anyone has guessed and that no one will have come close to guessing what really happened in *Prince* or what will happen in the seventh book.

Having said that, let me add a few ways that the story might be simpler than we expect.

For one thing, the story could conform pretty much to the ten-step trip Harry has taken every year since *Philosopher's Stone*. After *Goblet* and *Phoenix* I couldn't imagine how things could carry on as usual at Hogwarts in the following year. But they did. I'm going to assume the inertia of story telling patterns will win out again and that we will return to Hogwarts' happy confines one more time in the last book.

Further simplifying things would be Harry's discovery that all or almost all the Horcruxes are at Hogwarts and that they can be dispatched with or disarmed without losing an arm, if they haven't been "turned off" already. We know about the Ring, the Diary, and the Slytherin Necklace, which are either no longer functioning as Horcruxes or in the possession of the Order. We have been told pretty much flat-out that the Hufflepuff cup that Tom Riddle, Jr., stole is also a Horcrux. If we're right about Harry's scar and Lord Voldemort's wand, that comes to six Horcruxes, which, with the piece within Voldemort, brings us to seven.

I'll get to why I think Harry is a Horcrux in a minute and an idea about Voldemort's wand, too. My favorite ideas about potential Horcrux items besides these two come from Dr. Daniela Teodorescu, a French professor at Central Arkansas University, and from Maureen Lamson at the HogwartsProfessor.com discussion boards. Dr. Teo thinks the Mirror of Erised could be a Horcrux and Ms. Lamson thinks the Hufflepuff cup has been Transfigured into one of the pieces on display in the Hogwarts trophy room. You can read Dr. Teo's thoughts in *Who Killed Albus Dumbledore?* Ms. Lamson's remarkable detective work can be found at her Live Journal: http://felicitys-mind.livejournal.com/.

I like these two ideas because both objects can be found at Hogwarts so the Terrible Trio won't have to be doing a Marco Polo search of the Wizarding World for them. Even better, both the trophy and Mirror of Erised Horcrux possibilities underscore the literary alchemy of the books and the postmodern themes.

Unlike Ms. Lamson, I think the Transfigured Hufflepuff item has been made into the House Cup (she wrote that her best guess is Riddle's trophy of merit). It points to the alchemy in being a cup because a cup is one of the four suits representing the four elements. This is almost a given since it comes from a Hogwarts Founder. The cup also points to the postmodern themes of the books because, with the Sorting Hat, the House Cup is the primary vehicle of the divisive metanarrative at the school. Students identify themselves most with their houses in pursuit of the honor of winning the doggone Cup, which chase makes them into partisans with little sympathy for any house but their own.

You've got to think, too, that Voldemort had to love the idea of all the students at Hogwarts semiadoring his Horcrux, right?

The Mirror of Erised, Horcrux or not, would be a great addition to the finale. Not only was it a pivotal part of the climax of Stone we are likely to repeat in one form or another, but it is, in one object, an encapsulation of the alchemy and postmodern themes.

Literary alchemy is largely about the resolution of the contraries of human existence. The greatest of these contraries, even greater than male/female, are the poles of human thought, namely subject/object and inner/outer. All mirrors dissolve the subject/object distinction because the subject and object of a person looking at their reflection is the same. The Mirror of Erised takes this a step further by reflecting the interior of the person, their heart's desires, erasing the division of inner/outer.

Postmodern people have as their goal, heck, our goal to transcend as much as possible the shape our cultural metanarrative gives our thinking. Who wants to be a prejudiced drone or someone who believes they are what cultural "norms" and shared beliefs tell them they should be? Not me. I want to be self-actualizing, which is to say, I want to see myself as I am on the inside, as I really am, not as others imagine me because of my appearance and their pigeonholes.

The Mirror of Erised was made for this work, even if it has its downside. As Dumbledore says to young Harry in his first year:

"[T]his mirror will give us neither knowledge or truth. Men have wasted away before it, entranced by what they have seen, or been driven mad, not knowing if what it shows is real or even possible." (Stone, Chapter 12, p. 213)

As he explains in *Prince*, the Mirror of Erised acts as little more than a gauge of our desires, a tool for self-reflection on what sort of person we are. "The happiest man on earth would be able to use the Mirror of Erised like a normal mirror, that is, he would look into it and see himself exactly as he is" (*Stone*, op.cit.). The happiest man is the self-actualized person of postmodernism.

I suspect Harry will find a reason in the probable ambush at Godric's Hollow or at the alchemical wedding of Bill and Phlegm, I mean, Fleur, to return to Hogwarts, which, open for classes or not, will be the scene of his Horcrux searching or battle with the Dark Lord. The wand Voldemort himself, of course, will wait for destruction until the grand finale and last battle.

The questions I have been asked most often the last few months is why I think Harry is a Horcrux, what the other Horcruxes are, and whether Harry will survive. Before signing off to get in line to buy *Deathly Hallows*, let me take a shot at these maven stumpers.

Harry the Horcrux

Let's do a quick review of what a Horcrux is before jumping into why Harry's scar probably is one and how it could have been made as one.

The Horcrux, we are told in a memory of Horace Slughorn, is "the word used for an object in which a person has concealed part of their soul....[Y]ou split your soul, you see," said Slughorn, "and hide part of it in an object outside the body. Then, even if one's body is attacked or destroyed, one cannot die, for part of the soul remains earthbound and undamaged" (Chapter 23, p. 497). The "horror" in Horcrux is that splitting the soul is only possible "by an act of evil – the supreme act of evil. By committing murder. Killing rips the soul apart. The wizard intent upon creating a Horcrux would use the damage to his advantage. He would encase the torn portion" by a spell into an object (Chapter 23, p. 498).

The nightmare of Voldemort's immortality experiments is that he has six Horcruxes outside of his body for a total of seven soul fragments that must be destroyed to kill the Dark Lord.

The word "Horcrux," assuming it is a Rowling invention, is an interesting combination of Latin and French derivations. Ms. Rowling is both a classicist and former French teacher so this should not surprise us.

"Hor-crux" from the Latin would be "frightening or horrible" (horreo) and "cross" (crux) inviting the interpretation as a cross founded on murdering others rather than one's own ego concerns, in contrast to the way to immortality found in the life-saving sacrifice of Christ. The English reading from assonance ("whore cross") suggests the meaning of the Latin.

Mugglenet.com, a popular *Harry Potter* internet fan site, gives this definition from the French:

> The etymology of the word seems to be thus: a combination of "hors" from the French "dehors" meaning outside and "crux" meaning "essence." Thus, a horcrux is a device for keeping your soul (the essence) outside your body. ["Level 9: Mysteries Explained" section of http://www.mugglenet. com]

If the word "Horcrux" is a Rowling invention, the idea of encasing part of the soul or one's essence and power into a physical object apart from the body is not an innovation in literature, folk tales, and myth. It is the backdrop of Tolkien's *The Lord of the Rings* (Sauron's ring), the heart of the story in *Sir Gawaine and the Green Knight* (how the Green Knight survives a beheading), the secret of Korschei the *Deathless in the Firebird* saga (his heart hidden in seven layers of containers), and reflects obliquely the Christian teaching on the nature of a saint's incorrupt body at death (i.e., the grace-filled power of relics).

Rowling's brilliant spin on this literary topos or cliché is to say the soul is "rent" by sin and "split" by the greatest of sins against love for others (their murder, physically or spiritually). Lord Voldemort, the archvillain, pursues an individual immortality apart from God and His means to our salvation (the Cross) by means of a pouring of his soul into physical objects apart from his body. In this, Voldemort is simultaneously a materialist and a dualist. He also is no longer human, as Dumbledore says, because he fails to understand the power of a human being that is whole, an integer of body and soul, and pure (cf., Chapter 23, p. 511), which is to say, "not rent or split."

To destroy Voldemort, then, Harry must find and destroy the four remaining Horcruxes and Lord Voldemort while at the same time remaining "pure of heart." Dumbledore (or Snape-Dumbledore) warns Harry that, even after the Horcruxes are destroyed, "while his soul may be damaged beyond repair, his brain and his magical powers remain intact. It will take uncommon skill and power to kill a wizard like Voldemort even without his Horcruxes" (Chapter 23, p. 509). This power, Dumbledore tells Harry, is Harry's love.

Our clues about the possible Horcruxes have been summarized by Pat Henderson of Seattle this way (for which, "thank you, Pat!"):

> We know that Slytherin's Ring that belonged to Voldemort's grandfather was a Horcrux and that Dumbledore destroyed it, apparently at great injury to his wand hand.
>
> The second one was Tom Riddle's diary from *Chamber of Secrets* was a Horcrux, destroyed by Harry when he plunged the basilisk fang into it.
>
> One of the seven pieces of Voldemort's soul must still be inside Lord Voldemort to animate him – I don't know if that actually qualifies as a Horcrux or not. But that takes care of three out of the seven that are sure things.
>
> Moving from the realm of surety to speculation:
>
> We suspect that one of the Horcruxes is the Slytherin necklace that was in the basin in the cave, that was replaced. We suspect that it is now the locket that was in Grimmauld Place that they

found when they were cleaning – the one that no one could open. We aren't sure where it is – still there on the shelf, hidden away by Kreacher, or thrown away by Sirius, or nicked by Fred & George or Mundungus (and now in Hogsmeade with Aberforth).

That's four.

Helga Hufflepuff's cup is a likely one, but we don't know that for sure, and we don't know where it is. If it found its way back to Hepzebah Smith's family, it could be in Zacharia Smith's house somewhere – why else have him mentioned so many times when he was such a minor character?

That is five.

Number six and seven are the problems, as we don't really know what Harry is trying to find, nor does he.

Possibilities:

The Tiara in the Room of Requirement that Harry put on the statue when he hid his potions book there (the one that had been Snape's). We don't know of anything that belonged to Rowena Ravenclaw, but as the other founders have all been mentioned, I'm sure there is something of hers that Voldemort might have got hold of and made a Horcrux. Perhaps the Tiara in the Room of Requirement is hers.

......or it could be the Tiara that is mentioned when Molly says that Aunt somebody or other will lend it to Fleur when she marries Bill. Since the Weasleys are a pure-blood family and they were all in Gryffindor House, it's possible this could be the lost Gryffindor Horcrux. Or not.

That takes us to seven. And I've no idea. Harry or his scar? I don't think so, but many people do. Gryffindor's sword? Maybe. The Sorting Hat? Maybe.

The sword and hat both have the same sort of problem though. Both were brought to Harry to help him in the *Chamber of Secrets*. If part of Voldemort's soul was neatly tucked inside already, would those items have been positive things to help Harry? And the scar seems improbable because Voldemort wouldn't have made it intentionally.

Is there something else hidden at the Malfoy mansion? Wouldn't surprise me, but I've no idea what.

Or something else in Dumbledore's office or at Grimmauld Place or at Godric's Hollow – I'm guessing that Harry will find something important when he goes there, not just his parents' graves.

The only canon possibilities that Pat neglects are Dumbledore's speculation that Voldemort used Nagini, his pet snake, for a Horcrux or that there are more than six physical objects made into Horcruxes. After concluding that the Dark Lord had been frustrated in getting the objects from all four Hogwarts Founders he wanted, Dumbledore shares his suspicion with Harry (and Voldemort):

> "The snake?' said Harry, startled. "You can use animals as Horcruxes?"
>
> "Well, it is inadvisable to do so," said Dumbledore, "because to confide a part of your soul to something that can think and move for itself is obviously a very risky business. However, if my calculations are correct, Voldemort was still at least one Horcrux short of his goal of six when he entered your parents' house with the intention of killing you.
>
> "He seems to have reserved the process of making Horcruxes for particularly significant deaths. You would certainly have been that. He believed that in killing you, he was destroying the danger the prophecy had outlined. He believed he was making himself invincible. I am sure he was intending to make his final Horcrux with your death.
>
> "As we know, he failed. After an interval of some years, however, he used Nagini to kill an old Muggle man, and it might then have occurred to him to turn her into his last Horcrux. She underlies the Slytherin connection, which enhances Lord Voldemort's mystique; I think he is perhaps as fond of her as he can be of anything; he certainly likes to keep her close, and he seems to have an unusual amount of control over her even for a Parselmouth."
>
> "So," said Harry, "the diary's gone, the ring's gone. The cup, the locket, and the snake are still intact, and you think there might be a Horcrux that was once Ravenclaw's or Gryffindor's?"

"An admirably succinct and accurate summary, yes," said Dumbledore, bowing his head. (Chapter 23, pp. 506-507)

Evidence that Harry's Scar is a Horcrux

Nagini is a possibility in Dumbledore's mind I think only because he is trying to convince Voldemort he still has no idea about what the Horcruxes are. Assuming the snake Horcrux is a MacGuffin or red herring – it would make three Slytherin Horcruxes alongside the ring and the locket – and Ms. Rowling includes this passage as an instance of Snape/Dumbledore trying to deceive Voldemort into thinking they are clueless about Horcruxes or to make the point that Voldemort wanted to make a Horcrux after Harry's murder, we're left with the possibility that something went wrong with his plans that night and Harry's scar was made inadvertently as a Horcrux.

Why does this seem so likely a possibility? Because of all the questions answered by Harry's scar being a Horcrux. Here's a quick list:

Doppelganger connection: Harry has an amazing link to Lord Voldemort through his scar. Until *Half-Blood Prince*, it acted as something of a mood ring (a mood chain saw?) by which he could feel Voldemort's emotional state – joy, anger, etc. – or even see what Voldemort was seeing. As Cornelius Fudge noted at the end of *Goblet* in the infirmary wing, this scar doesn't behave like any other sort of curse scar ("You'll forgive me, Dumbledore, but I've never heard of a curse scar acting as an alarm bell before...." *Goblet*, Chapter 36, p. 706).

Beyond the mood ring effect, Harry is also a Parselmouth and has strange likenesses with Tom Riddle that both Riddle's Horcrux memory notes in the *Chamber of Secrets* (*Chamber*, Chapter 17, p. 317) and Dumbledore confirms in his end of year meeting (*Chamber*, Chapter 18, p. 333). They act the same, they have similar, rare powers, they even look alike. Dumbledore goes so far as to say outright to Harry:

> "Unless I'm much mistaken, [Voldemort] transferred some of his powers to you the night he gave you that scar. Not something he intended to do, I'm sure..."
>
> "Voldemort put a bit of himself in me?" Harry said, thunderstruck.
>
> "It certainly seems so." (op.cit.)

A scar Horcrux certainly answers the question of how it is that Harry and Voldemort are joined.

Sorting Hat confusion: The Sorting Hat has a hard time sorting Harry. It said when placed over his head:

> "Hmm," said a small voice in his ear. "Difficult. Very difficult. Plenty of courage, I see. Not a bad mind either. There's talent, oh my goodness, yes - and a nice thirst to prove yourself, now that's interesting.... So where shall I put you?"

In effect, the Sorting Hat balks at making a decision until Harry answers its question with the thought, "Not Slytherin, not Slytherin" (*Stone*, Chapter 7, p. 121). If Harry's scar contains a piece of Lord Voldemort's soul, a soul in direct descent from Salazar Slytherin, it is little wonder the Hat seemed to have been Confundus charmed.

Dementor madness for Harry: The dementors have an unusual taste for Harry Potter. If given a choice of targets (with the one exception of the attack in Little Whinging), they swarm to him or choose him before other possible targets. A scar Horcrux explains the preference; Harry is not just a one-souled creature, he is something of a dementor buffet table.

Ability to Outwill Lord Voldemort in Goblet's graveyard battle: Harry not only fights the Dark Lord to a standstill at the end of *Goblet*, he seems to outwill him when their wand-cores lock and the cage of Phoenix Song is created. I thought this was because of the effect of Phoenix Song on Good Guys and Bad Guys (cf., *Fantastic Beasts*, p. 32) until *Prince*; now it seems clear that it was because Harry's will and soul have a Horcrux supercharger exactly equivalent to one part that Voldemort is missing, a sum that gives Harry the edge in battles reduced to will power rather than magical skill.

This would also be the reason that Harry has such success resisting the Imperius charm Crouch/Moody puts on him in the DADA classroom in *Goblet*. "The voice in the back of Harry's head" that resists the curse is not a supercharged conscience but a secondthought courtesy of the soul fragment on board.

It should also be recalled that the "wand chooses the wizard." Both Harry and Voldemort have wands with Fawkes feather cores. A scar Horcrux is one explanation for why Harry's wand chose him; the same reason Tom Riddle, Jr.'s wand chose him.

Why Lord Voldemort stops manipulating Harry through their mind link in *Half-Blood Prince* or allow anyone to kill him: The Dark Lord traps Harry in the Department of Mysteries in *Phoenix* after planting a dream image via their mind link of this passage for the better part of a year. Incredibly, at the beginning of *Prince*, we learn that Harry's scar never hurts anymore and he isn't able to detect Voldemort's emotions or thoughts. The man who seems to be Dumbledore tells Harry it is Occlumency.

This is either a necessary plot device to allow Harry and Dumbledore the tutorial meetings that are essential to this book's closing events or a sign that Voldemort knows that Harry's scar is a Horcrux. After a year of learning how to use it to look through Harry the way Harry saw the attack on Mr. Weasley, the Dark Lord can see Harry's world in *Prince* without sending him into a rage like he did in *Phoenix*. By practicing Occlumency just as Dumbledore/Snape says!

Knowing that Harry is a Horcrux (and useful minicam in the camp of his enemies) is the reason Voldemort ordered his Death Eaters not to kill Harry, orders saying that, as Snape says, "Potter belongs to the Dark Lord – we are to leave him!" (Chapter 28, p. 603).

Harry's ability to destroy Horcruxes when Dumbledore can't: Harry thrusts a Basilisk fang into Riddle's Diary Horcrux at the end of their battle in *Chamber*. Nothing happens to Harry and the Horcrux dies in a blood-red bath of ink. If we believe the Headmaster's tale in *Half-Blood Prince*, it seems that Dumbledore, greatest living wizard™, tried to destroy the Ring Horcrux, and only the combined genius of Dumbledore and Snape could save him, even temporarily.

Dumbledore/Snape says that he is "much less valuable" than Harry at the Green Bird Bath in the Cave (Chapter 26, p. 570). Other than Harry's ability to destroy Horcruxes, I'm at a loss to see how Harry is more valuable in the war against Voldemort than Dumbledore. The Headmaster certainly doesn't buy into the idea that Harry is the only possible vanquisher because of the Prophecy – except for how the Dark Lord has marked him "as his equal." Harry's scar, if a Horcrux, could explain why the booby traps set on these items do not affect him.

Or it could just be that Harry's "greater value" is in his carrying a Scar-O-Scope through which the Dark Lord can be deceived into trusting Snape as his most faithful servant, the mistake that will create an opening for Snape to get him in the end.

How Lily's sacrificial love saved Harry: Dumbledore explains to Harry that his mother's love saved him and Riddle's memory says "So. Your mother died to save you. Yes, that's a powerful countercharm." But how does this wandless, wordless countercharm work if it is cast by a person having died? That something went wrong with the Dark Lord's death curse because of the sacrifice of Lily Potter means there may be a more satisfying explanation of how her death saved Harry, more satisfying at least than "Love conquers all."

Voldemort's Wand a Horcrux?

I hope that makes Harry being a Horcrux at least plausible to you. What about Voldemort's wand?

The man seeming to be Dumbledore explained to Harry that he believed the Dark Lord was collecting magical objects, preferring those "with a powerful magical history," "worthy of the honor" of serving as his soul depositories (Chapter 23, p. 504). Voldemort seems to have wanted a collection of Hogwarts Founders items to serve as Horcruxes. What could he have had in mind for the object to become a Horcrux after the Potter murders?

Logically, he had three options:

- something he always or already owned,
- something he had acquired before going to the Potters' home, or
- something he expected to find in the Potters' home.

Linda McCabe, a *Harry Potter* authority whose instincts I almost always defer to, suspects that it was either a Gryffindor relic Voldemort had found (i.e., stolen) or that he expected to find in the Godric's Hollow home of the Potters. There is nothing in the books to clue us in to what this might be (Dumbledore tells Harry the only known relic of Godric Gryffindor is the sword in Dumbledore's office, if we have been told the

Sorting Hat, too, once belonged to this Founder).

It might be something he stole from Hogwarts, perhaps on the day he visited Dumbledore to interview for a teaching position. In the Pensieve Harry sees Tom Riddle as he rises to leave the office reach for his wand: "He was sure that Voldemort's hand had twitched toward his pocket and his wand; but then the moment had passed, Voldemort had turned away, the door was closing, and he was gone" (Chapter 20, p. 446). This could be a sign of his frustration – or perhaps Voldemort got the drop on Dumbledore and went looking for Horcrux material? Not likely.

Again, Dumbledore says that Nagini is a likely Horcrux because the snake "underlies the Slytherin connection" and because his fondness for her means "he certainly likes to keep her close" (Chapter 23, pp. 506-507). If we eliminate as speculative the options of something he found and something he expected to find at the Potters' after he arrived, we are left with something he always had, something he "likes to keep close."

The obvious magical object that meets this requirement is Voldemort's wand.

Lord Voldemort's Wand

The Dark Lord's wand, we learn from Mr. Ollivander himself, is "Thirteen and-a-half inches. Yew. Powerful wand, very powerful, and in the wrong hands... well, if I'd known what that wand was going out into the world to do..." He laments to Harry, as he touches the scar on his eleven-year-old forehead, "I'm sorry to say I sold the wand that did it" (**Philosopher's Stone**, Chapter 5, p. 83). Dumbledore explains in Goblet again what Ollivander told Harry in his shop. Voldemort's wand has a Phoenix feather core, one of only two wands made from Fawkes' feathers, and that Voldemort's wand is in this respect the brother of Harry's eleven inch holly model (**Goblet**, Chapter 36, p. 697).

Lord Voldemort's wand meets every requirement Dumbledore thinks an object must have to become a Dark Lord Horcrux, namely:

- It is always with him;
- It is an object with a "powerful magical history;" and
- It is an object, in itself, "of a certain grandeur."

The key here is the core, Fawkes' feather. Simply being Lord Voldemort's wand might be sufficient to satisfy the necessity for "grandeur" given his high opinion of himself – but that the wand has a Phoenix feather, i.e., a core made from a Fantastic Beast who is immortal, and who is the pet of the greatest wizard living, gives it grandeur, history, and powerful magic all in one.

The wand may or may not be associated through Fawkes with Godric Gryffindor; we do not know Fawkes' prior "owners." It would be an impressive argument for its being a Horcrux object if we did know of this connection with a Hogwarts Founder, but, if it isn't, it is not a disqualifier.

The Diary and Nagini were thought by Dumbledore to be objects not because they were linked directly to Slytherin because they were owned by him but because they pointed to Riddle's relation with the Founder of Slytherin House. A wand in the four suits of playing cards ("clubs" in modern parlance) are tied to the Fire element as is the Phoenix, and Ms. Rowling in her description of the Four Houses of Hogwarts has told us that Gryffindor corresponds to the fire element. [We need a sword, a cup, and a ring for the set...]

Here I think Dumbledore's humility and our insistence that every relic be from a Founder blinds us to the "rightness" of a wand Horcrux. Lord Voldemort knew that Dumbledore was the greatest living wizard, the only wizard he ever feared, and that Fawkes was his familiar. Would he not have had some satisfaction in placing a Horcrux on a momento from his most dangerous adversary? Dumbledore gave Riddle the money he needed to buy his wand (Chapter 13, p. 274) and, Gryffindor pet or not, a Fawkes feather wand makes for a grand Voldemort Horcrux.

I have posted at HogwartsProfessor.com a long theory of how Harry became a Horcrux which involves the use of this wand (the post is called "Animampono"). I urge you to read Joyce Odell's Harry-Horcrux theory, too, that is at HogPro as "What Happened at Godric's Hollow." As fascinating as this back-story speculation is, thinking about what happens to Harry in *Deathly Hallows* gives us more material for talking about the Five Keys this book is about. Is Harry doomed to a sacrificial death? I certainly hope not.

Harry's Survival?

Here are two possible scenarios of the book's endings, one in which Harry dies and one in which he lives.

Harry dying to save the world or just to vanquish Voldemort has a certain messianic flair to it that has a great attraction to thoughtful readers. Certainly the number of times Harry dies a figurative death in this series points to the possibility that in the final book he takes a step beyond "figurative" into the great beyond. Linda McCabe's theory that he dies in an Arthur/Mordred death embrace with the Dark Lord, his psychological shadow and Hermaphroditic mirror, is the clearest way I can see this happening.

But I have never thought that Harry is a Christ figure for these books rather than an "Everyman" standing in for all human "seekers." It is easier to imagine Harry faking his death by beheading with a Headless Hat and the Draught of Living Death or some such chicanery than seeing him be "resolved" alongside his contrary in a killer bear hug. Certainly the sheer number of beheading references in the books (joined with a "faked death" or "seeming death" at Buckbeak's near execution) makes this possibility something to consider as an alternate to the Arthurian ending.

For one thing, I doubt that a bear hug would kill him. Completing the Gryffindor/Slytherin circuit with Voldemort is an agonizing thing, as we saw at the end of *Phoenix* when Lord Voldemort learned what joining up with Harry really meant, but it was worse for the bad guy than for our hero. If Severus and Harry, both Hermaphrodites and clean conductors of Love voltage, can both touch Voldemort, I think we have a de facto Love electrocution, which the two Dumbledore men should survive.

My big question is not whether Harry survives or not. Ms. Rowling has said there will be no sequels so he's dead to me either way, hard-hearted as that may sound. What tops my list of questions is the matter of how Harry and Severus resolve their agonies. Frankly, I don't see Harry buying Severus' argument that he had to play the sadist part or risk being discovered. He played the Harry Hating part very convincingly, and Harry is convinced his nemesis killed Dumbledore. Not very promising for a thoughtful exchange of ideas and reconciliation after Voldemort is vanquished.

Here are two possibilities. One, because Dumbledore really is dead, Fawkes flies to Professor Snape's shoulder as his familiar. Even Harry will have a hard time saying aloud or to himself that Fawkes could be deceived. This great denouement, sans Dumbledore, will have to come, as Joyce Odell has written, in a Shrieking Shack-like scene from *Prisoner*. The Red Hen even puts the scene in the Shrieking Shack because of the great importance she places on the "prank" that the Marauders played on Snape.

The second possibility is that we do get the Dumbledore denouement that every story except *Prince* left us with. Either Dumbledore settles all antagonisms before unstoppering and walking through the Veil on his adventure or the dying Dumbledore in *Prince* planned for a happy ending. He would certainly have foreseen the need for a way to convince Harry that Severus was not his enemy. I suspect that somewhere in Dumbledore's office, perhaps in the Pensieve closet, there is a small glass jar with a made-for-Harry memory taken from Hagrid's, Snape's, or Horace's head of Dumbledore's explanation of why it was necessary for Severus to do what he has done.

My "Headless Hat" prediction is that Lord Voldemort captures Hogwarts castle and Harry Potter. Before the Dark Lord can kill his prophesied Vanquisher, however, or before Harry can decapitate himself in his attempt to destroy his scar Horcrux (he has to finally figure this out, if he probably misses that Severus destroyed it), that the lowest of the low, Dumbledore's real secret Army, save Harry, defeat Dumbledore and the Death Eaters, and usher in a Metanarrative of Love.

Really.

How will Harry and friends overcome the combined forces of the Dark Lord, his Death Eaters, the Giants, the Goblins, and the rapidly-reproducing dementors?

Travis Prinzi, maven at the *Sword of Gryffindor* weBlog, has a theory that I think satisfies the Five Keys best, especially one of the postmodern requirements of the story, namely, that the periphery become the center, that the "other" becomes what is good and decisive in the central conflict. Travis' theory is that the house-elves in Hogwarts are Dumbledore's real Army; Ollivander has "disappeared" to arm them with wands and Dobby will lead them in combat against the Dark Lord they all despise to save their hero, Harry Potter. Travis' original post,

"What Happened to Ollivander," is worth reading in its entirety, but here is the part about the house-elves I find so striking:

> [The goals of S.P.E.W. as Hermione shares them in *Goblet* are:] fair wages, good working conditions, political representation, and ... wands. Wands! I don't think it's a coincidence that the same book that focuses so heavily on house-elf slavery also focuses so heavily on wands, and makes the point that the wizarding prejudice against house-elves is actually institutionalized, by forbidding them wands. We should probably conclude from this that, with wands in hand, house-elves would be powerful enough to be a threat to wizards.
>
> And a threat to wizards is exactly what we need, isn't it? Let's take up a quick assessment of Voldemort's army: (1) Voldemort himself, (2) Death Eaters, (3) Dementors (a vast and growing army), (4) innumerable Inferi, (5) werewolves, and (6) giants. Yikes. Compare that to (1) Harry, (2) the bungling MoM, (3) the leaderless Order, and (4) a bunch of kids from Hogwarts, and it's not much of a fight, is it? Something is going to have to give as full-scale war breaks out, which it will, now Dumbledore's out of the picture.
>
> So my theory is basically this: Ollivander's been hidden by Dumbledore, may be protected by a Fidelius charm (with Snape as the secret-keeper?), and he's got wands for an army of house-elves, ready to fight for their freedom.
>
> But they don't want...
>
> I know, I know. I've already established that a revolutionary change in house-elves' status is not something the house-elves themselves are ready for. So why would they voluntarily fight? The key to this lies with Dobby. Despite the fact that Dobby is held in ill-repute for wanting freedom and wages, he makes a point universal to house-elf experience in *Chamber of Secrets*: the house-elves were treated horribly during the first reign of Voldemort, and Harry is something of a hero to their kind. Let's hear Dobby's explanation:
>
> > Ah, if Harry Potter only knew...what he means to us, to

the lowly, the enslaved, we dregs of the magical world! Dobby remembers how it was when He-Who-Must-Not-Be-Named was at the height of his powers, sir! We house-elves were treated like vermin, sir! ... life has improved for my kind since you triumphed over He-Who-Must-Not-Be-Named. Harry Potter survived, and the Dark Lord's power was broken, and it was a new dawn, sir, and Harry Potter shone like a beacon of hope for those of us who thought the Dark days would never end, sir....(CS-10)

In short, then, Harry Potter may just be the person to inspire the house-elves to desire their freedom, especially if the alternative option is to return to the Dark days under Voldemort's reign. Dobby's words, combined with Dumbledore's urgency to teach Harry about the evils of prejudice against other magical brethren suggests that Harry will be something of a great uniter in Book 7, and house-elves certainly have the motivation to follow his lead.

But house-elves must obey their wizarding families, correct? How many families will agree to give up their house-elves to VoldWar II, or even command them to go into battle? Probably not many.

There are, however, at least a hundred house-elves at Hogwarts, and the school may not even be open in Book 7. I'm willing to bet a good number of them were refugees from Death Eater households who fled to sanctuary with Dumbledore after Voldemort was destroyed and the Death Eaters were rounded up after VoldWar I.

Consider this: Everything so far has foreshadowed an attempted Voldemort takeover of Hogwarts. In Books 1, 2, and 5, Dumbledore was tricked or forced entirely out of the castle. In Book 6, he was AK'd right out of the picture, and Death Eaters were loose in the school. "The only one he ever feared" is gone, and we learned from Book 6 that Hogwarts is the only place Voldemort ever truly had affection for. It's where he wants to be. Expect an attempted Voldemort takeover of Hogwarts in Book 7.

Harry feels the same way about Hogwarts, and he's not going

to give it up without a fight. I don't think the house-elves of Hogwarts would be too keen on having to submit to Voldemort himself, especially if many of them recall their days as slaves of Death Eaters. Look for a force of house-elves, finally armed with wands provided by Ollivander himself, in Book 7.

Travis Prinzi, Sword of Gryffindor

In terms of the Five Keys, this theory satisfies the postmodern theme requirement of losers being the greatest heroes, overlooked 'til the climactic end. There are many losers, outcasts, and significant "others" in this book, but no one or no breed is lower than the pathetic and oppressed house-elves. In terms of Sky High postmodern drama, we have to see a house-elf triumph and liberation. Fighting Voldemort for Harry Potter is the most likely road to that story ending.

For "Repeated Elements," the "House-elf Triumphant" scenario has what Travis points out in the several attempts throughout the series of Death Eaters and Voldemort himself attempting to remove the Headmaster and taking Hogwarts from Dumbledore's control from within. In *Stone*, it's Quirrelldemort, in *Chamber*, Dumbledore is removed from campus because of Riddle's memory and Malfoy's machinations, in *Goblet* a Death Eater joins the faculty at Hogwarts to attack from within, in *Phoenix*, Dumbledore is sacked again, and in *Prince*, we see Voldemort's first wave assault on the castle from the Room of Requirement. It would be odd if in Dumbledore's seeming absence that the Dark Lord wouldn't do what he could to move in. Voldemort and the Death Eaters, like the "good" wizards, are unlikely to give the Hogwarts house-elves any weight in their decision to attack what seems a defenseless school building.

In terms of "Literary Alchemy," House-elf Triumphant points to Harry's place as the only person who can unite the four Magical Brethren as quintessence. The goblins may be hard to bring on board, but the centaurs and house-elves, because of Harry's friendship with Firenze and Dobby, are strong possibilities.

Narrative Misdirection? You bet. As important as Dobby, Winky, and Kreacher have been in the storyline thus far and as involved as Hermione has been in her fantasy of liberating the oppressed housewives (I mean "elves"), no one takes the house-elves very seriously, do they?

House-elves are comic relief, and pathetic comic relief at that. For the house-elf slaves to be the deliverer and liberators of the world from Lord Voldemort is a possibility for which we are totally unprepared because of Harry's perceiving them as "other" and anything but "significant other." We saw Dobby blow away Lucius Malfoy without a wand at the end of *Chamber* but he is so bizarre and self-effacing that nothing clicks about what a powerful magic this pathetic guy can wield in a pinch.

But it is just this "overlooking" that is the strongest pointer to the likelihood of Mr. Prinzi's theory. Dumbledore doesn't overlook the strengths and possibilities in people or Magical Brethren.

On their first meeting in *Goblet of Fire*, Dobby says to Harry, Ron, and Hermione down in the kitchens that he and the other house-elves are delighted to be in the Headmaster's service. He goes so far as to say the house-elves know the Headmaster's secrets.

> "Tis part of the house-elf's enslavement, sir. We keeps their secrets and our silence, sir. We upholds the family's honor, and we never speaks ill of them – though Professor Dumbledore told Dobby he does not insist upon this. Professor Dumbledore said we is free to – to –"
>
> Dobby looked suddenly nervous and beckoned Harry closer. Harry bent forward. Dobby whispered. "he said we is free to call him a – a barmy, old codger if we likes, sir!"
>
> Dobby gave a frightened sort of giggle.
>
> "But Dobby is not wanting to, Harry Potter," he said, talking normally again, and shaking his head so that his ears flapped. "Dobby likes Professor Dumbledore very much, sir, and *is proud to keep his secrets and our silence for him.*"
> *Goblet*, Chapter 21, 'House-Elf Liberation Front,' page 380, emphasis added.

The biggest of these secrets seems to be his training them for more than cooking and cleaning duties. All possibilities that are way off the radar screen.

The Fifth Key, "Traditional Symbolism," is nailed down because of the wands Mr. Prinzi says the house-elves receive from Mr. Ollivander and the head of Dumbledore's kitchen Army. Ms. Rowling points to a traditional theocentric worldview, even Christocentric, in the power of wands. It is the cores. Felicity Lamson sent me this from Ms. Rowling's Radio City Question and Answer session in August, 2006:

> Samantha: In the Wizarding World there are many wandmakers, Ollivander's being the one we're most familiar with. How come Ollivander chose the three magical cores for the wands he makes to be phoenix feather, unicorn hair, and dragon heartstring? And how come he decided that these are the three most powerful cores as opposed to others such as veela hair?
>
> J.K. Rowling: Good question. Well, it is true that there are several wandmakers and in my notes about Harry I have many different cores for wands. Essentially I decided Ollivander was going to use **my three favorites**. So Ollivander has decided that those are **the three most powerful substances**. Other wandmakers might choose things that are particular to their country because countries as you know in my world have their own particular indigenous magical species so veela hair was kind of obvious for Fleur's wand. But um, yeah, good question. I've never had that one before (crowd applauds).
>
> An Evening with Harry, Carrie and Garp:
>
> Readings and questions #1, August 1, 2006

So the three wand-cores are Rowling's "favorites" and are Ollivander's preference because he "has decided that those are the three most powerful substances." How is the arming of the house-elves with Ollivander's wands a bit of traditional symbols?

The wand-cores that Ollivander thinks are "the three most powerful substances" are from symbols of Christ. The Phoenix or "resurrection bird" and Unicorn are symbols used in Christian art and literature as readily recognized stand-ins for Christ. But dragon-heart string? We need to look at the alchemical meaning of "dragon's blood."

A note from Lyndy Abraham's *A Dictionary of Alchemical Imagery*, from the end of the entry on 'blood:'

> At the final stage of the work, known as the rubedo, the image of blood symbolizes the precious red elixir or purple tincture [coming from the Stone]. The attainment of the red elixir (gold), after the white (silver), is sometimes compared to the dyeing or staining of white sheets with red blood (see rubedo). Paracelsus's *Aurora* called the purple tincture 'the blessed blood of Rosie colour' and Basil Valentine wrote that 'this Tincture is the Rose of our Masters, of purple hue, called also red blood' (HM, 1:330). Laurentius Ventura wrote of the fixation of the Stone: 'For the Stone must be kept in the fire, till it cannot any more be changed from one nature to another, from one color to another, but become like the Reddest blood running like wax in the fire, and yet diminishing nothing at all' (in ZC, 81). The divine tincture is thought to be capable of tingeing all metals to gold and of restoring man to perfect health and consciousness of God.
>
> The colour of the red tincture or Stone is sometimes compared to dragon's blood. A recipe for the tincture in Lancelot Colson's *Philosophia Maturata* instructs the alchemist to 'increase the fire, till it [the matter for the Stone] be perfect yellow, and then again increase the fire, until it be red as Dragon's blood'. (Abraham, pp. 28-29)

Dumbledore discovered the twelve uses of Dragon's Blood, Hermione has them memorized, and Hogwarts thinks it's important enough to know about Dragon's blood that it's in the first year's curriculum (assuming that Hermione is cramming for exams in **Stone**, Chapter 14, 'Norbert the Norwegian Ridgeback,' as the passage suggests, rather than just showing off). Dragon's blood, especially with the evident importance Slughorn, master Potions maker, and Dumbledore (Snape?), alchemist, give it in their curious asides in Chapter 4 of **Prince**, is pretty important stuff.

How important?

If dragon's blood is linked to the Elixir of Life that is the tincture of the Philosopher's Stone, a connection is made with the Eucharist, or, specifically, the Blood of Christ (the Philosopher's Stone is a traditional symbol of Christ in poetry and drama because it gives you eternal life and spiritual riches usually represented with gold). This suggests its powers must be somehow akin to the life-sustaining power of the unicorn's blood, another symbol of Christ in the stories. Ms. Rowling has Firenze almost quote from 1 Corinthians 11:29 when describing the effects of drinking unicorn's blood, establishing that link with the blood of Christ.

Why have Christ symbols in wand-cores? And what does this have to do with the house-elves?

It's all about Dumbledore's repeated explanations to Harry about the power of love. Love is the great mystery and power of Rowling's magical world, and, by the way, of all traditional cosmology. God is Love, as St. John tells us (1 John 4) and the Creative Principle driving and sustaining creation is one of polarity resolved, hence the complementary opposites that define life on earth (male/female, night/day, hot/cold, contraction/ expansion of heart, etc.). In Christian language, this Principle is God's Logos or Word that becomes a man as Jesus of Nazareth, the Christ.

Back to wand-cores.

What are the most powerful wand stuffers? Those that draw from or focus best the power that is the fabric of all things, seen and unseen, which power is Love. What better way would there be to represent this in story than to use pointers to Love Himself? We have that in Ollivander's preferences for Phoenix feathers (the Resurrection bird), Unicorn hair (traditional symbol in poetry, tapestry, and story for Christ), and, via its connection with the Dragon blood-red tincture of the Philosopher's Stone's Elixir, Dragon heart strings.

The house-elves are forbidden to have wands. They are magical but cannot have the tools they need to access the deeper magic in a focused way as they could with Christocentric wand-cores. Dumbledore or whoever arms the house-elves liberates them from their oppression by the metanarrative and "the last become first." Dobby has already blasted Malfoy. Look for him to be Voldemort's bane in *Deathly Hallows*.

Where's our Five Keys Scorecard? Let's connect the dots of back-story and Travis Prinzi's brilliant suggested ending.

Final Tallies on the Five Keys

Narrative Misdirection: It's all about narrative misdirection! Dumbledore and Severus are pulling the proverbial wool over Voldemort's eyes by doing to him in *Half-Blood Prince* what Ms. Rowling has done to us for six books. Trusting in the limited information we have from Harry is the big mistake we make alongside the Dark Lord because we never think that the white hats would be so devious and brilliant that they would stage events and leak information that would lead us to false conclusions. The house-elves, comic relief throughout the novels because wizard bigotry makes it hard to see them as anything but pets or domestic slaves however important they are in the storylines of four books, come out of nowhere to save the day at series' end.

Literary Alchemy: The rubedo or climactic stage of Deathly Hallows will reveal the transformations and mystery that have already happened in the albedo of *Half-Blood Prince*. Look for the symbolism of the alchemical wedding, philosophical orphan, the grave, and dragon's blood (the Elixir of the Philosopher's Stone) to play a big part in the finale as all contraries are resolved and peace – at a steep price in deaths – comes to the magical world.

Hero's Journey/Repeated Elements: The action almost certainly returns to Hogwarts and the repeated elements that disappeared in *Prince* will return in an avalanche in Deathly Hallows. Harry being a dummy taken in by his prejudices? The central place of the scar? Mistaken identies and faked deaths revealed? Oh, yeah. All that and the ten steps of the Journey, to include a figurative death and resurrection in the presence of a symbol of Christ, too. Not to mention the attempted takeover of Hogwarts.

Postmodern themes: The heroes will all be the good guy misfits nobody could love, most important, of course, being Severus Snape. Nothing will turn out as the storyline suggested was the truth, because that truth was hopelessly distorted by our prejudices and pro-Gryffindor biases. We will be stunned by our inability to see that Harry isn't even the superhero or the Chosen One (more on that in a second).

What will almost certainly happen is that the Founder's myth of Slytherin in opposition to Gryffindor will be subsumed by the poststructuralist's structure, namely Love. The Gryffindor/Slytherin antagonism will become or be revealed as the complementary contraries that they are, never fully themselves unless united with the other. Hence, peace, unity, harmony. In literary alchemy, this resolution happens via death. Mercutio and Tybalt, Romeo and Juliet, no doubt will have their equivalents in this simultaneously postmodern and alchemical drama.

Traditional Symbolism: Beyond the alchemical imagery of the transforming power of contraries resolving as Love and the symbols of Christ that are so much a part of the story already, the ending will include its share of grace-laden pointers. Look for the Mirror of Erised as mentioned above, dragons and dragon's blood, and sacrificial deaths, both a feigned death with that Draught of Living Death potion or a staged beheading and the real number, the Snape as Sydney Carton as Christ. At King's Cross? Hogwarts' Graveyard, the Deathly Hallows? Maybe, but certainly a death to save others and embracing love and life.

I'm rooting for a return of Norbert the Norwegian Ridgeback, both because of the symbolism of dragons and it would complete the circle of Hagrid's relation with Tom Riddle, Jr. Young Tom falsely accused Rubeus of opening the Chamber of Secrets and derailed Hagrid's life as a member of the wizard community. In *Stone*, he adds insult to this horrible injury by playing on his desires for a dragon to get him to betray a secret protecting the stone (Fluffy's love of music and a nap). Hagrid, though, loves the dragon hatched from Quirreldemort's egg and sets Norbert free. This love biting Lord Voldemort in the end would be more than fitting.

And there's Neville. Ms. Rowling is a classicist so you should know one thing about the prophecy: it almost certainly cannot be about Harry. Prophecies are never what they seem to be in classical drama and legend. Don't expect this one to be, either. That the Headmaster was talking to Harry and Voldemort when he said that it was almost certainly Harry the prophecy of the Vanquisher was about should give us pause. That and the critical five points awarded to Neville at the Leaving Feast in *Philosopher's Stone* that give the victory to Gryffindor over Slytherin. Look for Neville Longbottom to be the center and pinnacle of the story's climax. Riding Norbert for England? Maybe.

Need I add, "Don't forget the house-elves"?

The rest of the guesswork I leave for the many readers whose grasp of canon details and interview hints far surpass my own. My only advice is to follow the patterns as closely as you can, especially as they confirm and highlight the narrative misdirection, literary alchemy, the hero's journey repeated elements, traditional symbolism, and Ms. Rowling's postmodern themes. The final story will be told in the patterns of all the other stories.

Chapter 7

Afterword

This is the time to point out how weird what we are doing really is. Besides the rarity of having the opportunity to speculate about how a book will end, what is strange about we're doing in this book is how we're going about our business.

There are literally thousands of *Harry Potter* internet website on which millions of fans every day read the latest news about Harry and the Potterverse. Some of these sites reflect great thoughtfulness; I think immediately of *The Leaky Cauldron*, Steve Vander Ark's *The Harry Potter Lexicon*, Travis Prinzi's *Sword of Gryffindor*, Pauli Fry's *Muggle Matters*, Joyce Odell's *Redhen-publications.com*, and Maline Freden's *North Tower* and Daniela Teodorescu's *Two Way Mirror* essays on *Mugglenet.com*. Other sites include those that are simply fanzines or frightening examples of unbridled media and slash fan fiction. In contrast, there has only been a handful of scholarly works published which discuss *Harry Potter,* and these collections of essays by academics don't attempt to explore the series as a whole.

The reason for this scarcity of comprehensive criticism from professional literary types in our universities is probably just prudence. We don't have the whole series, so nothing definitive can safely be said about the books (beyond sociological reflections on Pottermania) in keeping with the empirical standards of the academy. Any one who dares risks being laughed at later.

I have tried here, prudence aside, to write a book that simultaneously (1) meets the need for serious critical parameters to evaluate the series at the conclusion of the final book and (2) satisfies the curiosity of fan-readers for ideas and clues about how the books will end. I also hope to have introduced Harry's avid followers in what is probably terra incognita to most (Literary alchemy? Narratological perspective? Metanarrative?) by daring to make plot-point predictions in the context of these ideas.

We have been using five literary keys that are invaluable, both for after-the-fact interpretation and for predicting what-will-happen-next. Outside of the wacky devices you see on late night infomercials that will gut your fish, clean your kitchen floor, and give you a killer workout for six-pack "abs," most tools don't do that kind of double duty.

Literary alchemy and analysis of the *Harry Potter* books as postmodern storytelling will play a large part in explaining the genius of the author and the popularity of the books when she is done. But using these tools to figure out what might happen before the stories are finished is a different story. If the interpretative tools are really good for revealing the patterns of the book in dramatic fashion, they should help with the speculation.

I'll be near the front of the line when the last *Harry Potter* book is published, and expect to be as surprised as anyone. I recognize her themes, symbols, and structures, from literary alchemy to postmodern realism, but in the end it is not enough to know what color paints a great artist has on her palette board. Who knows what she will draw? We can do little more than what we have done here, except look forward with anticipation of great delight for the final episode.

Further Reading:

For further reading on each of the Five Keys, I recommend the following brief pieces as excellent starting points:

· Narrative Misdirection: 'Control of Distance in Jane Austen's *Emma*,' Chapter 9 in Booth's *The Rhetoric of Fiction*;

· Literary Alchemy: "Abstract riddles of our stone": Ben Jonson and the Drama of Alchemy,' Chapter 5 of Linden's *Darke Hieroglyphicks*, and 'Insight into Alchemy,' Chapter 12 of Burckhardt's *Mirror of the Intellect*;

· Hero's Journey/Repeated Elements: Chapters 2, 3, and 5 in my *Looking for God in Harry Potter*;

· Postmodern Themes: Cahoone's 'Introduction' to his anthology *From Modernism to Postmodernism*; and

· Traditional Symbolism: 'What is Symbolism?,' Chapter 1 of Lings' *Symbol and Archetype*.

For more material on the Five Keys as they open up the meaning and artistry of Joanne Rowling's *Harry Potter* novels, visit my Blog www.HogwartsProfessor.com

Selected Bibliography:

ABRAHAM, LYNDY. *A Dictionary of Alchemical Imagery*. New York: Cambridge University Press, 1998.

AUSTEN, JANE. *The Oxford Illustrated Jane Austen: Emma*. New York: Oxford University Press, 1966.

AUSTEN, JANE. *The Oxford Illustrated Jane Austen: Mansfield Park*. New York: Oxford University Press, 1966.

AUSTEN, JANE. *The Oxford Illustrated Jane Austen: Pride and Prejudice*. New York: Oxford University Press, 1966.

BLOOM, HAROLD. *The Western Canon: The Books and School of the Ages*. New York: Harcourt Brace, 1994.

BOOTH, WAYNE C., *The Rhetoric of Fiction*. Chicago: The University of Chicago Press, 1983.

BROOKE, JOHN HEDLEY. *Science and Religion: Some Historical Perspectives*. New York: Cambridge University Press, 1991.

BURCKHARDT, TITUS. *Alchemy*. Baltimore: Penguin, 1972.
----. *Mirror of the Intellect: Essays on Traditional Science and Sacred Art*. Cambridge: Quinta Essentia, 1987.
----. *Sacred Art in East and West: Its Principles and Methods*. Bedfont: Perennial Books, 1967.

CAHOONE, LAWRENCE, ed. *From Modernism to Postmodernism: An Anthology*. Malden, MA: Blackwell Publishers, 2001.

CIRLOT, J. E. *A Dictionary of Symbols*. New York: Dorset Press, 1971

COOMARASWAMAY, ANANDA K. *Christian and Oriental Philosophy of Art*. New York: Dover, 1956.

CUTSINGER, JAMES S. *Advice to the Serious Seeker: Meditations on the Teaching of Frithjof Schuon*. Albany, NY: State University of New York Press, 1997.

DICKENS, CHARLES. *A Tale of Two Cities*. London: The Folio Society, 1985.

DOBSON, MICHAEL and STANLEY WELLS, eds. *The Oxford Companion to Shakespeare*. New York: Oxford University Press, 1991.

ELIADE, MIRCEA. *The Forge and the Crucible: The Origins and Structures of Alchemy*. Chicago: The University of Chicago Press, 1956.

----. *The Myth of the Eternal Return, or, Cosmos and History*. Princeton: Princeton University Press, 1971.

----. *The Sacred and the Profane: The Nature of Religion*. New York: Harcourt Brace, 1959.

EVANS, G. BLAKEMORE, ed. *The Riverside Shakespeare*. Princeton: Houghton Mifflin, 1974.

FRYE, NORTHRUP. *Anatomy of Criticism: Four Essays*. Princeton: Princeton University Press, 1957.

GILCHRIST, CHERRY. *The Elements of Alchemy*. Rockport, MA: Element Books, 1991.

GODWIN, JOSCELYN, trans. *The Chemical Wedding of Christian Rosenkreutz*. Grand Rapids, MI: Phanes Press, 1991.

GRANGER, JOHN. *Looking for God in Harry Potter*. Carol Stream, IL: Tyndale House, 2004.

----. *The Hidden Key to Harry Potter*. Wayne, PA: Zossima Press, 2002 (facsimile edition, 2007).

----, ed. *Who Killed Albus Dumbledore?* Wayne, PA: Zossima Press, 2006.

GUENON, RENE. *Fundamental Symbols: The Universal Language of Sacred Science*. Cambridge: Quinta Essentia, 1995.

----. *The Reign of Quantity & The Signs of the Times*. Ghent, NY: Sophia Perennis et Universalis, 1995.

HAEFFNER, MARK. *Dictionary of Alchemy*. San Francisco: Harper Collins, 1994.

KLOSSOWSKI DE ROLA, STANISLAS. *The Secret Art of Alchemy*. London: Thames and Hudson, 1973.

----. *The Golden Game: Alchemical Engravings of the Seventeenth Century*. New York: Thames and Hudson, 1988.

LEWIS, C. S. *An Experiment in Criticism*. Cambridge: Cambridge University Press, 1961.

----. *The Discarded Image: An Introduction to Medieval and Renaissance Literature*. Cambridge: Cambridge University Press, 1994.

LINDEN, STANTON J. *Darke Hierogliphicks: Alchemy in English Literature from Chaucer to the Restoration.* Lexington, KY: The University Press of Kentucky, 1996.

LINGS, MARTIN. *Ancient Beliefs and Modern Superstitions.* Cambridge: Quinta Essentia, 1991.

----. *Symbol and Archetype: A Study of the Meaning of Existence.* Cambridge: Quinta Essentia, 1991.

----. *The Eleventh Hour: The Spiritual Crisis of the Modern World in the Light of Tradition and Prophecy.* Cambridge: Quinta Essentia, 1987.

PARIS, JEAN. *Shakespeare.* New York: Grove Press, 1960.

PEARCEY, NANCY. *Total Truth: Liberating Christianity from Its Cultural Captivity.* Wheaton, IL: Crossway Books, 2004.

PERRY, WHITALL. *The Widening Breach: Evolutionism in the Mirror of Cosmology.* Cambridge: Quinta Essentia, 1995.

ROOB, ALEXANDER. *The Hermetic Museum: Alchemy & Mysticism.* New York: Taschen, 1996.

ROYLE, NICHOLAS, ed. *Deconstructions: A User's Guide.* New York: Palgrave/St. Martin's, 2000.

SCHWARTZ-SALANT, NATHAN, ed. *Jung on Alchemy.* Princeton: Princeton University Press, 2005.

SHEPARD, ODELL. *The Lore of the Unicorn.* New York: Dover, 1993.

SMITH, HUSTON. *Beyond the Postmodern Mind.* Wheaton, IL: Theosophical Publishing House, 1989.

TILLYARD, E. M. W. *The Elizabethan World Picture.* New York: Vintage, 1943.

VELIMIROVICH, NICOLAI. *The Universe as Symbols and Signs: An Essay on Mysticism in the Eastern Church.* Libertyville, IL: Serbian St. Sava Monastery, 1950.

YATES, FRANCES A. *The Art of Memory.* Chicago: The University of Chicago Press, 1966.

About the author

John Granger is an English and Latin teacher at Valley Forge Military Academy in Wayne, PA. He graduated from Phillips Exeter Academy and the University of Chicago with honors and was in the United States Marine Corps for six years, four of these years in Okinawa, Japan. John and his wife Mary have seven children, ages seven to nineteen, all of whom are self-directed learners ("home schoolers"). The Grangers are Orthodox Christians. John's previous books include *The Hidden Key to Harry Potter* and *Who Killed Albus Dumbledore?* (editor).

John is a popular speaker at academic and fan conferences about English literature, especially *Harry Potter,* and is a frequent guest for radio and television interviews. John is able to make difficult ideas accessible, meaningful, and fun for a variety of audiences. Check current speaking engagements or schedule him to speak at your event at *www.Zossima.com*

Also from Zossima Press

EVER YOURS, GEORGE MACDONALD $10

George MacDonald (1824-1905) is best known for his "wonder-stories" including *The Golden Key* and children's books such as *At The Back of the North Wind*. G.K. Chesterton called MacDonald's *The Princes and the Goblin* "the one book that made the difference to my whole existence." C.S. Lewis and J.R.R. Tolkien were influenced by MacDonald's writing and even the antiChristian writer Phillip Pullman writes of MacDonald with respect. MacDonald authored forty-nine books in his lifetime – novels, sermons, poetry, literary criticism, and fantasy stories. This CD is the most complete collection available with files of forty-eight books in both PDF and MS Word format.

Order directly at www.Zossima.com

Available Fall 2007

To Love Another Person
A Spiritual Journey through Les Miserables

Les Miserables, the Broadway musical based on the classic novel by Victor Hugo, is familiar to millions from Broadway performances or touring productions around the world. Author John Morrison leads readers on a journey to experience the great themes of passion and pain, love and redemption.

Printed in the United States
82244LV00007B/73-78